Digital Signal Processing and Control and Estimation Theory

The MIT Press Series in Signal Processing, Optimization, and Control
Alan S. Willsky, editor

1. *Location on Networks: Theory and Algorithms*, Gabriel Y. Handler and Pitu B. Mirchandani, 1979
2. *Digital Signal Processing and Control and Estimation Theory: Points of Tangency, Areas of Intersection, and Parallel Directions*, Alan S. Willsky, 1979

Alan S. Willsky

Digital Signal Processing and Control and Estimation Theory
Points of Tangency, Areas of
Intersection, and Parallel Directions

The MIT Press
Cambridge, Massachusetts, and London, England

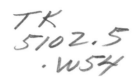

Second printing, December 1979
Copyright © 1979 by
The Massachusetts Institute of Technology

This book was printed and bound in the United States of America.

Library of Congress Cataloging in Publication Data

Willsky, Alan S
  Digital signal processing and control and estimation theory.
  (The MIT Press series in signal processing, optimization, and control; 2)
  Includes bibliographical references and index.
  1. Signal processing—Digital techniques. 2. Control theory. 3. Estimation theory. I. Title. II. Series.
TK5102.5.W54   621.38′043   78–26156
ISBN 0–262–23091–7

To my parents

Contents

Foreword

This book has grown out of an investigation over the past two years of the relationships between digital signal processing and control and estimation theory. I was motivated to undertake this study by a belief that there are enough similarities and differences in the philosophies, goals, and analytical techniques found in the two fields to indicate that a concentrated effort to understand these better might lead to a number of ideas for interaction and collaboration among researchers. One of the first conclusions, reached right at the start of this effort, was that this understanding could not be obtained by trying to study the two fields in the abstract. Rather, deep insight would come only from detailed examination of several specific topics, and this monograph is the result of those examinations.

Thus the goal of this book is to explore several directions of current research in the fields of digital signal processing and modern control and estimation theory. Our examination is in general not result oriented. Instead, I have been most interested in understanding the goals of the research and the methods and approach used. Understanding the goals may help us to see why the techniques used in the two disciplines differ. Inspecting the methods and approaches may allow us to see areas in which concepts in one field may be usefully applied in the other. The book undoubtedly has a control-oriented flavor, since it reflects my background and since the original purpose of this study was to present a control theorist's point of view at the 1976 Arden House Workshop on Digital Signal Processing. However, I have tried to explore avenues in both disciplines in order to encourage researchers in the two fields to continue along these lines.

I hope that these comments help explain the spirit in which this book was written. In reading through the monograph, the reader may find many comments that are either partially or totally unsubstantiated or that are much too black and white. I have included these points in keeping with the speculative nature of the study. However, I have attempted to provide background for my speculation and have limited these comments to questions that I feel represent exciting opportunities for interaction and collaboration. Clearly these issues must be studied at a far deeper level than is possible in this initial survey-oriented effort. To this end, I have included an extensive bibliography for the interested reader.

Nowhere in the book have I made a direct attempt to define the fields of digital processing and control and estimation. Rather, I hope that examining many of the issues of importance to workers in these fields will enable the reader to piece together a picture of the disciplines and their relationship to each other. As a preface to this examination and to provide the reader with some insight into the perspective of this book, let me mention several points concerning each field.

One of the crucial problems in digital signal processing is the design of an implementable system meeting certain specifications on its time or frequency response. Here the emphasis often is on the word *implementable*, with a fair amount of attention paid to issues such as the structure of the digital filter, its complexity in terms of architecture and computation time, the effect of finite word length on performance, and so on. Much of this attention is motivated by the need for extremely efficient systems to perform complex signal-processing tasks (the implementation of high-order recursive or nonrecursive filters) at very high data rates (such as those encountered in speech processing, where one runs into sampling rates on the order of 10 kHz).

The emphasis in control and estimation has been far less on implementation and more on developing methods for determining system design specifications for estimation or control systems. At one level these specifications are just a particular class of design guidelines that can be used to construct an implementable digital system. However, there are major differences between the systems arising in the control context and the typical digital-processing application. For one, the data rates for control systems are often far lower (in aircraft control systems, sampling rates on the order of 0.1 kHz are often encountered). More fundamentally, however, the signal processing to be done in a control system cannot be judged by itself, as can other signal-processing systems, since it is part of a feedback loop, and the effect of the processing must be studied in the context of its closed loop effects.

Many modern control and estimation techniques involve the use of a state-space formulation, as opposed to the input-output descriptions usually encountered in digital signal-processing applications. One implication of this difference is immediately evident. The use of a state-space description implies that the system is causal. In standard feedback control problems this is clearly the case, and thus state-space formulations make a great deal of sense. But there are digital signal-processing problems involving noncausal systems or systems in which the independent variable has nothing to do with time and for which causality has no intrinsic meaning. Thus, while we find several places in which state-space-concepts fit in naturally in the digital signal-processing context, we also find others in which that is decidedly not the case.

As I investigated the several topics discussed in the following chapters, I became convinced of the validity of my initial belief that much is to be gained from the interaction of researchers in digital signal processing and control and estimation theory. This monograph will be a success if I can convince others.

Acknowledgments

It is particularly appropriate that I acknowledge with gratitude the people who helped me during the writing of this book because I would never have undertaken this project without their substantial contributions. I am greatly indebted to Alan V. Oppenheim of MIT who invited me to give a lecture on this topic (before I really knew anything about it) at the 1976 IEEE Arden House Workshop on Digital Signal Processing. The original impetus for and much of the insight in this report is due to Al, and many of the ideas have grown directly out of an intensive set of discussions we held during the five months preceding Arden House and the nine months following. Those familiar with Professor Oppenheim's work and philosophy will see his influence in various parts of this book, and those familiar with my work can readily see the strong influence Oppenheim has had on my perspective and direction. Thanks Al.

During many of our discussions Al and I were joined by James McClellan of MIT. Fortunately Jim has a deep understanding of both disciplines—digital signal processing and modern estimation and control theory—and for long periods of time he not only provided useful insights but also served as an interpreter between Oppenheim and myself. I am particularly in Jim's debt for his valuable insights into the topics discussed in chapters 2 and 4 of this report.

As the research behind this book was begun, Wolfgang Mecklenbräuker of Phillips Research Laboratory was visiting MIT. I would like to express my deep appreciation to Wolfgang for his numerous suggestions in many of the areas explored in this monograph and in particular for his major contribution to my knowledge of the topic discussed in chapter 1.

I have also benefited from numerous discussions with many other colleagues. My conversations with the participants of the Arden House Workshop were of great value to me. Special thanks for discussions during and subsequent to this meeting go to Bradley W. Dickinson of Princeton University, Martin Morf of Stanford University, Thomas Parks of Rice University, Hans A. Schüssler of Erlangen University, Stephan Horvath of the Institute for Technical Physics in the ETH, Zürich, Switzerland, and Alfred Fettweis of Bochum University. In addition, I would like to express my appreciation to James W. Cooley, Ronald E. Crochiere, Daniel E. Dudgeon, Michael P. Ekstrom, Leland B. Jackson, James F. Kaiser, John Makhoul, Russell M. Mersereau, Lawrence Rabiner, Michael Sablatash, Ronald W. Schafer, Kenneth Steiglitz, and R. Viswanathan. I also am indebted to Thomas Kailath of Stanford University for his detailed comments on a preliminary version of this work.

Finally my thanks go to many of my MIT colleagues who aided in the development of these ideas. In particular, I would like to express my appreciation to David Chan for his contributions to chapters 3 and 4 and to Nils R. Sandell for listening to and talking about this stuff every day as we drove to and from MIT. That Nils is still talking to me may mean that there is something of interest in what follows.

I would also like to express my gratitude to Fifa Monserrate, Susanna Natti, Eleanor Stagliola, and Margaret Flaherty for their typing efforts and their patience and to Arthur Giordani for his help in drafting the illustrations for this book.

The work reported in this monograph was financially supported in part by NASA Ames Research Center under Grant NGL–22–009–124 and in part by the National Science Foundation under Grants GK-41647 and ENG 76–02860. The first two of these grants are with the MIT Electronic Systems Laboratory, while the third is with the MIT Research Laboratory of Electronics.

Digital Signal Processing and Control and Estimation Theory

1

Stability Analysis

1.1 The Basic Stability Problems

Of all the topics that we have investigated, we have found some of the clearest points of intersection and interaction between the disciplines in the area of stability analysis. In the field of digital signal processing, stability issues arise when one considers the consequences of finite word length in digital filters. Two problems arise (aside from the effects due to finite accuracy in filter coefficients [12, 75]). On the one hand a digital filter necessarily has finite range, and thus overflows can occur, while on the other one inevitably faces the problem of numerical quantization—roundoff or truncation. Since the filter has finite range (it is after all a finite-state machine), the question of the state of the filter growing without bound is irrelevant. However, the nonlinearites in the filter, introduced by whatever form of finite arithmetic is used, can cause zero-input limit cycles and discrepancies between the ideal and actual response of the filter to certain inputs. As discussed in [3, 15], the typical situation of concern is depicted in figure. 1.1. The filter is described (in state-variable form) by equations of the form

$$x(n + 1) = A\chi(n) + Bu(n), \qquad y(n) = Cx(n), \qquad \chi(n) = N(x(n)), \qquad (1)$$

where N is a nonlinear, memoryless function that accounts for the effects of overflow and quantization. If these effects were not present— if N were

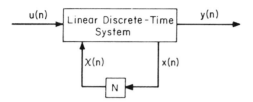

1.1
A digital filter with quantization and saturation nonlinearities.

the identity function—equation (1) would reduce to a linear equation. If one assumes that this associated linear system is designed to meet certain specifications, one would like to know how the nonlinearity N affects overall performance. One important question is, Assuming that the linear system is asymptotically stable, can the nonlinear system (1) sustain undriven oscillations and will its response to inputs deviate significantly from the response of the linear system? We will make a few remarks about this question in a moment. The survey papers [3, 5] and the other references at the end of the chapter provide more detailed descriptions of known results.

In control theory the question of system stability has long played a central role in the design and analysis of feedback systems. A typical feedback system, depicted in figure 1.2, is described by the functional equations

$$e_1 = u_1 - y_2, \qquad e_2 = u_2 + y_1$$
$$y_1 = G_1 e_1, \qquad y_2 = G_2 e_2, \tag{2}$$

where $u_1, u_2, e_1, e_2, y_1,$ and y_2 are functions of time (discrete or continuous) and G_1 and G_2 are operators (possibly nonlinear) describing the dynamics of the forward and feedback paths, respectively. In control theory one is interested in either the analysis or the synthesis of such systems. In the

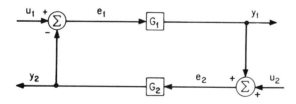

1.2
A typical feedback control system.

synthesis problem one is given an open-loop system G_1 and is asked to define a feedback system (2) such that the overall system has certain desirable stability properties. In stability analysis, with which we are most concerned here, one may be interested in either the driven or the undriven ($u_i = 0$) characteristics. In the driven case one wishes to determine, for example [42], whether bounded inputs lead to bounded outputs and whether the input-output relationship is continuous—that is, whether small changes in the u's lead to small changes in the y's. In the undriven case one wishes to determine whether the system response decays, remains bounded, or diverges when the only perturbing influences are initial conditions. The literature in this area is quite extensive, and we refer the reader to the texts [42, 44, 47], the survey paper [43], and to their references for more on these problems.

These descriptions clearly indicate some of the similarities and differences in the two topics.[1] In both areas one wants the answers to some qualitative questions: Is the system stable? Is it asymptotically stable? Is the system continuous [42] or does it exhibit "jumps" in response to small changes in the inputs [32, 43]? In addition, one often wants some quantitative answers. In digital filter design one is often interested in determining bounds on the magnitudes of limit cycles and how many bits are needed to keep the magnitudes of such oscillations within tolerable limits. In the study of feedback control systems one is interested in measures of stability as provided by quantities such as damping ratios and eigenvalues (poles). In addition, one is often interested in the shapes of these modes, that is in determining the state eigenvector corresponding to a particular eigenvalue.[2]

Not only are the goals of the two problem areas similar but similar bags of mathematical tricks have been used to obtain results. However, there are differences between the methods used and the results obtained in the two areas. The analysis of digital filters has been characterized by the study of systems containing quite specific nonlinearities. In addition, much of the work has dealt with specific filter structures. Second-order filters in particular have received a great deal of attention [2, 3, 11, 15, 18, 31] since more complex filters can be built out of series-parallel interconnections of such sections. The class of wave digital filters [6, 7, 8, 9, 10] has also been studied in some detail. Studies in these areas have yielded extremely detailed descriptions of regions of stability in parameter space [3] and numerous upper and lower bounds on limit cycle magnitudes [3, 4, 20, 26, 31, 35, 56, 59, 60, 63].

In control theory, on the other hand, the recent trend has been in the development of rather general theories, concepts, and techniques for stability analysis. Some powerful mathematical techniques have been developed, but not as much attention has been paid to obtaining tight bounds for specific problems. In addition, problems involving limit cycles have not received nearly as much attention in recent years as issues such as bounded-input, bounded-output stability and global asymptotic stability (although there clearly is a relationship between these issues and limit cycles).

In the rest of this chapter we briefly discuss the relationship between some of the results in the two fields. Our aim here is to point out areas in which researchers have used similar techniques, obtained similar results, or relied on similar concepts.

1.2 The Use of Lyapunov Theory

1.2.1 Basic Lyapunov Theory for Nonlinear Systems

The technique of constructing Lyapunov functions to prove the stability of dynamical systems has been used by researchers in both fields. The basic ideas behind Lyapunov theory are the following [47, 48, 52, 64]. Consider the dynamical system

$$x(k + 1) = f(x(k)), \qquad f(0) = 0, \tag{3}$$

where x is a vector. Suppose we can find a function $V(x)$ such that $V(0) = 0$ and the first difference along solutions satisfies

$$\Delta V(x) \triangleq V(f(x)) - V(x) \leq W(x) \leq 0. \tag{4}$$

Such a function is called a *Lyapunov function*. If this function has some additional properties, we can prove stability or instability of (3). (See [47, 48] for proofs.)

THEOREM 1.1 Suppose
  (i) V is positive definite; that is, there exists a continuous, nondecreasing scalar function α such that $\alpha(0) = 0$ and

$$V(x) \geq \alpha(|x|) > 0, \qquad \forall x \neq 0. \tag{5}$$

(ii) $\alpha(|x|) \to \infty$ when $|x| \to \infty$.   (6)

(iii) ΔV is negative definite; that is, there exists a continuous, nondecreasing scalar function γ such that

$$\Delta V(x) \le -\gamma(|x|) < 0.$$ (7)

Then all solutions of (3) converge to 0. ∎

In this result we can think of V as an "energy" function, and (5), (6) essentially state the intuitive idea that the larger the system state, the more energy is stored in it. With this interpretation the theorem states that if the system dissipates energy (7), the state will converge to 0. If we allow ourselves to consider energies that can take negative values, we can get instability results, such as theorem 1.2.

THEOREM 1.2 Suppose V satisfies (4) and suppose there exists an x_0 such that $V(x_0) < 0$. Then the system is not asymptotically stable in the large since the solution starting at x_0 does not converge to 0. ∎

The point here is that since energy decreases, once we arrive at a negative energy state, we can never reach the zero energy state.

Lyapunov stability has been used by many researchers. A crucial advantage of Lyapunov-type results is that the hypotheses for results such as theorems 1.1 and 1.2 can be checked using only the functions V and f; one does not have to construct explicit solutions of difference or differential equations. However, the major problem with the theory is the difficulty in finding Lyapunov functions in general. For linear systems a theory exists, and one can always find a quadratic Lyapunov function

$$V(x) = x'Qx$$ (8)

that will determine whether the system is asymptotically stable (in fact, a constructive procedure using the Lyapunov equation [47, 48] can be used). For nonlinear systems the construction of Lyapunov functions is much more difficult [47, 48].

1.2.2 Uses in Digital Filter Analysis

With respect to the limit cycle problem Willson [2, 13] has utilized Lyapunov functions (and essentially theorem 1.1) to determine conditions under which second-order digital filters will not have overflow limit cycles and will respond to "small" inputs in a manner that is asymptotically close to the ideal response. Parker and Hess [26] and Johnson and Lack [59, 60] have used Lyapunov functions to obtain bounds on the magnitude of limit cycles. In each of these the Lyapunov function used was a quadratic form that in fact proved asymptotic stability for the ideal linear system. Willson [13] was able to show that his results were in some sense tight by constructing counterexamples when his condition was violated. The bounds in [26, 59, 60] are not as good as others that have been found; Parker and Hess believe this may be due to the difficulty of determining which quadratic Lyapunov function to use. Claasen et al. point out [3] that it appears difficult to find appropriate Lyapunov functions for the discontinuous nonlinearities that characterize quantization (see appendix 1 for an example of the type of result one can find).

For one class of digital filters, wave digital filters (WDF), one can use Lyapunov techniques to prove stability [6, 7, 8, 9, 10]. Such filters have been developed by Fettweis so that they possess many of the properties of classical analog filters. Motivated by these analogies, Fettweis [8] defines the notion of instantaneous pseudopower, which is a particular quadratic form in the state of the WDF. By defining the notion of pseudopassivity for such filters, Fettweis introduces (in a very natural way for this setting) the notion of dissipativeness. With this framework the pseudopower becomes a natural candidate for a Lyapunov function, and Fettweis and Meerkötter [10] are able to apply standard Lyapunov arguments to obtain quite reasonable conditions on numerical operations that guarantee the asymptotic stability of pseudopassive WDFs. The concept of dissipativeness is often used in the study of stability [36], and a number of important stability results are based (at least from some points of view) on some notion of passivity. The use of passivity concepts and Lyapunov theory appear to be of some value in the development of new digital filter structures that behave well in the presence of quantization. For example, Meerkötter and Wegener [11] developed and analyzed a new second-order filter structure using pseudopower-Lyapunov arguments.

1.2.3 Uses in Control Theory

Lyapunov concepts have found numerous applications in control theory. Detailed studies of their use in system analysis are described in the important paper of Kalman and Bertram [48] and the texts [47], [52], and [64]. The construction of quadratic Lyapunov functions for linear systems is well understood and is described in detail in these texts. The key result in this area is the following theorem.

THEOREM 1.3 The discrete-time system

$$x(k + 1) = Ax(k) \qquad\qquad\qquad\qquad (9)$$

is asymptotically stable (all the eigenvalues of A lie inside the unit circle in the complex plane) if and only if for any positive definite matrix L, the solution Q of the (discrete) Lyapunov equation

$$A'QA - Q = -L \qquad\qquad\qquad\qquad (10)$$

is also positive definite. In this case the function

$$V(x) = x'Qx \qquad\qquad\qquad\qquad (11)$$

is a Lyapunov function satisfying the hypotheses of theorem 1.1; that is, it proves the asymptotic stability of (9). ∎

Equation (10) and its continuous-time analog [47] arise in several contexts in control theory. Note that theorem 1.3 provides a variety of choices for Lyapunov functions; we can choose any $L > 0$ in (10). Parker and Hess [26] obtain bounds on the magnitude of limit cycles by choosing $L = I$ (here (9) represents the ideal linear model). Tighter bounds might be possible with other choices of L; but it is not clear how one would go about finding a "better" choice other than by trial and error. The use of Lyapunov techniques to bound the magnitude of solutions of difference equations perturbed by nonlinearities has also been studied in the control literature, in particular, by Kalman and Bertram [48].

Specific applications of Lyapunov theory to linear and nonlinear systems appear in the references and in the literature (in particular the *IEEE Transactions on Automatic Control*). In the remainder of this section we concentrate on another use of Lyapunov concepts—as intermediate steps in the development of other results in control theory. An example of this occurs in the analysis of optimal control and estimation systems [64, 65, 66, 67]. Consider the linear system

$$x(k + 1) = Ax(k) + Bu(k), \qquad y(k) = Cx(k), \qquad\qquad (12)$$

and suppose we wish to find the control u that minimizes the cost

$$J = \sum_{i=0}^{\infty} y'(i)y(i) + u'(i)u(i). \tag{13}$$

This is a special case of the output regulator problem [66]. Here the cost (13) represents a trade-off between regulation of the output (the $y'y$ term) and conservation of control energy (the $u'u$ term). The following is the solution for a particular case.

THEOREM 1.4 Suppose the system (12) is completely controllable (any state can be reached from any other state by application of an appropriate input sequence) and completely observable (the state can be uniquely determined from knowledge of the input and output sequences). Then the optimal control in feedback form is

$$u(k) = -(R + B'KB)^{-1} B'KA \, x(k), \tag{14}$$

where K is the unique positive definite solution of the algebraic Riccati equation

$$K = A'KA + C'C - A'KB(R + B'KB)^{-1} B'KA. \tag{15}$$

One proof of this result proceeds along the following lines. Suppose we are presently in the state x. We can then define the *optimal cost to go* $V(x)$ as the minimum of J in (13) when we start in state x. With the aid of dynamic programming methods [66] one can show that V has the form

$$V(x) = x'Kx, \tag{16}$$

where K satisfies (15). The finiteness of V is proved using controllability, while observability guarantees that if $x \neq 0$, then y and u cannot both be identically 0; thus $J > 0$. Finally consider the closed-loop system (12), (14). One can show that this system is asymptotically stable [66]; in fact, the cost-to-go function $V(x)$ is a Lyapunov function that proves this result. Observability and controllability (and the somewhat weaker counterparts, detectability and stabilizability) are important concepts in the development of this result and many others. In fact, the concept of observability allows one to prove the following theorem [51].

THEOREM 1.5 Consider the system (9) and the function $V(x) = x'QX$. Suppose (i) $Q > 0$; (ii) $V(Ax) - V(x) = x'[A'QA - Q]x \leq x'C'Cx$; and

(iii) the system (9) is observable from the output $y(k) = Cx(k)$. Then (9) is asymptotically stable. ∎

Comparing theorems 1.3 and 1.5, we see that we have replaced the negative definiteness of $A'QA - Q$ with negative semidefiniteness and an observability condition. The intuitive idea is the following. Negative definiteness makes it clear that $V(x(k))$ strictly decreases along solutions whenever $x(k) \neq 0$, and from this we can deduce asymptotic stability; negative semidefiniteness says only that V does not increase. However, can V remain stationary indefinitely at a nonzero value? The answer is no, since if it did, we would be able to conclude that $Cx(j) = 0, j = k, k + 1$ $k + 2, \ldots$, and observability would require $x(k) = 0$. Thus V must decrease (not necessarily at every single step), and we can again deduce asymptotic stability.

Thus we see that Lyapunov concepts, combined with ideas from the theory of state-space models, can lead to important results concerning optimal designs of controllers and estimators. See [64, 65, 66, 67] for continuous time analogs of these results and dual results for estimators; in [68] the interplay of many of these ideas is discussed.

In addition to its use in studying design methods such as the regulator problem, Lyapunov theory has been used as a framework for the development of many more explicit stability criteria (Lyapunov theory in principle requires a search for an appropriate function). Examples of these are a number of the frequency domain stability criteria that have been developed in the last ten to fifteen years [1, 21, 22, 23, 24, 33, 37, 38, 39, 43, 44, 45]. Several of these results have analogs for the limit cycle problem. For example, Tsypkin's criteria [33, 21, 2] and [44, p. 194], which are analogs of the circle and Popov criteria in continuous time [43, 44], have counterparts in the theory of limit cycles [15, 16]. Instability counterparts of the Tsypkin-Popov type of result have been developed from a Lyapunov point of view [1, 39], and a thorough understanding of the basis for these results may lead to analogous results for limit cycles in digital filters.

In the next section we examine the interplay among a number of stability concepts (passivity, Lyapunov, Tsypkin, frequency domain analysis, positive real functions). The point here is that many stability results can and have been derived in a number of different ways, and an examination of these various derivations reveals a relationship among the various methods of stability analysis. Some of the most fundamental work in this area has been done by J. C. Willems [49, 50, 69].

1.3 Frequency Domain Criteria, Passivity, and Lyapunov Functions

1.3.1 Passivity and Frequency Domain Stability Criteria for Feedback Systems

We have already mentioned that passivity is important in stability theory and that Fettweis and Meerkötter used passivity notions to study certain digital filters with Lyapunov techniques. The relationship between passivity, Lyapunov functions, and many of the frequency domain criteria of stability theory is quite deep; in this section we wish to illustrate some of these ideas.

In recent years passivity has become one of the fundamental notions in the study of feedback stability. This notion, which is very much an input-output concept, is developed in detail by Willems [41, 42, 50, 69]; see also Holtzman's text [74]. We follow [42, 69][3]. Let U and Y be input and output sets, respectively, and let $\mathcal{U}$ and $\mathcal{Y}$ be sets of functions from a time set T into U and Y (T may be continuous or discrete [69]). Let $G: \mathcal{U} \to \mathcal{Y}$ be a dynamic system, mapping input functions $u \in \mathcal{U}$ into output functions $Gu \in \mathcal{Y}$ (we assume that G is a causal map [69]). Intuitively stability means that small inputs lead to small outputs, as the following definition makes precise.

DEFINITION 1.1 Let $\tilde{\mathcal{U}}$, $\tilde{\mathcal{Y}}$ be subspaces of $\mathcal{U}$ and $\mathcal{Y}$, respectively (these are our "small signals"). The system G is *I/O stable* if $u \in \tilde{\mathcal{U}}$ implies $Gu \in \tilde{\mathcal{Y}}$. Furthermore, if $\mathcal{U}$, $\mathcal{Y}$ are normed spaces, then G is *finite gain I/O stable* if there exists $K < \infty$ such that

$$\|Gu\| \le k\|u\|, \qquad \forall u \in \tilde{\mathcal{U}}. \tag{17}$$

A typical example is the case for which T is the positive integers, $\mathcal{U}$ and $\mathcal{Y}$ are all real sequences of numbers, and $\tilde{\mathcal{U}}$ and $\tilde{\mathcal{Y}}$ are all square-summable sequences. In this case *I/O* stability means

$$\sum_{i=1}^{\infty} u_i^2 < \infty \Rightarrow \sum_{i=1}^{\infty} y_i^2 < \infty, \tag{18}$$

and finite-gain *I/O* stability means

$$\sum_{i=1}^{\infty} u_i^2 < \infty \Rightarrow \left(\sum_{i=1}^{\infty} y_i^2\right)^{1/2} \leq K\left(\sum_{i=1}^{\infty} u_i^2\right)^{1/2}. \tag{19}$$

Note one property of this example. Let P_T be the operator

$$(P_T x)(t) = x(t), \qquad t \leq T, \\ = 0, \qquad t > T. \tag{20}$$

Then for any $u \in \mathcal{U}, y \in \mathcal{Y}$ we have $P_T u \in \tilde{\mathcal{U}}, P_T y \in \tilde{\mathcal{Y}}$. In this case $\mathcal{U}, \mathcal{Y}$ are called (*causal*) *extensions* of $\tilde{\mathcal{U}}, \tilde{\mathcal{Y}}$, and we assume this to be the case from now on. We now can define passive systems.

DEFINITION 1.2 Let $\mathcal{U} = \mathcal{Y}$, and assume that $\tilde{\mathcal{U}} = \tilde{\mathcal{Y}}$ is an inner product space. Then G is *passive* if

$$\langle P_T u, P_T G u \rangle \geq 0, \qquad \forall u \in \mathcal{U}, t \in T, \tag{21}$$

and *strictly passive* if there is an $\varepsilon > 0$ such that

$$\langle P_T u, P_T G u \rangle \geq \varepsilon \|P_T u\|^2. \tag{22}$$

In terms of our example G is passive if and only if

$$\sum_{i=1}^{N} u_i y_i \geq 0, \qquad \forall u_i, N, \tag{23}$$

and is strictly passive if and only if there exists an $\varepsilon > 0$ such that

$$\sum_{i=1}^{N} u_i y_i \geq \varepsilon \sum_{i=1}^{N} u_i^2, \qquad \forall u_i, N. \tag{24}$$

The motivation for the definition (23) stems from interpreting the left-hand side of (23) as the total energy input to the system. Thus a passive system always requires that a positive amount of energy be fed into it. This notion has extremely strong ties to the usual notions of passivity and dissipativeness for electrical networks and is, in fact, a natural generalization of these concepts [69, 73].

Much as with Fettweis's pseudopassive blocks, passive systems can be interconnected in feedback arrangements and remain passive. The following result of this type is one of the cornerstones of feedback stability theory [69].

THEOREM 1.6 Consider the feedback system of figure 1.2 where all inputs and outputs are elements of the same space $\mathcal{U}$ (for simplicity). The feedback system is strictly passive and finite-gain I/O stable if (i) G_1 is strictly passive and finite-gain I/O stable and (ii) G_2 is passive. ∎

Willems [69] outlines three basic stability principles—theorem 1.6, the small loop gain theorem (stability arises if the gains of G_1 and G_2 are each less than unity, a result used in the digital filter context in [72]), and theorem 1.7, which depends on the following definition.

DEFINITION 1.3 The conditions on $\mathscr{U}$, $\mathscr{Y}$ are as in definition 1.2. Let $a \leq b$ be given real numbers. Then G is inside (outside) the sector $[a, b]$ if

$$\langle (G - aI)u, (G - bI)u \rangle \leq 0 \quad (\geq 0), \qquad \forall u \in \tilde{\mathscr{U}}. \tag{25}$$

It is strictly inside (outside) the sector $[a, b]$ if there exists an $\varepsilon > 0$ such that

$$\langle (G - aI)u, (G - bI)u \rangle \leq -\varepsilon \|u\|^2 \quad (\geq \varepsilon \|u\|^2), \qquad \forall u \in \tilde{\mathscr{U}}. \tag{26}$$

We now state a variation of Willems' third stability condition [42].

THEOREM 1.7 Consider the feedback system of figure 1.2. This system is finite-gain stable if the following conditions are satisfied:
(1) G_2 is Lipschitz continuous; that is
$$\|G_2 u_1 - G_2 u_2\| \leq K \|u_1 - u_2\|$$
(2) For some $a \leq b > 0$, G_2 is strictly inside the sector $[a, b]$
(3) $I + \frac{1}{2}(a + b)G_1$ has a causal inverse on $\mathscr{U}$ (not necessarily $\tilde{\mathscr{U}}$)
(4) G_1 satisfies the following
    (i) $a < 0 \Rightarrow G_1$ is inside the sector $[-1/b, -1/a]$ on $\tilde{\mathscr{U}}$;
    (ii) $a > 0 \Rightarrow G_1$ is outside the sector $[-1/a, -1/b]$ on $\mathscr{U}$;
    (iii) $a = 0 \Rightarrow G_1 + (1/b)I$ is passive on $\mathscr{U}$. ∎

As developed by Willems [42, 69], this result leads to the circle criterion (in continuous time). Let us examine the third case in theorem 1.7 to sketch the derivation of one of Tsypkin's criteria. Consider the system in figure 1.3. Here G_2 is a memoryless nonlinearity, and we assume that f is in the sector $[0, k]$. We also take $\tilde{\mathscr{U}}$ to be all square-summable sequences. The system G_1 is a linear time-invariant system characterized by the transfer function $G(z)$, which we assume to be stable. Condition (iii) of theorem 1.7 then says that $(G_1 + 1/k)$ must be passive on $\mathscr{U}$; as discussed in [42, 69], this will be the case if and only if $G(z) + 1/k$ is *positive real*,

$$\mathrm{Re}(G(e^{j\omega})) + 1/k \geq 0, \qquad \forall \omega \in [0, 2\pi), \tag{27}$$

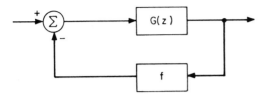

1.3
A linear system with memoryless nonlinear feedback.

which is precisely Tsypkin's condition [33]. The fact that $1 + \frac{1}{2} kG$ is invertible can be obtained by analogy with the continuous-time results in [42, ch. 5]; in fact, this result is a simple consequence of the Nyquist criterion when we observe that G is stable and take (27) into account.

Consider the feedback system in figure 1.2. It is clear that the input-output behavior of this system is the same as that for the system in figure 1.4, where M and N are operators (not necessarily causal). One can often find appropriate multipliers so that the modified forward and feedback systems satisfy the criteria of theorem 1.7 [42, 44]. This is in fact the basis for Popov's criterion [37], for its generalizations [38, 39, 40, 42, 43, 44, 45], and for Tsypkin's discrete-time version [23, 44].

Consider a nonlinear feedback system as in figure 1.3 but in continuous time (replace $G(z)$ with $G(s)$), and again suppose f is strictly inside the sector $[0, k]$. Using the multipliers $N = I$, $M = 1/(1 + \alpha s)$, we can show that the feedback path is also strictly inside the sector $[0, k]$; hence the modified forward loop must satisfy a passivity condition. Specifically, we obtain Popov's condition [38] that the feedback system is finite-gain I/O stable if G is stable (all poles in the left-hand plane) and if $(1 + \alpha s)G(s) + 1/k$ is positive real for some $\alpha \geq 0$, that is, if

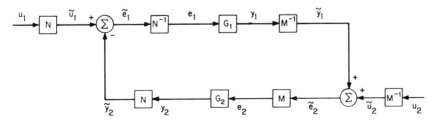

1.4
A feedback system with multipliers.

$\mathrm{Re}\left[(1 + \alpha j\omega)G(j\omega)\right] + 1/k \geq 0, \qquad \forall \omega.$

To obtain Tsypkin's result [23, 43], we must in addition assume that f is nondecreasing. In this case the discrete-time system is finite-gain I/O stable if there exists $\alpha \geq 0$ such that

$$\mathrm{Re}\left[(1 + \alpha(1 - e^{-j\omega}))G(e^{j\omega})\right] + 1/k \geq 0, \quad \omega \in [0, 2\pi]. \tag{28}$$

For extensions of Popov's criterion in continuous-time, see [42, 44, 45] and in particular [38]. As we shall see, some of the results on digital filter limit cycles resemble Tsypkin-type criteria.

1.3.2. Passivity and Frequency Domain Criteria for the Absence of Digital Filter Limit Cycles

Sector nonlinearity characteristics play a major role in the study of digital filter limit cycles [15]. Consider the roundoff quantizer in figure 1.5. This function is inside the sector [0, 2] (see [3,15] for other quantizers and their

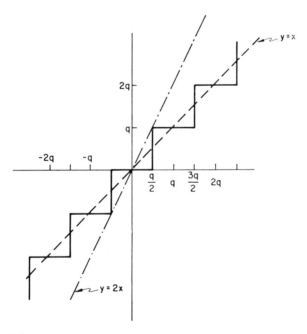

1.5
A roundoff quantizer.

sector characteristics). Using simply the sector nature of a nonlinearity, Claasen et al. [15] prove the following.

THEOREM 1.8   Consider the feedback system of figure 1.3, where f is in the sector $[0, k]$. Then limit cycles of period N are absent if

$$\text{Re}\left(G(e^{j2\pi l/N})\right) + 1/k > 0 \quad \text{for } l = 0, 1, \ldots, N - 1. \quad \blacksquare \tag{29}$$

If we also take the nondecreasing nature of f into account, we obtain [15] theorem 1.9.

THEOREM 1.9.   If f is inside the sector $[0, k]$ and is nondecreasing, then limit cycles of period N are absent from the system of figure 1.3 if there exist $\alpha_p \geq 0$ such that

$$\text{Re}\left\{\left[1 + \sum_{p=1}^{N-1} \alpha_p(1 - e^{j2\pi lp/N})\right] G(e^{j2\pi l/N})\right\} + 1/k > 0. \quad \blacksquare \tag{30}$$

If we take α_{N-1} to be the only nonzero α_p, we obtain the condition derived by Barkin [16] which is quite similar to Tsypkin's criterion (28). Note also the relationship between (29) and (27). The proofs given in [15] rely heavily on the passivity relations (29), (30). Theorem 1.8 then follows from an application of Parseval's theorem in order to contradict the existence of a limit cycle of period N. This last step involves the assumed periodicity in a crucial way, but the application of Parseval's theorem and the use of the positive real relationship (29) is reminiscent of stability arguments in feedback control theory [42]. The proof of theorem 1.9 uses the monotonicity of f in conjunction with a version of the *rearrangement inequality* [40, 42].

THEOREM 1.10   Let $\{x_n\}$ and $\{y_n\}$ be two sequences of real numbers that are similarly ordered; that is,

$$x_n \leq x_m \Rightarrow y_n \leq y_m. \tag{31}$$

If π is any permutation, then

$$\sum_n x_n y_n \geq \sum_n x_{\pi(n)} y_n. \quad \blacksquare \tag{32}$$

COROLLARY [40]   If f is a monotone function, then for any sequence $\{x_n\}$ and any permutation π

$$\sum_n f(x_n)[x_n - x_{\pi(n)}] \geq 0. \quad \blacksquare \tag{33}$$

Theorem 1.9 resembles the multiplier-type results of Popov and Tsypkin. In addition, Willems and Brockett [40, 42] utilize the rearrangement inequality to obtain a general multiplier stability result for discrete-time systems with single monotone nonlinearities. A thorough understanding of the relationships among these results might lead to new results on nonexistence of limit cycles. In addition, Claasen et al. [15] have improved (30) if f is also antisymmetric $(f(-x) = -f(x))$ and have devised linear programming techniques to search for the coefficients α_p in (30). This algorithmic concept may prove useful in developing search techniques for other, more complex multipliers. Cook [70] has recently reported several criteria for the absence of limit cycles in continuous-time systems. His results bear a strong relationship to those of Claasen et al. [15]. In particular, passivity conditions and Parseval's theorem are used in very similar ways in the two papers.

1.3.3 Relationships between Passivity and Lyapunov Functions

We now turn to the relationships between input-output concepts and questions of internal stability (the response to initial conditions). If we have an internal, state-space representation of a system with specific input-output behavior G (with $G(0) = 0$), we clearly cannot deduce asymptotic stability from input-output stability without some conditions on the state-space realization. For example, the map $G \equiv 0$ is input-output stable, but the realizations

$$\begin{aligned} \dot{x}(t) &= x(t), & y(t) &= x(t), \\ \dot{x}(t) &= x(t)+u(t) & y(t) &= 0, \end{aligned} \tag{34}$$

are clearly not asymptotically stable. In the first case the state space has an unstable mode, but if we start at $x(0) = 0$ (as we would to realize G), we can never excite this mode. Hence I/O stability can tell us nothing about it. In the second case we can excite the mode but we cannot observe it. These are precisely the difficulties that can arise; however, if one imposes certain controllability and observability conditions on the realization, one can deduce asymptotic stability from I/O stability. Thus controllability and observability play a crucial role in translating from I/O results to Lyapunov-type stability results. For a precise statement of the relationship between the two see [49, 69].

With this relationship established, it is natural to discuss the generation of Lyapunov functions for systems satisfying some type of passivity condition. Willems [49, 50, 69] has done some important work in this area. In [49, 69] he discusses the generation of Lyapunov functions for I/O stable systems. For passive systems he defines the notions of available and required energy as the solution of certain variational problems. If one then has a state-space realization satisfying certain controllability and observability conditions, one can use these functions as Lyapunov functions. This very general, physically motivated theory is further developed in [50]. Dissipative systems and the associated notions of storage function (an internal variable) and supply rate (input-output quantity) are defined; much as with Fettweis' pseudopassivity, dissipative systems have many appealing properties, such as preservation under interconnections. See [50, 69] for details of topics such as the construction of storage functions and their use as Lyapunov functions.

We mentioned that many frequency domain results can be derived with Lyapunov-type arguments. We have also seen that many of these results can be derived by using passivity arguments. Clearly the two are related, and the crucial result that leads to this relationship is the Kalman-Yacubovich-Popov lemma [61, 62, 69], which relates the positive realness of certain transfer functions to the existence of solutions to particular matrix equalities and inequalities. Kalman [62] utilized this result to obtain a Lyapunov-type proof of the Popov criterion, and Szegö [61; see also 33] used a discrete-time version to obtain a Lyapunov-theoretic proof of Tsypkin's criterion and several extensions when the derivative of the nonlinearity is bounded. Several other researchers [1, 38, 39] have utilized similar ideas to relate positive real functions to the existence of certain Lyapunov functions. It is beyond the scope of this book to discuss this problem in depth, but this area of research provides a number of insights into the relationships among various stability concepts. In addition, these results provide examples of nonlinear problems for which there exist constructive procedures for Lyapunov functions. The positive real lemma plays a crucial role in several other problems, including stochastic realization and spectral factorization [76] and the study of algebraic Riccati equations [67].

Many of these passivity-Lyapunov results have instability counterparts [1, 39]. The detailed development in [39] describes a Lyapunov-theoretic methodology for generating instability results. Such results may be useful in developing sufficient conditions for the existence of nonzero, undriven solutions such as limit cycles.

1.4 Concluding Remarks and Speculation

In this chapter we have considered some of the aspects of stability theory that deserve the attention of researchers in both disciplines. We have not, of course, been able to consider all the topics that one might investigate. For example, the "jump phenomenon" in which small changes in input lead to large changes in output is of interest in digital filter theory [32] and has been considered in feedback control theory [42, 43] where the concept of feedback system continuity is studied. In addition, Claasen et al. [31] have introduced the concept of accessible limit cycles; its relationship to concepts of controllability and to the structure of the state transition function of the filter is an intriguing question. We have not discussed the use of describing functions in digital filter analysis. There have been several attempts in this area [5, 29], but none has proven successful [30]. Except for the work of Parker and Hess [26] and Kalman and Bertram [48], we have not spoken about bounds on the magnitudes of responses. The digital filtering area includes a number of techniques for obtaining bounds [31, 35, 56]; the latter two references use an idea of Bertram's [58] as a starting point. In control theory the notion of I/O gain [42, 44] is directly tied to response magnitude bounds, although it is not clear how tight these would be in any particular case. Finally we have not discussed stability criteria for systems with multiple nonlinearities. There are some results in this area for digital filters [3,15], and the general framework considered for feedback systems allows one to adapt results such as theorem 1.7 to the multivariable case with little difficulty (hence one can readily obtain matrix versions of Tsypkin's criterion involving positive real matrices). The techniques of Lyapunov theory should also be of some use in obtaining stability results much like those in [2] for filters of higher order than the second-order section.

Many of the results in the two disciplines involve the use of very similar mathematical tools. On the other hand, the perspectives and goals of researchers in the two fields are somewhat different. The development of a mutual understanding of these perspectives and goals can only benefit researchers in both fields; in fact, such an understanding is absolutely crucial for the successful study of certain problems. For example, in the implementation of digital control systems one must come to grips with problems introduced by quantization. Digital controller limit cycles at frequencies near the resonances of the plant being controlled can lead to serious problems. In addition, the use of a digital filter in a feedback control loop creates new quantization analysis problems. Recall that limit cycles can occur only in recursive (infinite-impulse response) filters, while they do not occur in nonrecursive (finite-impulse response) filters. However, if a nonrecursive filter is used in a feedback control system, quantization errors it produces can lead to limit cycles of the closed-loop system [72]. How can one analyze this situation, and how does one take quantization effects into account in digital control system design? Questions such as these await further investigation.

1.5 Notes

1. One of the most trivial of these is the fact that control theorists put minus signs in their feedback loops, while there are none in the nonlinear digital filter of figure 1.1. The reader should be careful to make the proper changes of sign in switching between results.

2. This is of interest, for example, in the design of stability augmentation systems for aircraft. In this case one is quite interested in the shape of modes such as "Dutch roll," which involves both the bank and sideslip angles of the aircraft [71].

3. This development is by no means complete, since my intention is to relate several ideas and not to prove theorems. See the references, in particular [42], for a thorough treatment and for precise statements of the results described here. For example, I have not included a discussion of system well-posedness, which bears some similarities to the constraints on feedback paths imposed by Fettweis in his development of wave digital filters.

1.6 References

1. E. Noldus, "On the Instability of Nonlinear Systems," *IEEE Trans. Aut. Control* AC-18 (1973), pp. 404–405.

2. A. N. Willson, Jr., "Limit Cycles Due to Adder Overflow in Digital Filters," *IEEE Trans. Circ. Th.* CT-19 (1972), pp. 342–346.

3. T. A. C. M. Claasen, W. F. G. Mecklenbräuker, and J. B. H. Peek, "Effects of Quantization and Overflow in Recursive Digital Filters," *IEEE Trans. Acoust., Speech, and Sig. Proc.* ASSP-24 (1976), pp. 517–529.

4. I. W. Sandberg and J. F. Kaiser, "A Bound on Limit Cycles in Fixed-Point Implementation of Digital Filters," *IEEE Trans. Audio and Electroacoustics* AU-20 (1972), pp. 110–112.

5. J. F. Kaiser, "The Limit Cycle Problem in Digital Filters," to appear.

6. A. Fettweis, "Digital Filter Structures Related to Classical Filter Networks," *Archiv für Elecktronik und Übertrag.* 25 (1971), pp. 79–89.

7. A. Fettweis, "Some Principles of Designing Digital Filters Imitating Classical Filter Structures," *IEEE Trans. Circ. Th.* CT-18 (1971), pp. 314–316.

8. A. Fettweis, "Pseudopassitivity, Sensitivity, and Stability of Wave Digital Filters," *IEEE Trans. Circ. Th.* CT-19 (1972), pp. 668–673.

9. A. Fettweis, "Wave Digital Filters with Reduced Number of Delays," *Circuit Theory and Appl.* 2 (1974), pp. 319–330.

10. A. Fettweis and K. Meerkötter, "Suppression of Parasite Oscillations in Wave Digital Filters," *IEEE Trans. Circ. and Sys.* CAS-22 (1975), pp. 239–246.

11. K. Meerkötter and W. Wegener, "A New Second-Order Digital Filter without Parasitic Oscillations," *Archiv für Elektronik und Übertrag.* 29 (1975), pp. 312–314.

12. A. V. Oppenheim and C. J. Weinstein, "Effects of Finite Register Length in Digital Filtering and the Fast Fourier Transform," *Proc. IEEE* 60 (1972), pp. 957–976.

13. A. N. Willson, Jr., "Some Effects of Quantization and Adder Overflow on the Forced Response of Digital Filters," *Bell. Sys. Tech. J.* 51 (1972), pp. 863–887.

14. B. Eckhardt and W. Winkelnkemper, "Implementation of a Second Order Digital Filter Section with Stable Overflow Behaviour," *Nachrichtentechn. Z.* 26 (1973), pp. 282–284.

15. T. Claasen, W. F. G. Mecklenbräuker, and J. B. H. Peek, "Frequency Domain Criteria for the Absence of Zero-Input Limit Cycles in Nonlinear Discrete-Time Systems with Applications to Digital Filters," *IEEE Trans. Circ. and Sys.* CAS-22 (1975), pp. 232–239.

16. A. I. Barkin, "Sufficient Conditions for the Absence of Auto-Oscillations in Pulse Systems," *Automat. Remote Contr.* 31 (1970), pp. 942–946.

17. T. A. C. M. Claasen, W. F. G. Mecklenbräuker, and J. B. H. Peek, "On the Stability of the Forced Response of Digital Filters with Overflow Nonlinearities," *IEEE Trans. Circ. and Sys.* CAS-22 (1975), pp. 692–696.

18. T. Claasen and L. Kristiansson, "Necessary and Sufficient Conditions for the Absence of Overflow Phenomena in a Second-Order Recursive Digital Filter," *IEEE Trans. Acoust., Speech, and Sig. Proc.*, ASSP-23 (1975), pp. 509–515.

19. I. W. Sandberg, "A Theory Concerning Limit Cycles in Digital Filters," in *Proc. 7th Allerton Conf. on Circuit and System Theory*, sponsored by the Dept. of Elec. Eng. and the Coordinated Science Laboratory of the University of Illinois, Urbana-Champaign, October 1969, IEEE Catalog No. 69 C 48-CT, pp. 63–68.

20. L. B. Jackson, "An Analysis of Limit Cycles Due to Multiplication Rounding in Recursive Digital (Sub) filters," in *Proc. 7th Allerton Conf.*, Oct. 1969, Urbana, Illinois, pp. 69–78.

21. Ya. Z. Tsypkin, "Frequency Criteria for the Absolute Stability of Nonlinear Sampled Data Systems," *Automat. Remote Contr.* 25 (1964), pp. 261–267.

22. Ya. Z. Tsypkin, "Absolute Stability of a Class of Nonlinear Automatic Sampled Data Systems," *Automat. Remote Contr.* 25 (1964), pp. 918–923.

23. Ya. Z. Tsypkin, "A Criterion for Absolute Stability of Automatic Pulse Systems with Monotonic Characteristics of the Nonlinear Element," *Sov. Phys. Dokl.* 9 (1964), pp. 263–266.

24. E. I. Jury and B. W. Lee, "The Absolute Stability of Systems with Many Nonlinearities, " *Automat. Remote Contr.* 26 (1965), pp. 943–961.

25. I. W. Sandberg, "On the Boundedness of Solutions of Non-linear Integral Equations," *Bell Sys. Tech. J.* 44 (1965), pp. 439–453.

26. S. R. Parker and S. F. Hess, "Limit Cycle Oscillations in Digital Filters," *IEEE Trans. Circ. Th.* CT-18 (1971), pp. 687–697.

27. P. M. Ebert, J. E. Mago, and M. G. Taylor, "Overflow Oscillation in Digital Filters," *Bell Sys. Tech. J.* 48 (1969), pp. 2990–3020.

28. P. Vidal, *Non-Linear Sampled Data Systems*, Gordon and Breach, New York, 1969.

29. S. A. White, "Quantizer-Induced Digital Controller Limit Cycles," *IEEE Trans. Aut. Cont.* AC-14 (1969), pp. 430–432.

30. L. B. Jackson, "Comments on Quantizer-Induced Digital Controller Limit Cycles," *IEEE Trans. Aut. Contr.* AC-15 (1970), pp. 614–615.

31. T. A. C. M. Claasen, W. F. G. Mecklenbräuker, and J. B. H. Peek, "Some Remarks on the Classification of Limit Cycles in Digital Filters," *Philips Res. Repts.* 28 (1973), pp. 297–305.

32. L. Kristiansson, "The Jump Phenomenon in Digital Filters," *Electron. Lett.* 10 (1974), 14–15.

33. Ya. Z. Tsypkin, "Fundamentals of the Theory of Non-linear Pulse Control Systems," in *Proc. 2nd IFAC*, Basel, Switzerland, Butterworth & Co., Ltd., London (1964), pp. 172–180.

34. J. F. Kaiser, "Quantization Effects in Digital Filters," in Proc. Internat. Symp. Circ. Th. 1973, Catalog No. 73CHO 765-8CT, IEEE, New York (1973), pp. 415–417.

35. S. Yakowitz and S. R. Parker, "Computation of Bounds for Digital Filter Quantization Errors," *IEEE Trans. Circ. Th.* CT-20 (1973), pp. 391–396.

36. C. A. Desoer, "On the Relation between Pseudo-Passivity and Hyperstability," *IEEE Trans. Circ. and Sys.* CAS-22 (1975), pp. 897–898.

37. V. M. Popov, *Hyperstability of Control Systems*, Springer-Verlag, New York, 1973.

38. R. W. Brockett and J. L. Willems, "Frequency Domain Stability Criteria. I, II," *IEEE Trans. Auto. Contr.* AC-10 (1965), pp. 255–261, 401–413.

39. R. W. Brockett and H. B. Lee, "Frequency Domain Instability Criteria for Time-Varying and Nonlinear Systems," *Proc. IEEE* 55 (1967), pp. 604–619.

40. J. C. Willems and R. W. Brockett, "Some New Rearrangement Inequalities Having Application in Stability Analysis," *IEEE Trans. Aut. Contr.* AC-13 (1968), pp. 539–549.

41. J. C. Willems, "Stability, Instability, Invertibility, and Causality," *SIAM J. Control* (1969), pp. 645–671.

42. J. C. Willems, *The Analysis of Feedback Systems*, M.I.T. Press, Cambridge, Mass., 1971.

43. R. W. Brockett, "The Status of Stability Theory for Deterministic Systems," *IEEE Trans. Aut. Contr.* AC-11 (1966), pp. 596–606.

44. C. A. Desoer and M. Vidyasagar, *Feedback Systems: Input-Output Properties*, Academic Press, New York, 1975.

45. G. Zames, "On the Input-Output Stability of Nonlinear Time-Varying Feedback Systems. I, II," *IEEE Trans. Aut. Contr.* AC-11 (1966), pp. 228–238, 465–477.

46. I. W. Sandberg, "Some Results in the Theory of Physical Systems Governed by Nonlinear Functional Equations," *Bell Sys. Tech. J.* 44 (1965), pp. 871–898.

47. J. L. Willems, *Stability Theory of Dynamical Systems*, John Wiley and Sons, New York, 1970.

48. R. E. Kalman and J. E. Bertram, "Control Systems Analysis and Design via the Second Method of Liapunov. II: Discrete Systems," *Trans. ASME J. Basic Eng.* 82 (1960), pp. 394–400.

49. J. C. Willems, "The Construction of Lyapunov Functions for Input-Output Stable Systems," *SIAM J. Control* 9 (1971), pp. 105–134.

50. J. C. Willems, "Dissipative Dynamical Systems. I: General Theory; II: Linear Systems with Quadratic Supply Rates," *Archive for Rational Mechanics and Analysis* 45 (1972), pp. 321–343.

51. J. P. LaSalle, "An Invariance Principle in the Theory of Stability, Differential Equations and Dynamical Systems," in *Differential Equations and Dynamical Systems*, edited by J. K. Hale and J. P. LaSalle, Academic Press, New York, 1967, pp. 277–286.

52. W. Hahn, *Theory and Application of Liapunov's Direct Method*, Prentice-Hall, Englewood Cliffs, N. J., 1963.

53. B. C. Kuo, *Analysis and Synthesis of Sampled-Data Control Systems,* Prentice-Hall, Englewood Cliffs, N. J. ,1963.

54. A. Gelb and W. E. Vander Velde, *Multiple-Input Describing Functions and Nonlinear System Design*, McGraw-Hill, New York, 1968.

55. J. E. Gibson, *Nonlinear Automatic Control*, McGraw-Hill, New York, 1963.

56. S. R. Parker and S. Yakowitz, "A General Method for Calculating Quantization Error Bounds due to Roundoff in Multivariable Digital Filters," *IEEE Trans. Circ. and Sys.* CAS-22 (1975), pp. 570–572.

57. T. A. Brubaker and J. N. Gowdy, "Limit Cycles in Digital Filters," *IEEE Trans. Aut. Contr.* AC-17 (1972), pp. 675–677.

58. J. E. Bertram, "The Effect of Quantization in Sampled-Feedback Systems," *AIEE Trans (Appl. Ind.)* 77 (1958), pp. 177–181.

59. G. W. Johnson, "Upper Bound on Dynamic Quantization Error in Digital Control Systems the Direct Method of Liapunov," *IEEE Trans. Aut. Contr.* AC-10 (1965), pp. 439–448.

60. G. N. T. Lack and G. W. Johnson, "Comments on 'Upper Bound on Dynamic Quantization Error in Digital Control Systems Via the Direct Method of Liapunov,'" *IEEE Trans. Aut. Contr.* AC-11 (1966), pp. 331–334.

61. G. P. Szegö, "On the Absolute Stability of Sampled-Data Control Systems," *Proc. Nat. Acad. Sci.* 50 (1963), pp. 558–560.

62. R. E. Kalman, "Lyapunov Functions for the Problem of Lur'e in Automatic Control," *Proc. Nat. Acad. Sci.* 256 (1963), pp. 201–205.

63. G. A. Maria and M. M. Fahmy, "Limit Cycle Oscillation in a Cascade of First- and Second-Order Digital Sections," *IEEE Trans. Circ. and Syst.* CAS-22 (1975), pp. 131–134.

64. R. W. Brockett, *Finite Dimensional Linear Systems*, John Wiley and Sons, New York, 1970.

65. A. H. Jazwinski, *Stochastic Processes and Filtering Theory*, Academic Press, New York, 1970.

66. P. Dorato and A. H. Levis, "Optimal Linear Regulation: The Discrete-Time Case," *IEEE Trans. Aut. Contr.* AC-16 (1971), pp. 613–620.

67. J. C. Willems, "Least Squares Stationary Optimal Control and the Algebraic Riccati Equation," *IEEE Trans. Aut. Control* AC-16 (1971), pp. 621–634.

68. M. Athans, ed., "Special Issue on Linear-Quadratic-Gaussian Problem," *IEEE Trans. Aut. Contr.* AC-16 December (1971).

69. J. C. Willems, "Mechanisms for the Stability and Instability in Feedback Systems," *Proc. IEEE* 64 (1976), pp. 24–35.

70. P. A. Cook, "Conditions for the Absence of Limit Cycles," *IEEE Trans. Aut. Contr.* AC-21 (1976), pp. 339–345.

71. B. Etkin, *Dynamics of Atmospheric Flight*, John Wiley and Sons, New York, 1972.

72. A. Fettweis and K. Meerkötter, "On Parasite Oscillation in Digital Filters under Looped Conditions," *IEEE Trans. Circ. and Sys.* CAS-24 (1977), pp. 475–481.

73. B. D. O. Anderson and R. W. Newcomb, "Linear Passive Networks: Functional Theory," *Proc. IEEE* 64 (1976), pp. 72–88.

74. J. M. Holtzman, *Nonlinear System Theory*, Prentice-Hall, Englewood Cliffs, N. J., 1970.

75. A. V. Oppenheim and R. W. Schafer, *Digital Signal Processing*, Prentice-Hall, Englewood Cliffs, N. J., 1975.

76. P. Faurre, "Representation of Stochastic Processes," Ph.D. dissertation, Stanford University, 1967.

2

Parameter
Identification,
Linear Prediction,
Least Squares, and
Kalman Filtering

2.1 Basic Problems in Both Disciplines

A problem of great importance in many disciplines is determining the parameters of a model given observations of the physical process being modeled. In control theory this problem is often called the system identification problem, and it arises in many contexts. The special issue of the *IEEE Transactions on Automatic Control* [15] and the survey paper of Åström and Eykhoff [16] provide detailed discussions and numerous references on this problem. One of the most important applications of identification methods is adaptive estimation and control. Consider the situation depicted in figure 2.1 Here we have a physical process to be controlled or whose state is to be estimated. Many of the most widely used estimation and control techniques are based on a dynamic model (transfer function, state-space description) of the system. Hence it is necessary to obtain an appropriate model to apply these techniques. One can often perform tests on the process before designing the system and can apply an identification procedure to determine the system. On the other hand, in some cases the values of system parameters cannot be determined a priori or they vary during system operation. In such cases one may design a controller or estimator that depends explicitly on these parameters. In this manner we can adjust the parameters on-line as we perform real-time parameter identification. A number of such methods

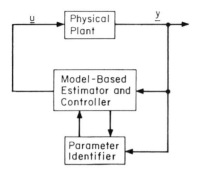

2.1
Conceptual diagram of an adaptive estimator-controller utilizing on-line parameter identification.

exist [15, 16, 80, 81, 98][1]. In addition to the problem of parameter identification, control engineers are sometimes concerned with the problem of identifying the appropriate structure for a parametric model of a process. We will not consider this issue in much detail in this chapter; see several of the papers in [15] on canonical forms and identifiability and the work of Rissanen and Ljung [79].

Parameter identification problems also arise in several digital signal-processing applications. Several examples of such problems are given in the special issue of the *Proceedings of the IEEE* [99]; the examples include (see [26]) seismic signal processing and the analysis, coding, and synthesis of speech. This latter application, which has received a great deal of attention in the past few years [24–26, 28–30, 44–55, 69–71, 74], forms a basis for our discussion of the identification question. We follow the work of Atal (48), Atal and Schroeder [70], Markel and Gray [44], and Makhoul [26]. Our presentation is necessarily brief and intuitive.

A popular and widely accepted model [44] for a discretized speech signal $\{y(k)\}$ is as the output of a linear system that can be considered time-invariant over short intervals of time

$$Y(z) = G(z)U(z), \tag{1}$$

where G represents the overall transfer function and $U(z)$ is the z-transform of the input, which is often taken as a periodic pulse train (whose period is the pitch period) for voiced sounds and as white noise for unvoiced sounds. In addition, a common assumption is that G is an all-pole filter

$$G(z) = 1/1 + \sum_{k=1}^{p} a_z z^{-k}. \tag{2}$$

This assumption has been justified in the literature under most conditions, although strong nasal sounds require zeros [44]. Note that under condition (2), equation (1) represents an autoregressive (AR) process

$$y(k) + a_1 y(k-1) + \ldots + a_p y(k-p) = u(k). \tag{3}$$

The problem now is to determine the coefficients $a_1, \ldots, a_p$. With these coefficients one can solve a number of speech analysis and communication problems. For example, one can use the model given by (2) to estimate formant frequencies and bandwidths, where the formants are the resonances of the vocal tract [55]. In addition, one can use equation (3) for efficient coding, transmission, and synthesis of speech [70]. As the model (1)–(3) indicates, the speech signal $y(k)$ contains highly redundant information, and a straightforward transmission of the signal requires high channel capacity for accurate reconstruction of speech. On the other hand, rearranging terms in (3)

$$y(k) = -\sum_{i=1}^{p} a_i y(k-i) + u(k), \tag{4}$$

we see that (4) represents a predictor, in which

$$\hat{y}(k) = -\sum_{i=1}^{p} a_i y(k-i) \tag{5}$$

is the one-step predicted estimate of y. Particularly in the speech problem, one often requires far fewer bits to code the prediction error u than to code the original signal y [70]. Thus one arrives at an efficient transmission scheme (linear predictive coding, LPC). Given y, estimate the a_i, compute u, transmit the a_i and u. At the receiver we then can use (4) to reconstruct y (of course, one must confront problems of quantization [119]). An alternative interpretation of this procedure is the following. Given y, estimate G in (2); pass y through the inverse, all-zero (moving average, MA) filter $1/G(z)$; transmit the coefficients in G and the output of the inverse filter. At the receiver we then pass the received signal through G to recover y (thus this procedure is causal and causally invertible).

The question that remains is how to estimate the a_i. The most widely used technique in the literature is *linear prediction*.[2] Interpreting $1 - 1/G(z)$ as a one-step predictor for the signal y, we wish to choose the coefficients $a_1, \ldots, a_p$ to minimize the sum of squares of the prediction errors[3]

$$J = \sum_n e^2(n), \qquad e(n) = y(n) - \hat{y}(n). \tag{6}$$

Here we assume that we are given $y(0), \ldots, y(N - 1)$. The range of n in the definition of J can be chosen in different manners, and different choices can lead to different results and to different interpretations. Some of these interpretations are given in [26, 44]. In the next two sections we consider two linear prediction methods—the autocorrelation and covariance methods—and we relate them to several statistical notions of importance in control and estimation applications. Following this we discuss several other identificantion methods and their relationship to the speech problem.

Before beginning these investigations, let us carry out the minimization required in linear prediction. Taking the first derivative of J with respect to the a_i and setting these equal to zero, we obtain the *normal equations*

$$\sum_{i=1}^{p} a_i c_{ik} = -c_{0k}, \qquad k = 1, \ldots, p, \tag{7}$$

where

$$c_{ik} = \sum_n y(n - i)y(n - k). \tag{8}$$

These equations are typical of equations that arise in linear, least-squares problems, and their efficient solution has been the topic of many research efforts.

2.2 The Autocorrelation Method, Kalman Filtering for Stationary Processes, and Fast Algorithms

2.2.1 The Toeplitz Normal Equations

Suppose we consider minimizing the sum-squared error in (6) over the infinite interval $-\infty < n < \infty$. Here we define $y(n) = 0$ for $n < 0$, $n \geq N$. In this case we find that

$$c_{ij} = \sum_{n=0}^{N-1-|i-j|} s(n)s(n + |i - j|) \triangleq r(|i - j|), \qquad (9)$$

and the normal equations become

$$Ta = c, \qquad (10)$$

where $a' = (a_1, \ldots, a_p)$, $c' = (-r(1), -r(2), \ldots, -r(p))$, and T is a symmetric Toeplitz matrix [37, 84, 91, 129] (the ijth element depends only on $|i - j|$)

$$T = \begin{bmatrix} r(0) & r(1) & \ldots r(p-1) \\ r(1) & r(0) & \ldots r(p-2) \\ r(2) & r(1) & \ldots r(p-3) \\ \vdots & & \\ r(p-1) & r(p-2) & \ldots r(0) \end{bmatrix}. \qquad (11)$$

Before we consider the solution to (10), let us derive equations of the same form from a probabilistic point of view [26]. Suppose that y is a stationary random process and that instead of (6) we are interested in minimizing

$$\tilde{J} = E(e^2(n)) \qquad (12)$$

where e and $\hat{y}$ are defined as before, although they now are random processes. Differentiating (12), we obtain the normal equations

$$\tilde{T}a = \tilde{c}, \qquad (13)$$

where $\tilde{c}' = (-R(1), -R(2), \ldots, R(p))$, $\tilde{T}$ is the symmetric Toeplitz matrix whose ijth element is $R(|i - j|)$, and $R(i)$ is the autocorrelation

$$R(i) = E(y(n)y(n + i)). \qquad (14)$$

From (9)–(14) we see that the two formulations are similar, and one can view (9) as a method for estimating the autocorrelation of an ergodic, stationary process [26] if we normalize (9) appropriately. This statistical point of view is extremely useful for obtaining certain insights into the approach and for connecting this method to certain recent results in linear estimation theory. Markel and Gray [44] provide several other interpretations of this method.

The solution to equations such as (10) and (13) has been the subject of a great deal of attention in the mathematical, statistical, and engineering literature [4, 7, 26, 34, 35, 36, 37, 50, 72, 84, 91, 94, 95, 96]. An efficient algorithm was proposed by Levinson [34], improved by Durbin [94], and studied in the speech-processing context by several authors, including Itakura and Saito [50]. The method essentially consists of solving forward and backward prediction problems of increasing size in a recursive manner and is known to be extremely efficient [26, 44]. That is, the algorithm computes the coefficients $a(1|i)$, ..., $a(i|i)$ for the best prediction of $y(n)$ based on $y(n - 1)$, ..., $y(n - i)$ and the coefficients $b(1|i)$, ..., $b(i|i)$ for the best prediction of $y(n - i - 1)$ based on $y(n - i)$, ..., $y(n - 1)$. The algorithm iterates on i. As a part of this algorithm, one computes the prediction error (for both forward and backward prediction), and thus one can determine when to stop based on the size of this quantity. Also, we must compute a coefficient k_i, which is known as the *partial correlation coefficient* [26, 44, 50]. We will mention this quantity again at the end of this section.

2.2.2 Probabilistic Interpretation and Relationship with the Kalman Filter
Let us now examine what this algorithm means from a statistical point of view. The first stage of the algorithm produces $a(1|1)$ and $b(1|1)$, which are the coefficients of the best one-step predictors

$$\hat{y}(1) = -a(1|1)y(0),$$
$$\hat{y}(0) = -b(1|1)y(1). \tag{15}$$

At the next stage we have $a(1|2)$, $a(2|2)$, $b(1|2)$, $b2|2)$, the coefficients of

$$\hat{y}(2) = -a(1|2)y(1) - a(2|2)y(0),$$
$$\hat{y}(0) = -b(1|2)y(1) - b(2|2)y(2). \tag{16}$$

After i steps we have the predictors

$$\hat{y}(i) = -\sum_{j=1}^{i} a(j|i)y(i - j), \tag{17}$$

$$\hat{y}(0) = -\sum_{j=1}^{i} b(j|i)y(j). \tag{18}$$

Thus the linear prediction solution gives us the *time-varying* coefficients of the weighting pattern of the optimal one-step predictor (17) or of the optimal initial time smoother (18). Note that these coefficients are in general time-varying in the following sense. From (17) we see that $a(j|i)$ is the coefficient that multiplies the data point occuring j units of time before the one whose value we wish to predict. If the filter were time-invariant, this would not depend on i. The reason that the predictor coefficients are time-varying is that although the y's are a stationary process, the mechanism of prediction is time-varying when the prediction is based on only a finite set of data (recall that the time-invariant Wiener filter assumes an infinite record of observations).

What does this mean for all-pole modeling through linear prediction? Not much. In the all-pole modeling problem we are interested only in designing a FIR filter, a prediction filter that produces the best estimate of $y(n)$ given the data window $y(n - 1), \ldots, y(n - p)$. The coefficients of such a filter are precisely $a(1|p), \ldots, a(p|p)$, and it does not matter (except from a computational point of view) that these coefficients were generated as part of a time-varying filter weighting pattern.

On the other hand, the time-varying weighting pattern interpretation is extremely important from a statistical point of view, especially if one wishes to design recursive predictors that are capable of incorporating all past measurements and not just a data window. One inefficient way to do this is to implement a nonrecursive filter that stores all past data $y(0), \ldots, y(n - 1)$, multiplies by the appropriate $a(i|n)$, and combines to form $\hat{y}(n)$. This method requires growing memory and is hardly appealing. How can one aviod such difficulties? An answer popular in state-space control and estimation theory arises if y has a Markovian representation

$$x(k + 1) = Ax(k) + w(k), \quad y(k) = c'x(k), \tag{19}$$

where x is a random n-vector ($x(0)$ is assumed to be zero mean), A is a constant $n \times n$ matrix, c is a constant n-vector, and w is a zero-mean uncorrelated sequence (uncorrelated with $x(0)$) with

$$E(w(k)w'(k)) = Q. \tag{20}$$

The correlation coefficients of y can be computed from the equations

$$E(y(k)y(j)) = c'E(x(k)x'(j))c \tag{21}$$

$$E(x(k)x'(j)) = \begin{cases} A^{k-j} \, \Pi(j), & k \geq j, \\ [E(x(j)x'(k))]', & k < j, \end{cases} \tag{22}$$

where Π is the covariance of x satisfying

$$\Pi(j + 1) = A\Pi(j)A' + Q. \tag{23}$$

In general $E(y(k)y(j))$ does not depend on $(k - j)$ alone. This type of dependence will occur and hence the process x will be stationary if and only if A is a stable matrix and $\Pi = \Pi(0)$ satisfies the Lyapunov equation

$$A\Pi A' - \Pi = -Q \tag{24}$$

(in which case both x and y are stationary).

Suppose now that (24) holds and that

$$R(|i - j|) = c'A^{|i-j|}\Pi c, \tag{25}$$

where the $R(i)$ are the quantities defined in (13)–(14). We now wish to design an optimal predictor for recursively estimating $y(n)$ given $y(0)$, . . . $y(n - 1)$. This is a standard state-space estimation problem [65], and the solution is the Kalman filter, which actually produces a prediction for the vector $x(n)$,

$$
\begin{aligned}
\hat{y}(n) &= c'\hat{x}(n),\\
\hat{x}(n) &= A\hat{x}(n - 1) + AK(n - 1)\gamma(n - 1),\\
\gamma(n - 1) &= y(n - 1) - \hat{y}(n - 1),\\
\hat{x}(0) &= 0,
\end{aligned}
\tag{26}
$$

where the time-varying gain satisfies[4]

$$K(n) = \frac{P(n|n - 1)c}{c'P(n|n - 1)c}. \tag{27}$$

Here $P(n|n - 1)$ is the covariance of the prediction error $x(n) - \hat{x}(n)$,

$$P(n + 1|n) = AP(n|n - 1)A' + Q - \frac{AP(n|n - 1)cc'P(n|n - 1)A'}{c'P(n|n - 1)c} \tag{28}$$

The *filter innovations* sequence $\gamma(n)$ is precisely the sequence of prediction errors, and the covariance of $\gamma(n)$ is $c'P(n|n - 1)c$, which is nothing more than (12). In the all-pole framework, we could alternatively view the prediction filter as specifying an inverse filter, which took the y's as inputs and produced the uncorrelated sequence of prediction errors as the output. In the context of the Kalman filter the analogous concept is the *innovations representation* (see representation IR-1 of [67]), in which we view the output of (26) as $\gamma(n)$. Note also that one can compute the predictor coefficients $a(j|i)$ as the weighting pattern of the filter

$$a(1|1) = -c'AK(0),$$

$$a(1|2) = -c'AK(1), \qquad a(2|2) = -c'A^2K(0) + c'AK(1)c'AK(0), \qquad (29)$$

$$\vdots$$

The Kalman filter and innovations representations have been the subjects of much research in the last fifteen years, and this technique has been studied in discrete and continuous time[5], for multiple-output systems, for time-varying systems, and for systems in which the actual observations are noisy versions of y's

$$z(n) = y(n) + v(n). \qquad (30)$$

There are many references on this subject, including, [7, 58, 67, 148].

2.2.3 Fast Algorithms
From (26)–(28) we see that the computation of the recursive filter coefficients requires the solution to the (discrete-time) Riccati equation (28). If x is an n-vector, then since P is symmetric, (28) represents $n(n + 1)/2$ equations. For reasonably large values of n this can be an extreme computational load, especially since all that is needed for the filter is the gain matrix K, which in the scalar-output case is an n-vector. If there are m outputs, K is $n \times m$ and as is often the case m is subtantially smaller than n and the number of parameters in K is much smaller than the number in P. Thus the question of computing K without P arises quite naturally. This issue—in both continuous and discrete time, in stationary and in some nonstationary cases—has been the subject of numerous papers in the recent past [1–8, 23, 39, 40, 56, 60, 64–66, 72, 73, 77].

It is not our intention to discuss these techniques in detail, but we want to point out that the underlying concepts leading to these "fast algorithms" (at least in the stationary case) are closely related to those leading to the Levinson algorithm. For some historical and mathematical perspective on this subject, see [4, 7, 63, 66]. The extension of the Levinson algorithm to the multivariable case is discussed in these papers (see also references [35, 36]). In this case, the matrix T in (10) or (12) is block-Toeplitz, and the extension to this case is nontrivial. For other methods of handling equations involving block-Toeplitz matrices see [37, 56, 84, 91, 95, 96]. In [4] it is shown that the derivation of the Levinson-type algorithms and Kalman gain equations in discrete and continuous time in the stationary case rely on the simultaneous solution of forward and backward filtering problems, thus introducing a backward innovation process representing backward prediction errors. This study also shows that both continuous and discrete algorithms can be obtained from the Bellman-Krein formulas [4, 7, 42, 43, 64, 65, 66], which describe the evolution of the weighting pattern of the optimal estimator of a stationary process. From this one can obtain the Levinson algorithm, its continuous analog, and some well-known relationships with orthogonal polynomials [4, 41]. If the process y has a Markovian representation, the Levinson-type equations and the state-space representation can be used to obtain fast algorithms for the Kalman gain. An excellent treatment of this is given in [4]; compare the discrete-time results in [4] to those in [26, 44] to see the relationship between the linear prediction equations and the version of the Levinson algorithm derived in [4]. For a thorough historical perspective we recommend the survey paper [7] and the insights provided in [130].

In this chapter we limit ourselves to a brief outline of one of the derivations in [4]. Let $y(n)$ be a vector-stationary, zero-mean process with covariance

$$R(t - s) = E(y(t)y(s)'). \tag{31}$$

We observe the process[6]

$$z(n) = y(n) + w(n), \tag{32}$$

where w is a zero-mean white process, uncorrelated with y, with covariance

$$E(w(n)w(n)') = I. \tag{33}$$

Let $\hat{y}(t|r)$ denote the wide-sense conditional mean of $y(t)$ given $z(0), \ldots, z(r)$; then [4]

$$\hat{y}(t|r) = \sum_{s=0}^{r} G_r(t, s)z(s), \tag{34}$$

where the weighting pattern is defined by

$$G_r(t, s) = E[\tilde{y}(t|r)\tilde{y}(s|r)'] = G_r(s, t)'. \tag{35}$$

Here $\tilde{y}(i|j)$ is the estimation error $y(i) - \hat{y}(i|j)$. The G_r satisfy the Toeplitz equations

$$G_r(t, s) + \sum_{i=0}^{r} G_r(t, i)R(i - s) = R(t - s),$$

$$G_r(t, s) + \sum_{i=0}^{r} R(t - i)G_r(i, s) = R(t - s). \qquad (36)$$

Note that $\hat{y}(t|t - 1)$ is the one-step prediction estimate, and from (34) we can identify (in the scalar case)

$$G_{t-1}(t, s) = -a(t - s|t). \qquad (37)$$

Comparing (36) and (37) with (7), (13), and (14), we see that we have similar equations; the first term on the left-hand side of (36) comes from the presence of w, but these equations can also be obtained when $w = 0$ if we can write $R = \tilde{R} + \varepsilon I$ for some positive semidefinite $\tilde{R}$ [9]. As [4] points out the Toeplitz equations are the counterparts of certain Fredholm resolvent equations that arise in the continuous case [64, 65].

Lindquist's derivation of the fast algorithms for computing $G_{t-1}(t, s)$ (one-step prediction) and $G_t(t, s)$ (filtering estimte) begins with the Bellman-Krein formulas:[7]

$$G_{r+1}(t, s) = G_r(t, s) - G_{r+1}(t, r + 1)G_r(r + 1, s),$$

$$G_{r+1}(t, s) = G_r(t, s) - G_r(t, r + 1)G_{r+1}(r + 1, s).$$

We next define the backwards weighting pattern

$$G_r^*(t, s) = G_r(r - t, r - s) \qquad (38)$$

and the matrix polynomials

$$\phi_t(z) = I - \sum_{s=1}^{t} z^s G_{t-1}^*(s - 1, -1), \qquad (39)$$

$$\phi_t^*(z) = z^t \left[I - \sum_{s=1}^{t} z^{-s} G_{t-1}(s - 1, -1) \right]. \qquad (40)$$

In the scalar case these polynomials are related to the Szegö polynomials [4]. If we let $\phi_{t,i}$ denote the coefficient of z^i in ϕ (similarly for ϕ^*), and if we use (34), (35), (38)–(40), we obtain the prediction and smoothing equations

$$\hat{y}(t|t-1) = - \sum_{i=0}^{t-1} \phi'_{t, t-i} z(i). \qquad (41)$$

$$\hat{y}(-1|t-1) = -\sum_{i=0}^{t-1}(\phi^*_{t,t-i-1})'z(i).\tag{42}$$

Thus if we can recursively compute ϕ_t and ϕ^*_t, we can recursively solve for the weighting pattern of the desired predictor. Utilizing the Bellman-Krein equations, Lindquist derives these recursions, which yield the multivariable Levinson equations

$$\phi_{t+1}(z) = \phi_t(z) - z\phi^*_t(z)\Gamma^*_t, \qquad \phi_0(z) = I,\tag{43}$$

$$\phi^*_{t+1}(z) = z\phi^*_t(z) - \phi_t(z)\Gamma_t, \qquad \phi^*_0(z) = I,\tag{44}$$

$$R_{t+1} = R_t - (\Gamma^*_t)'R^*_t\Gamma^*_t,\tag{45}$$

$$R^*_{t+1} = R^*_t - \Gamma'_tR_t\Gamma_t,\tag{46}$$

$$S_t = R(t+1) - \sum_{i=0}^{t-1}R(t-i)G_{t-1}(i,-1),\tag{47}$$

$$(\Gamma^*_t)'(R^*_t)' = S_t = R_t\Gamma_t.\tag{48}$$

Here R_t plays the role of forward prediction error, R^*_t is the backwards error, and Γ_t and Γ^*_t are the multidimensional analogs of the partial correlation coefficient. These relationships can be seen much more easily if one looks at the scalar case and uses the following special relationships that hold in this case.

$$\phi_t(z) = z^t\phi^*_t(z^{-1}), \qquad \Gamma^*_t = \Gamma_t.\tag{49}$$

Then the algorithm becomes

$$\phi^*_{t+1}(z) = z\phi^*_t(z) - z^t\phi^*_t(z^{-1})\Gamma_t,\tag{50}$$

$$R_{t+1} = R_t(1 - \Gamma^2_t),\tag{51}$$

$$\Gamma_t = \left[R(t+1) - \sum_{i=0}^{t-1}R(t-i)G_{t-1}(i,-1)\right]\bigg/R_t,\tag{52}$$

and the comparisons with the usual Levinson equations (equations (38a)–(38d) in [26] are clear. Note that in the scalar case the forward and backward predictors are essentially the same, a statement that is not true in the vector case.

Lindquist next considers the case in which the y's have a Markovian representation. Using the algorithm (43)–(48), he obtains a fast algorithm for the Kalman gain. For the details of this derivation see [4] .

It is worth noting that the starting point for this extremely efficient algorithm for solving Toeplitz normal equations is the empirical correlation function (9) or a statistically specified one (14). Once one has these correlations, the fast algorithms greatly reduce the remaining computational burden in obtaining the optimal predictor coefficients. However, if we must first calculate $r(i)$ as in (9), the computational load of the overall linear prediction procedure is greatly increased, and the effect of using the Levinson algorithm is not as dramatic. This point is important in assessing the true impact of these fast algorithms.

Numerous physical and mathematical relationships between fast algorithms have been derived in a number of disciplines. The auxiliary variable k_i in the scalar Levinson algorithm[8] can be interpreted as a reflection coefficient [26, 44]. This fact has been utilized in speech processing, in which these coefficients specify certain parameters in an acoustic model of the speech process [26, 44], and in geophysics to model the acoustic transmission response of the earth [139]. Casti and Tse [40], Kailath [6, 7], and Sidhu and Casti [117] have shown that the fast Kalman gain algorithms are closely related to the work of certain astrophysicists, in particular Chandrasekhar [38], who devised algorithms for solving finite-time Wiener-Hopf equations arising in radiative transfer. Relationships between linear filtering and scattering theory have been brought to light in recent papers [77, 101, 102]. Seeing these algorithms from several perspectives allows us to gain insight into their properties, potentials, and limitations.

For a good overview of some of the mathematical relationships see [7, 125, 129]. In addition, a great deal of work is being done in exploring and exploiting the mathematical relationships. An approach to the efficient inversion of general matrices is given in [142]. This technique can be viewed as a generalization of the Levinson algorithm because the efficiency of the inversion process is directly related to how nearly Toeplitz the matrix to be inverted is. In addition, in [140, 141] the Chandrasekhar fast algorithms are tied in with square-root filtering algorithms, and extremely efficient methods for solving for the Kalman gain are developed. See these papers and the references in them for more on square-root algorithms; see [140] for a concise picture of the Chandrasekhar equations.

2.3 The Covariance Method, Recursive Least-Squares Identification, and Kalman Filters

2.3.1 Solving the Symmetric Normal Equations

Consider again the normal equations (7), (8). We now consider the range of n to be only as large as the actual data allow; in equation (3), $k, k - 1$, ..., $k - p$ must all be within the range $0, ..., N - 1$. Thus the range for n is

$$p \leq n \leq N - 1. \tag{53}$$

In this case the normal equations become

$$Sa = -d, \tag{54}$$

where $d' = (c_{01}, c_{02}, ..., c_{0p})$ and S is the symmetric matrix whose ijth element is c_{ij}. Note that c_{ij} is not in general a function of $i - j$, and thus S is not Toeplitz.

This method also has several interpretations. Makhoul [26] shows that one can obtain equations of identical form as the linear least-squares predictor for a nonstationary process. In addition, if one makes a Gaussian assumption, then the covariance method produces the conditional maximum likelihood estimate of a, given $y(0), ..., y(p - 1)$. See [44] for several other interpretations of the covariance method.

The fast methods described in the preceding section do not carry over quite so nicely for solving (54), since S is not Toeplitz. Markel and Gray [44] describe a method analogous to the Levinson routine; this method iterates on the order of the predictor filter and computes forward and backward predictors simultaneously. However, it is not nearly as efficient for solving the normal equations as the Levinson Algorithm is in the autocorrelation case, because (49) does not hold in this case even for the one-dimensional problem. The solution to the autocorrelation and covariance equations can be viewed as a Cholesky decomposition, or equivalently a Gram-Schmidt orthogonalization, of T and S [44]. In the Toeplitz case very fast algorithms exist for Cholesky decomposition [37, 72], while this procedure is somewhat slower for symmetric, non-Toeplitz matrices. Recently, however, Morf et al. [71] have obtained fast algorithms for the covariance method by exploiting the fact that S, though not Toeplitz, is the product of Toeplitz matrices (see equations (56)–(59)).

See [71] for the details of several algorithms that essentially embed the original scalar prediction problem into a multidimensional problem to which the fast-vector Levinson algorithm can be applied.

2.3.2 Recursive Least-Squares Interpretation and the Tracking of Parameters

Let us look at the covariance method from a slightly different point of view. Recall that the Levinson algorithm and its analog for the covariance method involve recursions on the order of the filter given a fixed set of data. Now we consider a recursion for updating coefficients of a fixed-order filter given more and more data. To do this, we refer to the survey paper [16], where the covariance method, termed the "least-squares method," is discussed.[9] Given the data $y(0), \ldots, y(N-1)$, the covariance method attempts to find a least-squares fit to the equation

$$L_{N-1} a = f_{N-1}, \tag{55}$$

where

$$L_{N-1} = \begin{bmatrix} -y(p-1) & -y(p-2) & \cdots & -y(0) \\ -y(p) & -y(p-1) & \cdots & -y(1) \\ -y(p+1) & -y(p) & \cdots & -y(2) \\ \vdots & & & \vdots \\ -y(n-2) & -y(N-3) & \cdots & -y(N-p-1) \end{bmatrix},$$

$$a = \begin{bmatrix} a_1 \\ \vdots \\ a_p \end{bmatrix}, \quad f_{N-1} = \begin{bmatrix} y(p) \\ y(p+1) \\ \vdots \\ y(N-1) \end{bmatrix},$$

The least-squares solution is given by

$$(L'_{N-1} L_{N-1})\, \hat{a} = L'_{N-1} f_{N-1}, \tag{56}$$

which is identical to (54). Thus the covariance method computes

$$\hat{a}(N-1) = (L'_{N-1} L_{N-1})^{-1} L_{N-1} f_{N-1}. \tag{57}$$

Suppose we have $\hat{a}(N-1)$, and we now obtain the new data point $y(N)$. We would like to update our estimate to $\hat{a}(N)$ more efficiently than solving

(56) from scratch. Following standard recursive least-squares (RLS) procedures [16], we note that incorporation of $y(N)$ into (55) adds a new equation; that is it adds a last row to L_{N-1}

$$l'(N) = (-y(N-1), -y(N-2), \ldots, -y(N-p))$$

and a last element $y(N)$ to f_{N-1}. Thus (55) takes the form

$$\begin{bmatrix} L_{N-1} \\ l'(N) \end{bmatrix} a = \begin{bmatrix} f_{N-1} \\ y(N) \end{bmatrix}, \tag{58}$$

and (57) becomes

$$\hat{a}(N) = [L'_{N-1}L_{N-1} + l(N)l'(N)]^{-1}[L'_{N-1}f_{N-1} + l(N)y(N)]. \tag{59}$$

With the aid of the matrix inversion lemma [146], we can rewrite (59) as

$$\hat{a}(N) = \hat{a}(N-1) + K(N)[y(N) - l'(N)a(N-1)], \tag{60}$$

where

$$K(N) = \frac{P(N-1)l(N)}{1 + l'(N)P(N-1)l(N)} \tag{61}$$

and

$$P(N) = (L'_N L_N)^{-1} = P(N-1) - \frac{P(N-1)l(N)l'(N)P(N-1)}{1 + l'(N)P(N-1)l(N)}. \tag{62}$$

These equations represent a Kalman filter [17]. In fact, they are precisely the Kalman filter equations used by Gibson et al. in speech processing [24, 47]. They consider the dynamic equations

$$a(k+1) = a(k), \tag{63}$$

$$y(k) = z'(k)a(k) + v(k), \tag{64}$$

where

$$z'(k) = -(y(k-1), y(k-2), \ldots, y(k-p)) \tag{65}$$

and $v(k)$ is a zero-mean, white process with

$$E(v^2(k)) = \Psi. \tag{66}$$

Setting Ψ to 1 gives the solution to the covariance equations. In this formulation $P(N)$ can be interpreted as the covariance of the estimation error $a - \hat{a}(N)$.

Note some of the properties of the recurisve solution (60)–(62). From (60) we see that the increment in our estimate $\hat{a}$ is proportional to the error (innovations) in predicting the latest value of y using preceding values and our previous estimate of a. This suggests that the residuals

$$r(N) = y(N) - l'(N)\hat{a}(N - 1) \tag{67}$$

can be monitored to help detect abrupt changes in the predictor coefficients[10] or the presence of glottal excitation in voiced sounds. In this manner one may be able to improve the estimation of a. Whether such a procedure would be of value is a matter for future study. Such techniques have been developed and successfully applied to a variety of problems including the detection of arrhythmias in electrocardiograms [103, 104]. Also, the filter can be made more responsive to changes in the coefficients by using one of several methods available for adjusting Kalman filters [146]. These include exponentially age-weighting old data in favor of the more recent pieces of information or modeling a as a slowly varying Markov process

$$a(k + 1) = Aa(k) + w(k), \tag{68}$$

where A is a stable matrix and w is zero-mean white noise with covariance Q. In this case equations (60)–(62) become

$$\hat{a}(N) = A\hat{a}(N - 1) + K(N)[y(n) - l'(N)A\hat{a}(N - 1)], \tag{69}$$

$$K(N) = \frac{P(N|N - 1)l(N)}{1 + l'(N)P(N|N - 1)l(N)}, \tag{70}$$

$$P(N|N - 1) = AP(N - 1|N - 1)A' + Q, \tag{71}$$

$$P(N|N) = P(N|N - 1) - \frac{P(N|N - 1)l(N)l'(N)P(N|N - 1)}{1 + l'(N)P(N|N - 1)l(N)}. \tag{72}$$

Again, the utility of such a procedure is not clear; further thought and experimentation are necessary.

Let us now consider the computational complexity of (60)–(62). We do not have to compute the correlation coefficients (elements of S in (54)), but we do have to calculate $K(N)$ at every stage, and if we solve for the gain from the Riccati equation (62), there are on the order of p^2 multiplications per stage. This computational burden has so far kept recursive methods such as recursive least squares from being adopted in speech processing. However, Morf et al. [71] and Morf and Ljung [120] have exploited the structure of the equations to obtain fast algorithms for the direct computation of K. Thus the results in [71, 120] give us efficient recursive procedures for the covariance method as we increase either the order p of the predictor or the number N of data points (or both simultaneously). The most efficient procedure is to use $p = 1$ and process the data points successively. At the end of this procedure p can be increased until an acceptable prediction error is obtained [71, 120].

Gibson et al. [47] have proposed a filter of the same structure as (60)–(62) but requiring far fewer multiplications per stage (the order of p). This procedure is based on stochastic approximation methods and replaces (61)–(62) with

$$K(N) = \frac{gl(N)}{100 + l'(N)\,l(N)}, \tag{73}$$

where g is a gain to be determined by experimentation [47][11]. See [24, 47] for details and experimental results.

Finally we turn to the relative merits of the autocorrelation and covariance methods. Makhoul points out [115, 143] that the autocorrelation method guarantees the stability of the resulting all-pole filter; however, the method's reliance on setting $y(i) = 0$ outside the available range of data leads to spectral distortion. The covariance method avoids the distortion problem because it does not consider points outside the given range, but it need not lead to a stable filter. Stability for these methods is guaranteed if and only if all the reflection coefficients have magnitude less than one [30, 115], and a number of modified covariance-type methods that have this property have been devised. This work is related to the so-called lattice and ladder forms for all-pole models. These structures explicitly involve the partial correlation coefficients in their implementation. Itakura and Saito [30] were among the first to use such structures with a modified covariance algorithm for speech processing, and recently a number of researchers have examined this type of formulation [143, 147] One of the best known is Burg's maximum entropy spectral estimation algorithm [145]. Taking this as a starting point, Morf et al. [144, 146, 147] have performed detailed studies on ladder forms, and they have developed efficient algorithms for solving for the reflection coefficients and methods for recursively updating these coefficients as more data become available.

Makhoul presents a particularly nice overview of the ideas behind lattice methods and develops a class of new algorithms guaranteeing stability [143]. Morf et al. [71] point out that if we use a hybrid method—define $y(i) = 0$, $N + 1 < i < N + p$ but do not use $y(j)$, $j < 0$—we can guarantee the stability of the resulting filter and still obtain fast algorithms as the covariance matrix is the product of Toeplitz matrices.

2.4 Design of a Predictor as a Stochastic Realization Problem

2.4.1 The Basic Problem and Its Relationship to Spectral Factorization

A problem that has attracted a great deal of attention in the control and estimation literature is the stochastic realization problem [7, 11, 13, 15, 20, 21, 22, 37, 63, 67, 72, 85, 90, 105]. A special version of the stochastic realization problem asks the following. Given a stationary Gaussian random process y (taken as a scalar here for simplicity[12]) with correlation function $R(n)$, find a Markovian representation

$$x(n + 1) = Ax(n) + w(n), \qquad y(n) = c'x(n), \tag{74}$$

where w is a zero-mean white noise process with covariance Q. Referring to (19)–(25), we see that this is equivalent to finding a factorization of R of the form

$$R(i) = c'A^ib, \tag{75}$$

where

$$b = Pc, \qquad APA' - P = -Q. \tag{76}$$

From (75) and (76) we see that the algorithm falls naturally into two steps: (i) find a triple (A, b, c) satisfying (75); (ii) find P and Q satisfying (76). One of the best-known studies of this problem is that of Faurre [21, 57, 85]. As he pointed out, the first step of the algorithm is simply the well-known deterministic realization problem given the weighting pattern $R(0)$, $R(1)$, $R(2)$, ... The problem has been widely studied in the literature [9, 10, 11, 12, 13, 14, 72, 106, 107]. Before we discuss the numerical aspects of the first step or the details of the second, let us see what the first part yields in the frequency domain [63]. Define the power spectral density

$$S_y(z) = \sum_{i=-\infty}^{+\infty} R(i)z^{-i}. \tag{77}$$

Then since $R(-i) = R(i)$, the factorization (75) yields[13]

$$S_y(z) = c'(zI - A)^{-1}zb + c'(z^{-1}I - A)^{-1}Ab. \tag{78}$$

Noting the form of (78) and defining

$$\alpha(z) = \det (zI - A), \tag{79}$$

we see that the first step in the algorithm yields[14]

$$S_y(z) = \frac{p(z)}{\alpha(z)\alpha(z^{-1})}. \tag{80}$$

That is, we have factored the denominator of S_y. If we can also factor the numerator

$$S_y(z) = \frac{\mu\beta(z)\beta(z^{-1})}{\alpha(z)\alpha(z^{-1})} \qquad (\mu > 0), \tag{81}$$

we will have determined the desired transfer function[15]

$$G(z) = \beta(z)/\alpha(z) \tag{82}$$

which, when driven by white noise with spectrum $\mu^{1/2}$, yields the spectrum $S_y(z)$. It is clear from (74) that the second part of the spectral factorization is accomplished by the second step of the stochastic realization algorithm. Finally note that the model (82) contains both poles and zeros (it is an autoregressive-moving-average (ARMA) model).

2.4.2 The Two-Step Algorithm

There are several methods for performing the second step of the algorithm. Faurre [21, 85] showed that (76) could be solved for some values of P inside a given range

$$P_* \leq P \leq P^* \tag{83}$$

(here inequality is in the matrix sense), and he identified the smallest such covariance P_* as that arising from an innovations representation of y—that is, a Kalman filter (see Gevers-Kailath [67] for a full description). This representation is of the form

$$\xi(n + 1) = A\xi(n) + K\varepsilon(n + 1), \tag{84}$$

$$y(n) = c'\xi(n),\tag{85}$$

where ε is an innovations process with covariance

$$R_\varepsilon = c'b - c'P_*c\tag{86}$$

and P_* is the solution of the algebraic Riccati equation

$$P_* = AP_*A' + \frac{A[b - P_*c][b - P_*c]'A'}{c'b - c'P_*c}.\tag{87}$$

Then the Kalman gain is given by

$$K = \frac{[b - P_*c]}{c'b - c'P_*c}.\tag{88}$$

Comparing this with (26), we see several differences. First in (26) we had an equation of the form

$$\hat{x}(n + 1) = A\hat{x}(n) + AK\varepsilon(n), \qquad y(n) = c'\hat{x}(n) + \varepsilon(n).\tag{89}$$

The differences between (84) and (89) can be explained by noting that (84) is a representation based on the filtered estimate of $x(n)$ given $y(0), \ldots, y(n)$ and (89) is the one-step predicted estimate of $x(n)$ given $y(0), \ldots, y(n - 1)$. It is easy to pass from one representation to the other [67].

Thus from (84)–(88) we see that the second step of the algorithm consists of solving the equations defining a steady-state Kalman filter. Again the most difficult step is solving for the covariance—in this case P_*—from the nonlinear equation (87). However, P_* is not needed in (84). All we really need are R_ε and K. Thus an alternative procedure is to use the fast algorithms of section 2.2 [63, 69]. These will produce the time-varying histories of K and R_ε. If we let the transients (due to the finite data with which the filter must work to produce an estimate) die out, we will obtain K and R_ε. Although this approach involves solving for K and R_ε recursively (in time), this procedure may be much faster than direct solution of (86)–(88).

Once we have K, we have determined the optimal recursive predictor or filter; comparing (26) and (89), we can readily turn the innovations representation into a one-step predictor. This model is causal and causally invertible [67, 69]. Hence the method can be interpreted as an inverse filter approach to the identification of $G(z)$; that is, we have equivalently determined the optimal predictor or a whitening filter. This method also allows for zeros in the model. Morf et al. proposed a method of this type [69] and suggested that one might benefit from the use of the time-varying innovations representation (before it reaches steady state). See [69, 72] for more on the time-varying problem.

There is an alternative approach to the Kalman filter method for finding a factorization of the numerator of $S_y(z)$. Suppose we pass the process y in (80) through the all-zero filter $\alpha(z)$. The resulting process η has power spectral density $p(z)$; it is a finitely correlated (moving average) process. Given its correlation function $p(z)$, we wish to factor it

$$p(z) = \sum_{i=-m}^{m} p_i z^i = \left(\sum_{i=0}^{m} \beta_i z^i \right) \left(\sum_{i=0}^{m} \beta_i z^{-i} \right)$$
$$= \beta(z)\beta(z^{-1}).$$
(90)

This is equivalent to factoring the infinite symmetric Toeplitz matrix [11, 13, 37, 56] with finitely many nonzero diagonals

$$P = \begin{bmatrix} p_0 & p_1 & \cdots & p_m & 0 & 0 & \cdots \\ p_1 & p_0 & & p_{m-1} & p_m & 0 & \\ \vdots & & & & & & \\ p_m & p_{m-1} & & p_2 & p_1 & p_0 & \\ 0 & p_m & & p_3 & p_2 & p_1 & \\ \vdots & & & & & & \end{bmatrix}$$
(91)

into the product of an upper triangular matrix and its transpose. Recursive procedures for this are discussed in [37], and clearly the Levinson-type algorithm can be used in this scalar case. As the recursion proceeds, certain elements of the Cholesky factor converge to the desired β_i [13]. Clearly an alternative to this procedure is to find the innovations representation of η using the fast algorithms of section 2.2. This method is closely related to the fast Cholesky algorithms [63, 72]. For a detailed discussion and new results on the use of the Riccati equation for spectral factorization see [112, 132].

2.4.3 Numerical Aspects and Approximate Realizations

Let us now turn to the numerical aspects of this two-stage procedure. We concentrate here on the first stage, the computation of the factorization

(75). The algorithms of Rissanen [11] and Ho [106] are based on examination of the Hankel matrix

$$
H_N = \begin{bmatrix} R(0) & R(1) & R(2) & \cdots & R(N-1) \\ R(1) & R(2) & R(3) & \cdots & R(N) \\ \vdots & & & & \\ R(N-1) & R(N) & R(N+1) & & R(2N-2) \end{bmatrix}. \tag{92}
$$

It is well-known [107] that R admits a factorization (75) if and only if there is some integer n such that

$$\text{rank } H_N \leq n, \quad \forall N. \tag{93}$$

Ho's original algorithm yielded a minimal realization (dim A in (75) is as small as possible) if a bound n was known in advance. A far more critical question from a practical point of view is the partial realization question. Here we take into account that we have only a finite number of correlations $R(0)$, $R(1)$, . . . , $R(N-1)$, and we would like to obtain the minimal factorization that matches these. We can use Ho's algorithm, but it is not recursive; if we incorporate $R(N)$, we must re-solve the whole problem. Fortunately, Rissanen [11] and Dickinson et al. [9] have developed efficient, recursive procedures (the latter is based on the Berlekamp-Massey algorithm [10], which was developed for the scalar case). These algorithms essentially solve the Padé approximation problem.

Thus efficient algorithms exist for spectral factorization, and one would expect good results *if the process y truly has a Markovian representation and if one has the exact values of the correlations*. This points out a conceptual difference between linear prediction and the stochastic realization procedure. Linear prediction makes no pretense about exactly matching a model. All that is wanted is a least-squares fit, and thus one would expect this procedure to be relatively robust when one uses a finite record of real data to estimate the correlation function which is then used in the linear prediction procedure. On the other hand, an infinitesimal perturbation of H_N in (92) can make it have full rank. In this case the partial realization procedures—which in essence are looking to match a model exactly—yield a system of extremely high dimension. Thus it appears that these algorithms are inherently sensitive to errors in estimates of the correlation coefficients. In addition, if y has no Markovian representation, the linear prediction approach still works but the partial realization procedures, which are based on exact model matching, may very well run astray as they try to fit the data "too closely."

Does this mean that this procedure is useless in identifying parameters in a speech model? Perhaps not. What is needed is a modification of the first step of the stochastic realization algorithm. This version is too sensitive. In fact, De Jong [108] has shown that these methods are numerically unstable; the inexact minimal realization supplied by these algorithms, as implemented on a finite-word-length computer may not be a "numerical neighbor" of the sequence $\{R(i)\}$ that is to be factored. Much of the difficulty exists because the problem of finding the rank of the Hankel matrix is ill posed. By rephrasing the algorithm in terms of the ε-rank (the least rank of all systems within an ε-neighborhood of the given sequence), De Jong obtains a slower algorithm that is similar to Rissanen's but numerically stable. This approach is extremely appealing for two reasons. First, within this framework we can seek minimal realizations in the ε-neighborhood of a sequence $\{R(i)\}$ that is not realizable by a finite-dimensional system. Second, we can seek the "nearest" reduced-order realization of given dimension of a given system. These two properties may help overcome some of the sensitivity problems with the two-step procedure. In addition, Kung [133] discusses another variation of the Berlekamp-Massey algorithm that may lead to improvements in numerical stability.

In addition to the work of De Jong, a number of other methods have been proposed for "approximate" Padé approximations, and any of these could be used as the first step in the algorithm. McDonough and Huggins [113] propose to approximate a time function $f(t)$ by a sum of (possibly complex) exponentials

$$f_a(t) = \sum_{i=1}^{N} A \exp\{s_i t\}.$$

They study numerical methods for the iterative determination of the A_i and s_i that minimize $\int_0^T e^2(t)dt$, where e is the signal error $e(t) = f(t) - f_a(t)$. One needs iterations because this is a nonlinear problem. This is closely related to the discrete-time problem of finding $\{A, b, c\}$ with $A\, n \times n\, (n$ fixed) to minimize some function of the error $e(i) = R(i) - cA^i b$. Some effort has been put into this problem [19, 75, 110], and one possibility, of course, is the all-pole approximations. For example, we might perform linear prediction with the $R(i)$ as the observed signal (regarded as the impulse response of some filter). This would require computing the correlation of $R(i)$ or, in other words, the correlation of the correlation of the $y(i)$! Note that the all-pole assumption for $R(i)$ would not necessarily lead to an all-pole model for $G(z)$ in (82).

Another possible method has been proposed by Burrus and Parks [114]. They consider approximating

$$r(z) = R(0) + R(1)z^{-1} + R(2)z^{-2} + \ldots$$

by

$$G(z) = \frac{a_0 + a_1 z^{-1} + \ldots + a_{N-1}z^{-N+1}}{1 + b_1 z^{-1} + \ldots + b_{M-1}z^{-M+1}} = \frac{a(z)}{b(z)}.$$

In addition to specifying some exact realizability conditions on $\{R(i)\}$ (which can easily be reduced to Hankel matrix conditions and statements), they suggest the following. We would like $r(z) \simeq a(z)/b(z)$. Multiplying by $b(z)$, we obtain $b(z)r(z) \simeq a(z)$, and if we attempt to minimize some norm on the difference between these quantities (called the equation error), we can obtain linear approximation algorithms [114].

Initial results [109, 111] utilizing the two-step stochastic realization procedure indicate the potential of the approach. In particular, the work at IRIA [109] has produced good results for the design of whitening (inverse) filters. Given this limited success, it appears that the utility of the two-step stochastic realization procedure merits further investigation.

2.5 Some Other Issues in System Identification

2.5.1 Recursive Methods for Pole-Zero Modeling

It is appropriate to mention several other identification procedures. In section 2.3 we saw that the covariance method is equivalent to a Kalman filter when we recursively update our estimates of the predictor coefficients. Several other recursive identification schemes can also be considered Kalman filter–type algorithms [17]. One of these is the instrumental variables approach, which is similar to the least-squares algorithm and leads to Toeplitz equations in the stationary case [91]. Akaike [91] points out how to devise Toeplitz Yule-Walker equations to determine the poles (AR part) in an ARMA model.[16] Because this requires knowledge of the order of the MA part, it is more likely to lead to the sensitivity problems that arise in techniques based on the assumption that the data obeys certain constraints (as in the first step of the stochastic realization algorithm). In addition, we are no longer guaranteed that the solution to the Yule-Walker equations leads to a stable inverse filter.

The methods of least squares (covariance) and instrumental variables, as described in [17], are used for all-pole models when the input is unknown and assumed to be noisy. However, if the input is known, both the usual least squares and the instrumental variables can easily be modified for the identification of zeros. Consider the model

$$
\begin{aligned}
y(k + 1) &+ a_1 y(k) + \ldots + a_p y(k - p + 1) \\
&= b_0 u(k) + b_1 u(k - 1) + \ldots + b_m u(k - m) + \varepsilon(k),
\end{aligned}
\tag{94}
$$

where we measure both the y's and u's (here $\varepsilon(k)$ is the driving noise, or the equation error). In this case let

$$
\theta' = (-a_1, \ldots, -a_p, b_0, \ldots, b_m),
\tag{95}
$$

$$
\phi'(k) = (y(k), \ldots, y(k - p + 1), u(k), \ldots, u(k - m)).
\tag{96}
$$

Then the recursive least-squares procedure reduces to a Kalman filter for the system

$$
\theta(k + 1) = \theta(k), \qquad y(k + 1) = \phi'(k)\theta(k) + \varepsilon(k).
\tag{97}
$$

Although this known input model is not of interest in the speech problem, it is important in control applications in which one wants to manipulate the system through the input u. See [17] for the analogous development for the instrumental variables method.

Two other algorithms in [17] are of interest. These methods allow zeros both in the deterministic input-output response and in the noise-output response; that is, they can be used to identify ARMA models. Both algorithms are recursive (in the data), both are approximate maximum likelihood methods, and both are of the Kalman filter type. The second of these (RML2 in [17]) is discussed in detail in [18]. The first of these, RML1, is in some sense an approximation to RML2, and we outline the basic idea. Consider the ARMA model

$$
\begin{aligned}
y(k + 1) &+ a_1 y(k) + \ldots + a_p y(k - p + 1) \\
&= e(k) + c_1 e(k - 1) + \ldots + c_q e(k - q).
\end{aligned}
\tag{98}
$$

We can rewrite (98) as

$$\theta(k + 1) = \theta(k), \qquad y(k + 1) = \phi'(k)\theta(k) + e(k), \tag{99}$$

where

$$\begin{aligned}\theta' &= (-a_1, \dots, -a_p, c_1, \dots, c_q), \\ \phi'(k) &= (y(k), \dots, y(k - p + 1), e(k - 1), \dots, e(k - q)).\end{aligned} \tag{100}$$

If ϕ were known, we could again devise a Kalman-filter structure for the estimate $\hat{\theta}$. However, the noises e are not known. As suggested in [17, 82, 83] a natural approximation is to replace $e(j)$ in (100) by its estimated value—the residual

$$\varepsilon(j) = y(j + 1) - \hat{\phi}'(j)\hat{\theta}(j). \tag{101}$$

If we do this, we obtain the following recursive scheme,

$$\hat{\theta}(j + 1) = \hat{\theta}(j) + K(j + 1)\varepsilon(j) \tag{102}$$

$$K(j + 1) = \frac{P(j)\hat{\phi}(j)}{1 + \hat{\phi}'(j)P(j)\hat{\phi}(j)} \tag{103}$$

$$P(j + 1) = P(j) = \frac{P(j)\hat{\phi}(j)\hat{\phi}(j)'P(j)}{1 + \hat{\phi}'(j)P(j)\hat{\phi}(j)} \tag{104}$$

$$\hat{\phi}(j)' = (y(j), \dots, y(j - p + 1), \varepsilon(j - 1), \dots, \varepsilon(j - q)) \tag{105}$$

Söderström et al. [17] provide a detailed description of this and several other algorithms, and they consider uniqueness of stationary points and the stability of these algorithms. In particular, they show that RLS is stable and has a unique solution, that RML1 and RML2 have unique solutions for ARMA models, that RML2 always converges, and that RML1 converges for MA models, for first-order ARMA models, but that it may diverge in higher-order cases (an example is given). See [120] for fast on-line algorithms for these identification schemes. These methods are analogous to the fast algorithms for recursive least squares discussed in section 2.3.2.

2.5.2 Nonrecursive Approaches to Pole-Zero Modeling
The methods described in section 2.5.1 in principle allow one to identify zeros as well as poles. In addition, several other methods for zero modeling have been described in the literature [26, 68, 100, 113, 114, 123]. The method

in [68] is based on cepstral analysis. Let $Y(z)$ be the z-transform of a signal y, which we wish to model as the impulse response of an ARMA model

$$Y(z) = N(z)/D(z). \tag{106}$$

Usual linear prediction (with care taken to avoid the zeros [26, 68, 100]) will identify D. Suppose now we define the complex cepstrum $\hat{y}(n)$ so that $\hat{Y}(z) = \log Y(z)$. Then the z-transform of $n\hat{y}(n)$ is

$$-z \frac{d\hat{Y}(z)}{dz} = -z \frac{D(z)N'(z) - N(z)D'(z)}{N(z)D(z)}, \tag{107}$$

and thus linear prediction on $n\hat{y}(n)$ will identify the zeros and the poles of y [26, 68]. A second use of cepstral analysis is given in [126] in which it is used for homomorphic deconvolution to obtain a nonparametric estimate of a section of the impulse response of a system, and this estimate is then fit with a rational spectrum.

Several other nonparametric approaches have been suggested for pole-zero modeling. For example, the generalized Padé methods in [113, 114, 123, 128] can be used for pole-zero modeling directly (as well as for the first step of the two-step procedure of section 2.4). Also Atashroo and Boll [121] have suggested a multistep procedure in which one uses linear prediction to obtain the poles, inverse filters to obtain a finitely correlated sequence, linear prediction again to obtain a high-order all-pole model of this sequence, and then a third linear prediction to obtain a lower order all-zero inverse of the all-pole model. Another method for fitting pole-zero models as in (106) is the iterative prefiltering approach of Steiglitz and McBride [87], discussed in detail in [127]. From Parseval's theorem the optimal least-squares solution for the coefficients of N and D can be obtained by minimizing

$$\int_0^{2\pi} \left| Y(e^{j\omega}) - \frac{N(e^{j\omega})}{D(e^{j\omega})} \right|^2 d\omega.$$

Since this is a nonlinear problem, we attempt to find a solution iteratively. Suppose we have computed $N_i(z)$ and $D_i(z)$; then the $(i + 1)$st iteration consists of finding N_{i+1} and D_{i+1} to minimize

$$\int_0^{2\omega} \frac{1}{D_i(e^{j\omega})} \left| Y(e^{j\omega})D_{i+1}(e^{j\omega}) - N_{i+1}(e^{j\omega}) \right|^2 d\omega.$$

This is a linear problem, which can be solved readily. Although no proof of convergence is known, this algorithm has worked well in practice [87, 127].

2.6 Concluding Remarks

In this section we have examined a number of aspects of the identification-estimation problem, and we have pointed out a number of similarities between the goals and techniques of the two disciplines. We have also seen some of the differences, but we have not discussed others. In particular, we have treated identification for its own sake. In control system design, identification is often simply a means toward efficient control [16]. Thus in many control applications the value of identification is not measured by the accuracy of the parameter estimates, but by the performance of the overall system. This is discussed somewhat in [17] and in the study of self-tuning regulators [80, 81]. In addition, in control there are several types of identification problem, since the system can be excited through inputs. The problems are different if the system is operating open loop, in a time-invariant closed-loop mode, or in an adaptive closed-loop mode [15, 17, 134]. In addition, the number of parameters to be identified in many on-line control problems is not very large—four or five. In fact, one of the key problems in practical adaptive control is choosing which few parameters to identify. Finally, in the control context, we often deal with systems for which we are interested in determining system structure as well as identifying the parameters of a model. The issues involved here are complex [15, 16].

On the digital filtering side, we are often interested in the accuracy of the parameter estimates. This is important, for example, if we are attempting to design an all-pole filter that matches a given impulse response in a least-squares sense, or if we are attempting to estimate formants from an all-pole speech model. On the other hand, for linear predictive coding, the accuracy of the parameters may be of secondary interest, while the primary concern is more efficient coding of speech data. In this case accuracy is important only insofar as it makes the coding scheme more efficient. In this regard an important question involves the quantization of the predictor specifications; that is, what is the most efficient method for transmitting the specifications of the all-pole model. The reflection coefficients (from which one can construct the filter) offer the most efficient parametrization from a quantization point of view [119]. Finally, in the speech problem we are usually dealing with many unknown parameters, between 12 and 16 [44].

The linear prediction approach appears particularly well-suited to the speech problem. The all-pole model is a good one in many cases (from a physical point of view);[17] the algorithms are fast, the intermediate variables in the algorithm (the partial correlation coefficients) have useful physical interpretations, the linear prediction procedure tends to match the spectral envelope, and so on. (See [26] for many of the properties of linear prediction and [116] for some of its statistical properties.) Finally and most important, linear prediction has worked well on speech signals; further work is needed before we can say with confidence that any of the other techniques described in this chapter can improve this performance.

Thus we see that there are a surprising number of relationships, similarities, and differences among the techniques and goals of researchers in both disciplines who are concerned with parameter identification. The possibilities for collaboration and interaction seem particularly abundant in this area. We have barely touched the relative merits of the methods or the problems that a method addresses and does not address. In addition, a number of the stochastic identification algorithms that we have discussed may prove valuable in solving problems in speech analysis, such as the enhancement of noise-degraded speech and the identification of time-varying speech models.[18] We have also pointed out a number of questions concerning some of these methods, such as the need for detailed numerical analyses of the many fast algorithms.

Finally, one further issue that we have not discussed is the determination of an appropriate order for the parametric model to be identified. Clearly, as we allow more free parameters, we can get a better fit, but we would expect a diminishing return beyond a certain number of parameters. Åström and Eykhoff [16] propose one test criterion, while Akaike [32, 92; 15, p. 716; see also 26] proposed an information-theoretic criterion that provides a direct trade-off between the value of the log-likelihood function and the number of free parameters in the model. Recently Rissanen and Ljung [79] have obtained a related criterion that incorporates the assumed model structure as well as the number of parameters. A thorough investigation of the value of these results and the other questions raised in the speech context remains.

2.7 Notes

1. Elliott, et al. [98] discuss a variety of adaptive control techniques all applied to the control of the F-8C aircraft and thus provide some insight into the similarities, differences, advantages, and disadvantages of the techniques. All these projects were sponsored by NASA Langley. This "fly-by-wire" adaptive control program is still in its evolutionary stages, and new methods and concepts are still being developed.

2. Linear prediction is an example of a prediction error identification method. For discussions of such methods in a fairly general context see [135, 136].

3. One can modify the linear prediction formulation to take into account the quasi-periodic nature of speech for voiced sounds. In [70] such a procedure is developed in which one also obtains an estimate of the pitch period. An alternative approach to this problem is to solve the linear prediction problem as outlined in sections 2.2 and 2.3, pass the speech through the inverse filter, and analyze the resulting signal to determine the pitch [25, 44]. Recently Steiglitz and Dickinson [100] have described a method for improving pole estimation by completely avoiding the part of a voiced speech signal that is driven by glottal excitation.

4. Note that we require $c'P(n|n-1)c \neq 0$. This requires the positivity of the covariance $R(i)$, which is clearly related to the statement that $y(n)$ is not a deterministic function of $y(0), \ldots, y(n-1)$ for any n [67].

5. In continuous time the problem is somewhat more difficult; we do not consider one-step prediction and in fact run into difficulties if we assume we observe y as opposed to a noise-corrupted version. See [67] and the references therein for more on this problem.

6. As before we can take $w = 0$ if R is positive definite. Lindquist discusses this in [4].

7. The existence of two such formulas is related to the existence of both a one-step prediction and a filtering estimate, in clear distinction to the continuous-time case, in which we only have one such formula and filter. Indeed, the discrete-time problem leads to a number of innovations representations [67] and to more complex equations for the weighting pattern and gain. See [4, 67, 101, 102] for more on the differences between the continuous- and discrete-time cases.

8. In the multivariable case the k_i have two matrix counterparts (Γ_i^* and Γ_i in [4]) which in general coincide only in the scalar case, because the covariance matrix R is only block-Toeplitz. This also leads to the differences between the forward and backward predictors, which in turn leads to an increase in computational complexity in the vector case. Morf et al. [131] have shown how to write the vector algorithm in terms of a single reflection-coefficient matrix, providing a natural generalization of the scalar result.

9. In this survey paper the autocorrelation method, called the corrrelation method is compared to least squares.

10. Bergland [124] has suggested monitoring the residuals of a linear predictor to determine when to update the estimates of the predictor coefficients.

11. In [47] the gain $K(N)$ is calculated in a slightly different way because of the inclusion of quantization effects.

12. The algorithms discussed in this chapter have been extended, in most cases nontrivially, to the vector case.

13. If we had realized $\frac{1}{2} R(0)$, $R(1)$, $R(2)$, . . . , instead of $R(0)$, $R(1)$, $R(2)$, . . ., we would have a more symmetrical version of (78) [63]. Note that the equality of (77) and (78) is as formal power series.

14. The assumption that we can factor R as in (75) implies (and is implied by) the fact that $S_y(z)$ is a rational function.

15. We choose β and α to consist of the poles and zeros of $S_y(z)$ that lie within the unit circle. This guarantees the stability of G and of its inverse [63].

16. This method is similar in spirit to the Burrus-Parks generalized Padé equation error approach for the determination of the denominator of a pole-zero model [114].

17. This may be a weakness with stochastic realization-type methods for speech processing. Since the pole locations (the formants) are of such importance, we would like a system that gives us particularly robust estimates of their locations. It is not clear that the stochastic realization procedures do this. Identification schemes that are more directly geared to identifying system poles (eigenvalues) may prove superior in the speech context.

18. For examples of time-varying speech models see [137, 138].

2.8 References

1. M. Morf, G. S. Sidhu, and T. Kailath, "Some New Algorithms for Recursive Estimation in Constant, Linear, Discrete-Time Systems," *IEEE Trans. Aut. Contr.* AC–19 (1974), pp. 315–323.

2. A. Lindquist, "A New Algorithm for Optimal Filtering of Discrete-Time Stationary Processes," *SIAM J. Contr.* 12 (1974), pp. 736–746.

3. A. Lindquist, "Optimal Filtering of Continuous-Time Stationary Processes by Means of the Backward Innovation Process," *SIAM J. Contr.* 12 (1974), pp. 747–755.

4. A. Lindquist, "On Fredholm Integral Equations, Toeplitz Equations, and Kalman-Bucy Filtering," *Applied Math and Opt.* 1 (1975), pp. 355–373.

5. A Lindquist, "Some Reduced-Order Non-Riccati Equations for Linear Least Squares Estimation: The Stationary, Single-Output Case," *Int. J. Control*, to appear.

6. T. Kailath, "Some New Algorithms for Recursive Estimation in Constant Linear Systems," *IEEE Trans. Inf. Th.* IT-19 (1973), pp. 750–760.

7. T. Kailath, "A View of Three Decades of Linear Filtering Theory," *IEEE Trans. Inf. Th.* IT-20 (1974), pp. 146–181.

8. J. Rissanen, "A Fast Algorithm for Optimum Linear Predictors," *IEEE Trans. Aut. Contr.* AC-18 (1973), p. 555.

9. B. W. Dickinson, M. Morf, and T. Kailath, "A Minimal Realization Algorithm for Matrix Sequences," *IEEE Trans. Aut. Contr.* AC-19 (1974), pp. 31–38.

10. J. L. Massey, "Shift Register Synthesis and BCH Decoding," *IEEE Trans. Inf. Th.* IT-15 (1969), pp. 122–127.

11. J. Rissanen, "Recursive Identification of Linear Systems," *SIAM J. Contr.* 9 (1971), pp. 420–430.

12. L. Silverman, "Realization of Linear Dynamical Systems," *IEEE Trans. Aut. Contr.* AC-16 (1971), pp. 554–467.

13. J. Rissanen and T. Kailath, "Partial Realization of Random Systems," *Automatica* 8 (1972), pp. 389–396.

14. A. J. Tether, "Construction of Minimal Linear State-Variable Models from Finite Input-Output Data," *IEEE Trans. Aut. Contr.* AC-15 (1970), pp. 427–436.

15. T. Kailath, D. Q. Mayne, and R. K. Mehra, eds., Special Issue on System Identification and Time-Series Analysis, *IEEE Trans. Aut. Contr.* AC-19 December 1974, pp. 637–951.

16. K. J. Åström and P. Eykhoff, "System Identification—A Survey," *Automatica* 7 (1971), pp. 123–162.

17. T. Söderström, L. Ljung, and I. Gustavsson, "A Comparative Study of Recursive Identification Methods," Report 7427, Lund Institute of Technology, Dept. of Aut. Contro., Lund, Sweden, December 1974.

18. T. Söderström, "An On-Line Algorithm for Approximate Maximum Likelihood Identification of Linear Dynamic Systems," Report 7308, Lund Institute of Technology, Dept. of Aut. Contr., Lund, Sweden, March 1973.

19. H. P. Zeiger and A. J. McEwen, "Approximate Linear Realizations of Given Dimension via Ho's Algorithm," *IEEE Trans. Aut. Contr.* AC-19 (1974), p. 153.

20. H. Akaike, "Markovian Representation of Stochastic Processes and Its Application to the Analysis of Autoregressive Moving Average Processes," *Ann. Inst. Statist. Math.*, to appear.

21. P. Faurre, Representation of Stochastic Processes, Ph.D. dissertation, Stanford University, 1967.

22. B. Anderson, "The Inverse Problem of Stationary Covariance Generation," *J. Stat. Phys.* 1 (1969), pp. 133–142.

23. G. S. Sidhu, T. Kailath, and M. Morf, "Development of Fast Algorithms via Innovations Decompositions," in *Proc. Seventh Hawaii Internat. Conf. on Systems Sciences,* Western Periodicals Co., North Hollywood, Calif. (1974), pp. 192–195.

24. J. D. Gibson, J. L. Melsa, and S. K. Jones, "Digital Speech Analysis Using Sequential Estimation Techniques," *IEEE Trans. Acous. Speech, and Sig. Proc.* ASSP-23 (1975), pp. 362–369.

25. B. Atal and S. L. Hanauer, "Speech Analysis and Synthesis by Linear Prediction of Speech Wave," *J. Acoust. Society of America* 50 (1971), pp. 637–655.

26. J. Makhoul, "Linear Prediction: A Tutorial Review," *Proc. IEEE,* 63 (1975), pp. 561–580.

27. G. E. P. Box and G. M. Jenkins, *Time Series Analysis: Forecasting and Control,* Holden-Day, San Francisco, 1970.

28. F. Itakura and S. Saito, "Analysis Synthesis Telephony Based on the Maximum Likelihood Method," in *Rep. 6th Int. Congr. Accustics,* edited by Y. Kohasi, Paper C-5-5, August 1968, pp. C17–C20.

29. F. Itakura and S. Saito, "A Statistical Method for Estimation of Speech Spectral Density and Formant Frequencies," *Electron. Commun. Japan* 53-A (1970), pp. 36–43.

30. F. Itakura and S. Saito, "Digital Filtering Techniques for Speech Analysis and Synthesis," *Conf. Rec. 7th Int. Cong. Acoustics,* Budapest, Paper 25 C 1, 1971.

31. J. C. Chow, "On Estimating the Orders of an Autoregressive Moving-Average Process with Uncertain Observations," *IEEE Trans. Aut. Contr.* AC-17 (1972), pp. 707–709.

32. H. Akaike, "Maximum Likelihood Identification of Gaussian Autoregressive Moving Average Models," *Biometrika* 60 (1973), pp. 255–265.

33. S. A. Tretter and K. Steiglitz, "Power-Spectrum Identification in Terms of Rational Models," *IEEE Trans. Aut. Contr.* AC-12 (1967), pp. 185–188.

34. N. Levinson, "The Wiener RMS Error in Filter Design and Prediction," Appendix B in N. Weiner, *Extrapolation, Interpolation and Smoothing of Stationary Time Series,* MIT Press, Cambridge, Mass., 1942.

35. P. Whittle, "On the Fitting of Multivariate Autoregressions and the Approximate Canonical Factorization of a Spectral Density Matrix," *Biometrica* 50 (1963), pp. 129–134.

36. R. A. Wiggins and E. A. Robinson, "Recursive Solutions to the Multichannel Filtering Problem," *J. Geophys. Res.* 70 (1965), pp. 1885–1891.

37. J. Rissanen, "Algorithms for Triangular Decompositions of Block Hankel and Toeplitz Matrices with Applications to Factoring Positive Matrix Polynomials," *Mathematics of Computation* 27, (1973), pp. 147–154.

38. S. Chandrasekhar, *Radiative Transfer*, Dover Publications, Inc., N.Y., 1960.

39. J. Casti, R. Kalaba, and V. K. Murthy, "A New Initial Value Method for On-Line Filtering and Estimation," *IEEE Trans. Inf. Th.* (1972), pp. 515–517.

40. J. Casti and E. Tse, "Optimal Linear Filtering Theory and Radiative Transfer: Comparisons and Interconnections," *J. Math. Anal. and Appl.* 40 (1972), pp. 45–54.

41. L. Ya. Geronimus, *Orthogonal Polynomials*, Consultant Bureau, New York, 1961.

42. R. Bellman, "Functional Equations in the Theory of Dynamic Programming. VII: A Partial Differential Equation for the Fredholm Resolvent," *Proc. Amer. Math. Soc.* 8 (1957), pp. 435–440.

43. M. Krein, "On a New Method for Solving Linear Integral Equations of the First and Second Kinds, "*Dokl. Akad. Nauk. SSSR* 105 (1955), pp. 637–640.

44. J. D. Markel and A. H. Gray, Jr., *Linear Prediction of Speech,* Springer-Verlag, New York, 1976.

45. B. S. Atal and M. R. Schroeder, "Predictive Coding of Speech Signals," in *Proc. 1967 Conf. Commun. and Process.*, pp. 360–361.

46. S. F. Boll, "A Priori Digital Speech Analysis," Ph.D. dissertation, University of Utah, 1973.

47. J. D. Gibson, S. K. Jones, and J. L. Melsa, "Sequentially Adaptive Prediction

and Coding of Speech Signals," *IEEE Trans. Comm.* COM-22 (1974), pp. 1789–1797.

48. B. S. Atal, "Speech Analysis and Synthesis by Linear Prediction of the Speech Wave," *J. Acoust. Soc. Amer.* 47 (1970), p. 65.

49. J. L. Flanagan and L. R. Rabiner, ed., *Speech Synthesis*, Dowden, Hutchinson, and Ross, Stroudsburg, Pa., 1973.

50. F. Itakura and S. Saito, "Speech Analysis-Synthesis Based on the Partial Autocorrelation Coefficient," presented at Acoust. Soc. of Japan Meeting, 1969.

51. F. Itakura and S. Saito, "On the Optimum Quantization of Feature Parameters in the PARCOR Speech Synthesizer," in *Conf. Record IEEE* 1972 Conf. Speech Commun. and Process,. New York, Paper L4, 1972, pp. 434–437.

52. F. Itakura, S. Saito, Y. Koike, H. Sawabe, and M. Nishikawa, "An Audio Response Unit Based on Partial Correlation," *IEEE Trans. Commun.* COM-20 (1972), pp. 792–797.

53. H. Wakita, *Estimation of the Vocal Tract Shape by Optimal Inverse Filtering and Acoustic/Articulatory Conversion Methods*, SCRL Monograph No. 9, Speech Comm, Res. Lab., Santa Barbara, Calif., 1972.

54. J. D. Markel, "Digital Inverse Filtering: A New Tool for Formant Trajectory Estimation," *IEEE Trans. Audio and Electroacoust.* AU–20 (1972), pp. 129–137.

55. J. D. Markel, "Basic Formant and F_0 Parameter Extraction from a Digital Inverse Filter Formulation," *IEEE Trans. Audio and Electroacoust.* AU–21 (1973), pp. 154–160.

56. J. Rissanen and L. Barbosa, "Properties of Infinite Covariance Matrices and Stability of Optimum Predictors," *Inform. Sci.* 1 (1969), pp. 221–236.

57. P. Faurre and J. P. Marmorat, "Un Algorithme de Realization Stochastique," *C. R. Acad. Sci. Paris Ser. A* 268 (1969), pp. 978–981.

58. T. Kailath and R. Geesey, "An Innovations Approach to Least Squares Estimation. IV: Recursive Estimation Given the Covariance Function," *IEEE Trans. Aut. Contr.* AC–16 (1971), pp. 720–727.

59. M. Pagano, "An Algorithm for Fitting Autoregressive Schemes," *J. Royal Statist. Soc. Series C (Applied Stat.)* (1972), pp. 274–281.

60. A. Lindquist, *Linear Least-Squares Estimation of Discrete-Time Stationary*

Processes by Means of Backward Innovations, Lec. Notes in Econ. and Math. Sys., vol. 107. Springer-Verlag, New York, 1975, pp. 44–63.

61. D. Q. Mayne, "A Solution of the Smoothing Problem for Linear Dynamic Systems," *Automatica* 4 (1966), pp. 73–92.

62. D. C. Fraser and J. E. Potter, "The Optimum Linear Smoother as a Combination of Two Optimum Linear Filters," *IEEE Trans. Aut. Contr.* 14 (1969), pp. 387–390.

63. B. W. Dickinson, T. Kailath, and M. Morf, "Canonical Matrix Fraction and State-Space Descriptions for Deterministic and Stochastic Linear Systems," *IEEE Trans. Aut. Contr.* AC–19 (1974), pp. 656–667.

64. T. Kailath, "Application of a Resolvent Identity to a Linear Smoothing Problem," *SIAM J. Contr.* 7, (1969), pp. 68–74.

65. T. Kailath, "Fredholm Resolvents, Wiener-Hopf Equations and Riccati Differential Equations," *IEEE Trans. Inf. Th.* IT–15 (1969), pp. 665–672.

66. G. S. Sidhu and T. Kailath, "The Shift-Invariance Approach to Continuous-Time Fast Estimation Algorithms," in *Proc. 1974 Conf. on Decision and Control,* Catalog No. 74CH0900-ICS, *IEEE,* New York (1974), pp. 839–845.

67. M. Gevers and T. Kailath, "An Innovations Approach to Least-Squares Estimation. VI: Discrete-Time Innovations Representations and Recursive Estimation," *IEEE Trans Aut. Contr.* AC–18 (1973), pp. 588–600.

68. A. Oppenheim and J. M. Tribolet, "Pole-Zero Modeling Using Capstral Prediction," Res. Lab. Electronics, MIT, Cambridge, Mass., QPR 111, 1973, pp. 157–159.

69. M. Morf, T. Kailath, and B. Dickinson, "General Speech Models and Linear Estimation Theory," in *Speech Recognition,* Academic Press, New York, 1975.

70. B. S. Atal and M. R. Schroeder, "Adaptive Predictive Coding of Speech Signals," *Bell. Sys. Tech. J.,* 49 (1970), pp. 1973–1986.

71. M. Morf, B. Dickinson, T. Kailath, and A. Vieira, "Efficient Solutions of Covariance Equations for Linear Prediction," *IEEE Trans. Acoust., Speech, and Sig. Proc.* ASSP–25 (1977), pp. 429–433.

72. M. Morf, "Fast Algorithms for Multivariable Systems," Ph. D. dissertation, Stanford University, Stanford, Calif., 1974.

73. G. S. Sidhu, "A Shift-Invariance Approach to Fast Algorithms for Estimation and Control," Ph. D. dissertation, Standford University, 1974.

74. F. Itakura, "Extraction of Feature Parameters of Speech by Statistical Methods," in *Proc. 8th Symp. Speech Information Processing*, February 1972.

75. R. Parthasarathy and H. Singh, "On Suboptimal Linear System Reduction," *Proc IEEE* 63 (1975), pp. 1610–1611.

76. F. Bauer, "Ein Directes Iterationsverfahren zur Hurwitz-Zerlegung eines Polynoms," *AEÜ* 9 (1955), pp. 285–290.

77. L. Ljung, T. Kailath, and B. Friedlander, "Scattering Theory and Least Squares Estimation. I: Continuous-Time Problems; II: Discrete-Time Problems," in *Proc. 1975 IEEE Conf. on Descision and Control*, Catalog No. 75CH1016-5CS, IEEE, New York (1975), pp. 55–58.

78. L. C. Pusey and A. B. Baggeroer, "The Role of the Stationarity Equation of Least-Squares Linear Filtering in Spectral Estimation and Wave Propagation," presented at 1974 IEEE Symp. on Inf. Th., Notre Dame, Indiana, October 1974.

79. J. Rissanen and L. Ljung, "Estimation of Optimum Structures and Parameters for Linear Systems," in *Mathematical Systems Theory*, edited by G. Marchesini and S. K. Mitter, Lec. Notes in Econ. and Math. Sys., No. 131, Springer-Verlag, New York, 1976, pp. 92–110.

80. K. J. Åström and B. Wittenmark, "On Self-Tuning Regulators," *Automatica*, 9 (1973), pp. 185–199.

81. L. Ljung and B. Wittenmark. "Asymptotic Properties of Self-Tuning Regulators," Rept. 7404, *Div. Aut. Contr.*, Lund Inst. Tech., Lund, Sweden, 1974.

82. V. Panuska, "An Adaptive Recursive Least Squares Identification Algorithm," in *Proc. IEEE Symposium on Adaptive Processes (8th), Decision and Control*, Catalog No. 69 C 52–AC, IEEE, New York (1969), pp. 6e1–6e5.

83. P. C. Young, "The Use of Linear Regression and Related Procedures for the Identification of Dynamic Processes," *Proc. 7th IEEE Symp. on Adaptive Processes*, UCLA, 1968.

84. J. J. Cornyn, Jr. "Direct Methods for Solving Systems of Linear Equations Involving Toeplitz or Hankel Matrices," Rept. AD/A–002 931, prepared for Office of Naval Research, October 1974; also S. M. thesis, University of Maryland, College Park, Md.

85. P. Faurre, "Réalisations Markoviennes de Processus Stationnaires," Rept. No. 13, IRIA, Rocquencourt, France, March 1973.

86. D. W. Clarke, "Generalized-Least Squares Estimation of the Parameters of

a Dynamic Model," presented at IFAC Symp. on Identif. in Autom. Control Sys., Prague, 1967.

87. K. Steiglitz and L. E. McBride, "A Technique for the Identification of Linear Systems," *IEEE Trans. Aut. Contr.* AC–10 (1965), pp. 461–464.

88. L. H. Zetterberg, "Estimation of Parameters for a Linear Difference Equation with Application to EEG Analysis," *Math. Biosci.* 5 (1969), pp. 227–275.

89. J. M. Mendel, "Multistage Least-Squares Parameter Estimators," *IEEE Trans. Aut. Contr.* AC–20 (1975), pp. 775–782.

90. H. Akaike, "Markovian Representation of Stochastic Processes by Canonical Variable," *SIAM J. Control* 13 (1975), pp. 162–173. (See also [15], p. 667].

91. H. Akaike, "Block Toeplitz Matrix Inversion," *SIAM J. App. Math.* 24 (1973), pp. 234–241.

92. H. Akaike, "Information Theory and an Extension of the Maximum Likelihood Principle," in *Proc. 2nd Symp. Inf. Th.,* Akadémiai Kiadó, Budapest, 1973, 267–281; see also [15, p. 716].

93. B. Wittenmark, "A Self-Tuning Predictor," *IEEE Trans Aut. Contr.* AC–19 (1974), pp. 848–851.

94. J. Durbin, "The Fitting of Time-Series Models," *Rev. Inst. Internat. Statist.* 28 (1960), pp. 233–244.

95. W. F. Trench, "An Algorithm for the Inversion of Finite Toeplitz Matrices," *SIAM J. Appl. Math* 12 (1964), pp. 515–521.

96. S. Zohar, "Toeplitz Matrix Inversion: The Algorithm of W. F. Trench," *J. Assoc. Comput. Mach.* 16 (1967), pp. 592–601.

97. H. B. Aasnaes and T. Kailath, "An Innovations Approach to Least-Squares Estimation VI: Some Applications of Vector Autoregressive-Moving Average Models," *IEEE Trans. Aut. Contr.* AC–18 (1973), pp. 601–607.

98. J. Elliott, "Adaptive Control of the F-8C Digital-Fly-By-Wire-Aircraft," in *Proc. of 1975 Conf. on Decision and Control,* Catalog No. 75CH1016–5CS, IEEE, New York, 1975, pp. 217–237.

99. A. V. Oppenheim, ed., Special Issue on Digital Signal Processing, *Proc. IEEE* 63, April 1975.

100. K. Steiglitz and B. Dickinson, "The Use of Time-Domain Selection for Improved Linear Prediction," *IEEE Trans. Acoust., Speech, and Sig. Proc.* ASSP–25 (1977), pp. 34–39.

101. L. Ljung, T. Kailath, and B. Friedlander, "Scattering Theory and Linear Least Squares Estimation. I: Continuous Time Problems," *Proc. IEEE* 64 (1976), pp. 131–139.

102. B. Friedlander, T. Kailath, and L. Ljung, "Scattering Theory and Linear Least Squares Estimation. II: Discrete-Time Problems" *J. Franklin Inst.* 301 (1976), pp. 71–82.

103. A. S. Willsky, "A Survey of Failure Detection Methods in Linear Dynamic Systems," *Automatica* 12 (1976), pp. 601–611.

104. D. L. Gustafson, A. S. Willsky, J.-Y. Wang, M. C. Lancaster, and J. H. Triebwasser, "A Statistical Approach to Rhythm Diagnosis of Cardiograms," *Proc. IEEE* 65 (1977), pp. 802–804.

105. G. Picci, "Stochastic Realization of Gaussian Processes," *Proc. IEEE* 64 (1976), pp. 112–122.

106. B. L. Ho and R. E. Kalman, "Effective Construction of Linear State Variable Models from Input-Output Functions," *Regelungstechnik* 14 (1966), pp. 545–548.

107. R. E. Kalman, P. L. Falb, and M. A. Arbib, *Topics in Mathematical System Theory*, McGraw-Hill, New York, 1969.

108. L. S. DeJong, "Numerical Aspects of Realization, Recursive Algorithms," *SIAM J. Cont. and Opt.*, Vol. 16, No. 4, July 1978, pp. 646–659.

109. Private communication with Dr. F. Levieux (Institut de Recherche en Informatique et Automatique, Domaine de Voluceau, Rocquencourt, 78150 Le Chesnay, France) concerning ongoing research project at IRIA.

110. M. F. Hutton and B. Friedland, "Rough Approximations for Reducing Order of Linear, Time-Invariant Systems," *IEEE Trans. Aut. Contr.* AC–20 (1975), pp. 329–337.

111. P. E. Caines and S. Sinha, "An Application of the Statistical Theory of Feedback to Power System Identification," in *Proc. 1975 IEEE Conf. on Dec. and Contr.*, Catalog No. 75CH1016–5CS, IEEE, New York, 1975, pp. 584–589.

112. D. J. Clements and B. D. O. Anderson, "Polynomial Factorization via the Riccati Equation," *SIAM J. Appl. Math.* 31 (1976), pp. 179–205.

113. R. N. McDonough and W. H. Huggins, "Best Least-Squares Representation of Signals by Exponentials," *IEEE Trans. Aut. Contr.* AC–13 (1968), pp. 408–412.

114. C. S. Burrus and T. W. Parks, "Time Domain Design of Recursive Digital Filters,' 'IEEE Trans. Audio and Electroacoustics AU-18 (1970), pp. 137–141.

115. J. Makhoul, "New Lattice Methods for Linear Prediction," presented at 1976 Int. Conf. on Acoustics, Speech and Sig. Proc., Philadelphia, Pa., April 1976.

116. A. B. Baggeroer, "Confidence Intervals for Regression (MEM) Spectral Estimates," IEEE Trans. Inf. Th., to appear.

117. G. S. Sidhu and J. L. Casti, "A Rapprochement of the Theories of Radiative Transfer and Linear Stochastic Estimation," Appl. Math. and Comp. 1 (1975), pp. 295–323.

118. P. R. Graves-Morris, ed., Pade Approximants and Their Applications, Academic Press, New York, 1973.

119. R. Viswanathan and J. Makhoul, "Quantization Properties of Transmission Parameters in Linear Predictive Systems," IEEE Trans. Acous., Speech, and Sig. Proc. ASSP-23 (1975), pp. 309–321.

120. M. Morf and L. Ljung, "Fast Algorithms for Recursive Identification," Proc. 1976 IEEE Conf. on Dec. and Cont., Clearwater Beach, Fl., December 1976; also IEEE Trans. Aut. and Control, to appear.

121. M. A. Atashroo and S. F. Boll, "Pole-Zero Modeling Using Autocorrelation Prediction," presented at 1976 Arden House Workshop on Digital Signal Processing, Harriman, N. Y., February 1976.

122. L. E. McBride, "Iterative Methods for Systems Identification," Tech. Rept No. 15, Communications Lab., Dept. of E. E., Princeton Univ., Princeton, New Jersey, June 1966.

123. F. Brophy and A. C. Salazar, "Considerations of the Padé Approximant Technique in the Synthesis of Recursive Digital Filters," IEEE Trans. Audio Electroacous. AU-21 (1973), pp. 500–505.

124. G. Bergland, "Stuttered Sampling-Rate Speech Encoding," presented at 1976 IEEE Arden House Workshop on Digital Signal Processing, Harriman, N. Y., February 1976.

125. G. Szegö, Orthogonal Polynomials, American Mathematical Society, New York, 1959.

126. G. E. Kopec, A. V. Oppenheim, and J. M. Tribolet, "Speech Analysis by Homomorphic Prediction," IEEE Trans. Acoust., Speech, and Sig. Proc. ASSP-25 (1977), pp. 40–49.

127. K. Steiglitz, "On the Simultaneous Estimation of Poles and Zeroes in Speech Analysis," *IEEE Trans. Acoust., Speech, and Sig. Proc.* ASSP-25 (1977), pp. 229–234.

128. R. Hastings-James and S. K. Mehra, "Extensions of the Padé-Approximant Technique for the Design of Recursive Digital Filters," *IEEE Trans. Acoust., Speech, and Sig. Proc.* ASSP–25 (1977), pp. 501–509.

129. T. Kailath, A. Vieira, and M. Morf, "Inverses of Toeplitz Operators, Innovations, and Orthogonal Polynomials", *SIAM Review* 20 (1978), pp. 106–119.

130. T. Kailath, "Some New Results and Insights in Linear Least-Squares Estimation Theory," *IEEE-USSR Workshops Proceedings*, Catalog No. 75CH1167-61T, IEEE, New York (1975).

131. M. Morf. A. Vieira, and T. Kailath, "Covariance Characterization by Partial Auto-Correlation Matrices," *Ann. of Statistics*, to appear.

132. B. D. O. Anderson and P. J. Moylan, "Spectral Factorization of a Finite-Dimensional Nonstationary Matrix Covariance," *IEEE Trans. Aut. Conf.* AC–19 (1974), pp. 680–692.

133. S. -Y. Kung, "Multivariable and Multidimsenional Systems: Analysis and Design," Ph.D. dissertation, Stanford University, 1977.

134. I. Gustavsson, L. Ljung, and T. Söderström, "Identification of Processes in Closed-Loop—Identifiability and Accuracy Aspects," *Automatica* 13 (1977), pp. 59–75.

135. P. E. Caines, "Prediction Error Identification Methods for Stationary Stochastic Processes," *IEEE Trans. Aut. Control,* AC–21 (1976), pp. 500–505.

136. P. E. Caines, "Linear and Non-Linear System Identification via Prediction Error Methods," submitted to 1978 Conf. of Internat. Fed. of Automatic Control, Helsinki, Finland, June 1978.

137. L. A. Liporace, "Linear Estimation of Nonstationary Signals," *J. Acoust. Soc. Am.* 58 (1975), pp. 1268–1295.

138. M. Hall, A.V. Oppenheim, and A. S. Willsky, "Time-Varying Parametric Modeling of Speech," in *Proc 1977 Conf. on Dec. and Control*, Catalog No. 77CH1269–OCS, IEEE, New York (1977), pp. 1085–1091.

139. J. F. Claerbout, "Synthesis of a Layered Medium from Its Acoustic Transmission Response," *Geophysics* 33 (1968), pp. 264–269.

140. A. Vieira, T. Kailath, and M. Morf, On the Fast Chandrasekhar and Square-Root Algorithms, submitted to *IEEE Trans. Aut. Control.*

141. M. Morf, J. R. Dobbins, B. Friedlander, and T. Kailath, "Square-Root Algorithms for Parallel Processing in Optimal Estimation," presented at *Int. Symp. on Inf. Th.,* Cornell University, Ithaca, New York, October 1977.

142. T. Kailath, S. -Y. Kung, and M. Morf, Some Aspects of the Computational Complexity of Matrix Inversion, submitted to *SIAM Review.*

143. J. Makhoul, "Stable and Efficient Lattice Methods for Linear Prediction," *IEEE Trans. Acous., Speech and Sig. Proc.* ASSP–25 (1977), pp. 423–428.

144. M. Morf, A. Vieira, and D. T. Lee, "Ladder Forms for Identification and Speech Processing," in *Proc. 1977 IEEE Conf. on Dec. and Contr.,* Catalog No. 77CHI269–OCS, IEEE, New York (1977), pp. 1074–1078.

145. J. Burg, "Maximum Entropy Spectral Analysis," Ph.D. dissertation, Stanford University, May 1975.

146. M. Morf, D. T. Lee, J. R. Nickolls, and A. Vieira, "A Classification of Algorithms for ARMA Models and Ladder Realizations," in *Proc. 1977 IEEE Conf. on Acoust., Speech, and Sig. Proc.* Catalog No. 77CH1197–3 ASSP, IEEE, New York (1977), pp. 13–19.

147. M. Morf, A. Vieira, D. T. Lee, and T. Kailath, "Recursive Multichannel Maximum Entropy Method," *Proc. 1977 Joint. Aut. Cont. Conf.,* Catalog No. 77CHI220-3CS, IEEE, New York (1977), pp. 113–117.

148. A. H. Jazwinski, *Stochastic Processes and Filtering Theory,* Academic Press, New York, 1970.

3

Synthesis, Realization, and Implementation

3.1 Different Meanings for Design

In this chapter we investigate one area in which the differences in perspective between the two disciplines are most apparent. Specifically we consider the question of design. However, our discussion does not deal with design methods as much as with the meaning of design to researchers in the two disciplines and the sorts of problems their techniques are equipped to handle.

Perhaps the most obvious difference between the fields is in the system representations used. Digital signal processing emphasizes input-output descriptions. while control and estimation theory emphasizes state-space models. This difference stems from the different questions addressed by researchers in the two disciplines. In digital signal processing one is interested in the implementation of a system with a specified input-output behavior (hence the need for an input-output description). Questions such as efficient implementation and number of bits needed to achieve the desired level of accuracy are of great importance.

In control and estimation theory implementation is not considered to nearly the same extent. Realization techniques address the question of constructing a state-space realization that leads to a specified input-output behavior, but such techniques do not address many of the major issues involved in implementation. In fact, viewed as implementable algorithms, state-space realizations do not include some of the most important system structures used in digital system design. Nevertheless state-space models do play an important role in control and estimation system design. A state-space model for a given physical system is necessary in the application of a number of techniques for the analysis of system performance and for the design of feedback control or estimation systems (the specification of the desired input-output behavior of a control or estimation system).

Thus we see some fundamental differences between the perspectives of researchers in the two disciplines. Clearly there are also several areas for interaction between the fields—to develop useful multiple-input, multiple-output structures (a marriage of digital implementation and multivariable realization concepts), to utilize state-space techniques to analyze the performance of digital filter structures, and to consider the digital implementation of state-space control and estimation system designs.

3.2 State-Space Realizations and State-Space Design Techniques

3.2.1 Fundamentals of Realization Theory

State-space concepts and methods have a number of uses for design. Let us first recall some of the basic concepts from realization theory [2–13, 91–93]. We follow [93] and state several results in the continuous-time framework, but analogous results hold for the discrete-time problem. We are interested in time-varying linear system representations of the form

$$\dot{x}(t) = A(t)x(t) + B(t)u(t), \qquad x(t_0) = x_0,$$
$$y(t) = C(t)x(t), \tag{1}$$

where $x(t) \in R^n$, $u(t) \in R^m$, $y(t) \in R^p$, and A, B, C are matrices of appropriate dimension. From an input-output point of view the system (1) is equivalent to the representation

$$y(t) = C(t)\Phi(t, t_0)x_0 + \int_{t_0}^{t} C(t)\Phi(t, \tau)B(\tau)u(\tau)\, d\tau, \tag{2}$$

where Φ is the $n \times n$ state-transition matrix

$$\dot{\Phi}(t, \sigma) = A(t)\Phi(t, \sigma), \qquad \Phi(\sigma, \sigma) = I, \tag{3}$$

and the matrix

$$H(t, \tau) = C(t)\Phi(t, \tau)B(\tau), \quad t \geq \tau, \tag{4}$$

is the impulse-response matrix. As pointed out in [93], in many control and estimation problems we are interested in the weighting pattern matrix[1]

$$K(t, \tau) = C(t)\Phi(t, \tau)B(\tau), \quad \forall t, \tau. \tag{5}$$

If A, B, and C are constant, then Φ and K have particularly nice expressions

$$\Phi(t, \tau) = e^{A(t-\tau)}, \quad K(t, \tau) = Ce^{A(t-\tau)}B, \quad \forall t, \tau, \tag{6}$$

and in this case, given the dependence on $t - \tau$ only, we write $K(t, 0) = K(t)$, $H(t, 0) = H(t)$. An equivalent input-output representation is provided by the Laplace transform of $H(t)$, the transfer function

$$G(s) = \mathscr{L}[H(t)] = C(Is - A)^{-1}B. \tag{7}$$

The realization problem, then, is to obtain a recursive description of the form (1) when we are given the weighting pattern, impulse-response function, or transfer function. If a realization exists, then many solutions exist. For example, we obtain the same weighting pattern as (1) if we take $\xi = 2x$ to be our state variable

$$\dot{\xi}(t) = A(t)\xi(t) + 2B(t)u(t), \quad y(t) = \tfrac{1}{2}C(t)\xi(t),$$

or if we take $\eta' = (x, 0)$ as our state

$$\dot{\eta}(t) = \begin{bmatrix} A(t) & 0 \\ 0 & \alpha(t) \end{bmatrix}\eta(t) + \begin{bmatrix} B(t) \\ \beta(t) \end{bmatrix}u(t),$$
$$y(t) = [C(t), \gamma(t)]\eta(t),$$

where α is arbitrary and either β or γ is identically zero. These two examples illustrate the two basic issues that arise. In the first case ξ and x are in some sense equivalent, since they contain identical information and one can be obtained from the other via an invertible linear transformation. This is not the case in the second example, in which η carries superfluous information (from an input-output standpoint) in its last component η_{n+1}. If $\beta = 0$ the input can never affect η_{n+1} (a controllability problem); while if $\gamma = 0$ the output never sees η_{n+1} directly or indirectly since η_{n+1} is decoupled from the other state components) (an observability problem).

Thus, one of the key issues in realization theory involves the characterization of minimal realizations—those containing no superfluous information in their state variables. See the references, in particular [93], for the full development of realization theory for time-invariant multivariable systems. As one might guess, the concepts of controllability and observability are closely tied to the minimality of a state-space realization. For the sake of brevity we state the major results only for the time-invariant case (stationary weighting pattern and constant realizations of it).

DEFINITION 3.1   A realization (time-varying or time-invariant) of a weighting pattern or transfer function is *minimal* if any other realization has a state vector of dimension at least as large.

DEFINITION 3,2.   A constant linear system in state space form (1) is *controllable* if for every state $x \in R^n$ and any $T > 0$ there exists an input function $u(t)$, $t \in [0, T]$ that drives the system from $x(0) = 0$ to $x(T) = x$.[2]

DEFINITION 3.3   A constant linear system in state-space form (2) is *observable* if for any $T > 0$, given $u(t)$ and $y(t)$, $t \in [0, T]$ we can uniquely determine $x(t)$ in this interval.

THEOREM 3.1   Suppose we are given a stationary impulse-response matrix $H(t)$ or its transfer function $G(s)$. This system has a state-space representation of the form (1) if and only if $G(s)$ is a matrix of rational functions of s, each of which is proper (degree of the denominator > degree of the numerator).[3] In this case $G(s)$ has a minimal, constant realization. In fact, a realization

$$\dot{x}(t) = Ax(t) + Bu(t), \tag{8}$$

$$y(t) = Cx(t) \tag{9}$$

is minimal if and only if it is controllable and observable. In addition, any minimal constant realization can be obtained from a given one via an invertible linear transformation of the state variable $\xi = Px$, or equivalently

$$(A, B, C) \longrightarrow (PAP^{-1}, PB, CP^{-1}). \tag{10}$$

Finally, if dim $x = n$, the realization (8), (9) is controllable if and only if

$$\text{rank}[B, AB, \ldots, A^{n-1}B] = n, \tag{11}$$

and it is observable if and only if

$$\text{rank}[C', A'C', \ldots, (A')^{n-1}C'] = n. \quad \blacksquare \tag{12}$$

Essentially the same result holds in discrete time, in which we have the (z-transform) transfer function $G(z)$ and we wish to represent it as

$$G(z) = C(Iz - A)^{-1}B, \tag{13}$$

which is equivalent to the state-space description

$$x(k + 1) = Ax(k) + Bu(k), \qquad y(k) = Cx(k). \tag{14}$$

From (7) and (13) we see that any algorithm that realizes the continuous-time system $G(s)$ is also a valid realization algorithm for the discrete-time system $G(z)$ and vice versa. We thus turn to the discrete-time framework for a moment to gain some insight into the realization question.

There are relatively simple algorithms for obtaining controllable or observable realizations of $G(z)$, if we assume that it is in rational form so that we can compute the least common denominator of all of the elements of G [2, 91, 93–95]. Ho's algorithm [94, 95] and that of Silverman and Meadows [13] provide methods for extracting minimal constant realizations from the Hankel matrix. In this approach we write $G(z)$ in series form

$$G(z) = \sum_{i=1}^{\infty} T_i z^{-i}, \tag{15}$$

and we recognize that $\{T_i\}$ is the impulse-response sequence. Referring to (13), we see that the realization problem is equivalent to finding A, B, C so that

$$T_i = CA^{i-1}B, \qquad \forall i. \tag{16}$$

One can find such a factorization if and only if the ranks of the Hankel matrices

$$H_N = \begin{bmatrix} T_1 & T_2 & \cdots & T_{N-1} \\ T_2 & T_3 & & T_N \\ \vdots & & & \\ T_{N-1} & T_N & & T_{2N-3} \end{bmatrix} \tag{17}$$

are bounded by some integer [91, 94, 95], and then the maximal rank of the H_N is the dimension of the minimal realization of G. If G is proper rational, one can show that this is indeed the case and, given the degree of the least common multiple of the denominators of elements of G, can find a particular H_N that achieves the maximal rank. From this matrix one can then extract the minimal realization [13, 93–95] (see [11, 12, 91] for a procedure based on partial fraction expansions). However, if we are given G in the form (15) instead of the rational form, in general we cannot easily determine whether G is rational or, equivalently, if the ranks of H_N are bounded. In this case the partial realization algorithms discussed in section 2.4 are of use. These algorithms essentially produce minimal-dimension systems of the form (14) that match the expansion (15) up to some specified power of (z^{-1}); that is, these systems match the impulse response out to some specified point. But these algorithms have numerical difficulties that must be overcome.

Thus the realization problem can in principle solve certain questions related to system synthesis. The input-output description (2) for continuous systems or the analogous one for time-invariant, discrete-time systems

$$y(n) = \sum_{i=0}^{n-1} T_{n-i} \, u(i) \tag{18}$$

is nonrecursive; equation (18) implies an algorithm in which all the past input vectors $u(0), \ldots, u(n-1)$ are multiplied at each point in time by the appropriate impulse-response matrices and then summed. Clearly such an approach is feasible only if the system to be implemented has a finite impulse response (FIR), where $T_i = 0 \; \forall i >$ some integer. In general, however, (18) requires growing memory, and even in the FIR case the nonrecursive implementation may require exorbitant amounts of storage. In this case recursive implementations are called for, and the state-space realization (14) provides an answer to this question. In fact, the computation of minimal realizations allows one to determine the minimal amount of storage needed in any linear, recursive realization. One of the most important aspects of the state-space approach is that it allows one to consider multiple-input, multiple-output systems and time-varying systems. The ability to handle multivariable and time-varying systems is one of its most important assets for synthesis.

3.2.2 The Uses of State-Space Models for Design and Analysis
State-space realization theory has played a major role in network synthesis for both time-invariant and time-varying circuits. A number of papers have been written in this area [3–9 and the references therein]; in

some of this work [4] realization concepts are tied together with some concepts concerning dissipative systems to yield useful results in network synthesis.

We will not discuss analog network synthesis further because our major concern is with relationships with the implementation of digital filters. For discrete-time systems, the state-space approach tells us the minimal amount of storage (the minimal number of delays) needed to realize a given transfer function. In addition, we know how to obtain any minimal state-space realization from a given one; we apply (10) for any invertible P. Also, any recursive linear realization can be written in vector difference-equation (state-space) form by keeping track of all memory updates. This does not mean that state-space realization theory solves the digital filter design question. Many issues besides minimal storage are involved in choosing a "good" filter structure (algorithm). However, we can obtain any minimal state-space realization algorithm by choosing an invertible matrix P and applying (10). Still this does not mean that selecting a good filter structure is equivalent to finding a good P. The primary reason that this is not so is the distinction between interpreting a state-space realization as a description of dynamical behavior and as an algorithm (see section 3.3.3).

State-space realizations play a major but indirect role in a number of important design problems in control theory, as such realizations are needed in order to use the powerful state-space methods. We illustrate a few of these here. Consider the system pictured in figure 3.1. We are given an open-loop $p \times m$ transfer function $G(z)$ and we wish to design a feedback compensator that has certain properties. For example, we may wish to design a feedback system so that all the modes of the closed-loop system have time constants in a specified range. For scalar systems ($p = m = 1$) (frequency domain) techniques for solving this problem have been avail-

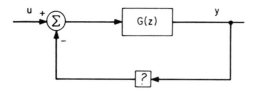

3.1
A feedback design problem.

able for a number of years [2, 96], and frequency domain techniques for the multivariable case have been derived by Wolovich [97] and Rosen-brock [98]; their methods stand as a middle ground between state-space and classical frequency domain methods [99]. However, if one uses a state-variable description of the system, one can obtain a solution in the general multivariable setting [2]. We briefly outline a method discussed in [14]. Suppose that $G(z)$ is proper, rational, and reduced (no element of G has common poles and zeros) and that we have constructed a realization

$$x(k + 1) = Ax(k) + Bu(k), \qquad y(k) = Cx(k). \tag{19}$$

We note that the poles of $G(z)$ are precisely the eigenvalues of A if and only if (19) is minimal. Suppose we implement a control law of the form

$$u(k) = -Kx(k). \tag{20}$$

Then the closed-loop poles are just the eigenvalues of $(A - BK)$. We can find a K to place these eigenvalues wherever we want if and only if (19) is controllable [14]. A constructive algorithm is given in [14].

Suppose we cannot implement (20); that is, we have only u and y at our disposal. One might then consider the design of a system that estimates x from u and y. A natural structure for such an observer [14, 15] is

$$\hat{x}(k + 1) = A\hat{x}(k) + Bu(k) + H(y(k) - C\hat{x}(k)). \tag{21}$$

If $x(k) = \hat{x}(k)$, then $x(n) = \hat{x}(n)$ for all $n > k$, and the error $e(k) = x(k) - \hat{x}(k)$ obeys the equation

$$e(k + 1) = (A - HC)e(k). \tag{22}$$

Also the poles of $A - HC$ can be placed arbitrarily if and only if (19) is observable.[4] If we then implement the control law

$$u(k) = -K\hat{x}(k), \tag{23}$$

we find that the poles are just the eigenvalues of $(A - BK)$ and $(A - HC)$, and we have solved the pole placement problem. This procedure illustrates one of the crucial aspects of many state-space design methods—that the solution to design problems is an algorithm, which in some cases can be implemented on a general-purpose computer.[5]

There are algorithmic, state-space solutions for a wide variety of other problems: decoupling (design a feedback law so that the ith input affects only the ith output [16]), invertibility (when can we design a system that

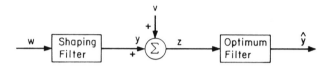

3.2
An optimum filtering problem.

takes the output of our given system and recovers the input [17, 82]), and so on. The special issue of the *IEEE Transactions on Automatic Control* [92] provides an overview of the design methods that have been developed. Some of these techniques allow us to solve quantitative optimization problems. The linear-quadratic optimal control problem is an example of this, as is the design of a Wiener filter as a steady-state Kalman filter [18, 92, 100]. Consider the estimation problem illustrated in figure 3.2. We have a Gaussian stationary process y with given rational power spectral density $\Phi_y(s)$ and we observe the signal z, which consists of the sum of y and a Gaussian white-noise process v. We wish to design a causal filter that minimizes the variance of the estimation error

$$e(t) = y(t) - \hat{y}(t). \tag{24}$$

If we assume that we have an infinite record length on which to operate, the solution to this problem is the Wiener filter [18–21], which can be obtained by performing a certain spectral factorization. We also know [18] that the Kalman filter can be used to solve this problem. Given that y has a rational power spectral density, we can find a minimal representation ("shaping filter")

$$\dot{x}(t) = Ax(t) + w(t), \qquad y(t) = Cx(t), \qquad z(t) = y(t) + v(t). \tag{25}$$

Here $E(w(t)w'(\tau)) = Q\delta(t - \tau)$, $E(v(t)v'(\tau)) = R\delta(t - \tau)$, and w and v are independent. If we assume stationarity, $x(0)$ is zero mean with covariance P_0, which satisfies the (continuous-time) Lyapunov equation

$$AP_0 + P_0A' = -Q. \tag{26}$$

Then it is well known [18] that the optimal filter is given by

$$\dot{\hat{x}}(t) = A\hat{x}(t) + K(t)[z(t) - C\hat{x}(t)], \qquad \hat{x}(0) = 0, \qquad \hat{y}(t) = C\hat{x}(t), \tag{27}$$

where

$$K(t) = P(t)C'R^{-1} \tag{28}$$

and P is the solution to the Riccati equation

$$\dot{P}(t) = AP(t) + P(t)A' - P(t)\,C'R^{-1}CP(t) + Q, \qquad P(0) = P_0. \tag{29}$$

Equivalently, we could use one of the fast algorithms discussed in section 2.2.3 to obtain $K(t)$ directly.

Suppose we let $t \to \infty$; that is, we consider the limit of an infinite record length. One can show [18, 100] that the algorithms for $K(t)$ (Riccati or the fast algorithms) converge to

$$K = P_\infty C'R^{-1}, \tag{30}$$

where P_∞ is the unique positive definite solution of the algebraic Riccati equation

$$AP_\infty + PA' - P_\infty C'R^{-1}CP_\infty + Q = 0. \tag{31}$$

Thus the state-space formulation provides several algorithms that solve the Wiener filtering spectral factorization problem to yield the optimal transfer function (from z to $\hat{y}$)

$$G(s) = C(Is - A + P_\infty C'R^{-1}C)^{-1}P_\infty C'R^{-1}. \tag{32}$$

Thus we see that realization theory, by providing a state-space model for the system to be controlled or the signal to be estimated, plays an important role in allowing us to utilize powerful state-space algorithms for the specification of designs that possess certain performance characteristics. All these algorithms lead to designs specified in terms of a state space model (27) or a transfer function (32). Then if the system is to be implemented in digital form, the issues raised in section 3.3 must be considered in evaluating the performances of the overall system.

In addition to providing a framework for the specification of designs, the state-space framework allows us to analyze the performance characteristics of the overall system after it has been implemented. For example, the techniques described in chapter 1 can be used to study the stability characteristics of the system. A subject of much interest is the sensitivity of such designs [23; references in 22]. The major emphasis here is that designs from state-space algorithms are model-based, and deviations between true and assumed parameter values and the fact that the assumed model is often an idealization of true system behavior inevitably lead to variations in the performance of the optimal design. Issues such as these have led to sensitivity studies and to the development of design methods that are adaptive or inherently robust [24, 25]; methods used to overcome sensitivity problems for Kalman filters are discussed in [100].

Another analytical tool used to study system performance is *covariance analysis*. For linear systems we consider the model

$$x(k + 1) = Ax(k) + w(k), \qquad y(k) = Cx(k) + v(k), \tag{33}$$

where w and v are zero-mean, independent white noises

$$E(w(k)w(j)') = Q\delta_{kj}, \qquad E(v(k)v(j)') = R\delta_{kj}. \tag{34}$$

These noises may represent actual noise sources or the effects of small nonlinearities (such as quantization noise), unmodeled phenomena, and so on. If we assume $x(0)$ is zero mean with covariance $P(0)$, then a simple calculation yields an equation for the covariances $P(k)$ and $S(k)$ of $x(k)$ and $y(k)$, respectively:

$$P(k + 1) = AP(k)A' + Q, \qquad S(k) = CP(k) C' + R. \tag{35}$$

If A is a stable matrix, we can evaluate the steady-state covariances P and S by solving the Lyapunov equation [6]

$$APA' - P = -Q. \tag{36}$$

In the nonlinear case a number of approximate methods eixist [100, 26]. See [27] for the discussion of one widely used method based on describing functions.

In implementing the designs that arise from state-space methods, we must consider a number of issues that digital signal processors have studied in detail. On the other hand, some of the state-space analysis methods mentioned may be useful in evaluating the performance of different system implementations.

3.3 The Implementation of Digital Systems and Filters

3.3.1 Basic Aspects of Digital System Design

The design of digital systems consists of three steps: (1) specification of desired properties, (2) approximation or realization of these properties by a causal, discrete-time system, and (3) implementation of the system using finite precision arithmetic [1]. From this point of view the methods of section 3.2 deal with the first two issues. Design procedures such as pole allocation and Kalman filtering specify desired input-output behavior for feeback compensators or optimal estimation. Realization procedures clearly play an indirect role in these techniques by providing the state-space models on which the design techniques are based. But what about realizations from the point of view of system synthesis and implementation? As we shall see, state-space realizations can play some role in implementation, but they are far from providing the entire solution.

The digital filter design techniques that we wish to consider are discussed in detail in [1, 28–33, 101], and the major emphasis of these methods is on the second and third tasks in digital filter design. The techniques for the second task [1] take as their starting point the specification of certain frequency-response or impulse-response characteristics. The role of the second task is then to take these specifications and produce a scalar transfer function that meets these design specifications. An excellent description of the range of available techniques for this problem is given in [1, ch. 5]. A number of methods are based on transformation of analog filter transfer functions. One of these is the impulse-invariance method in which one samples a continuous-time impulse response to obtain a discrete-time impulse response. This method suffers from aliasing problems if the analog frequency response is not strictly band-limited. A somewhat more complex procedure that avoids the aliasing problem is the bilinear transformation

$$s(z) = k(1 - z^{-1})/(1 + z^{-1}). \tag{37}$$

This invertible transformation of the z-plane into the s-plane maps the inside of the unit circle in the z-plane onto the open left-half plane of the s-plane, thus preserving stability. One can then transform an analog transfer function $H(s)$ into a digital function

$$\tilde{H}(z) \triangleq H(s(z)). \tag{38}$$

If H is rational, so is $\tilde{H}$. This transformation introduces nonlinear distortion in the frequency domain (the mapping of the unit circle in z onto the imaginary axis in s), and care must be taken in achieving a design with the desired frequency response.

In addition to these methods that yield closed-form solutions, there are a number of computer-aided design methods. These include minimizing the mean-squared error between the actual frequency response and the desired response at a selected (finite) set of frequencies. Linear prediction can be used to fit an all-pole model to a desired impulse response, and the Padé approximation–partial realization algorithms described in [93, 102–104] can be used to find least-order pole-zero transfer functions that match a certain number of terms of a desired impulse response.

There are also a number of methods used to design FIR filters. Many of these involve windows, in which one multiplies a desired impulse response by a finite duration window. The usual rectangular window leads to the well-known Gibbs phenomenon; more sophisticated windows have been devised to reduce this effect. See [1] for more on windowing and computer-aided methods for FIR filter design. A good discussion of the overall design problem and the design of optimum filters that approximate a given frequency response in the Chebyshev (L_∞) sense can be found in [101]. As these references indicate, a number of filter design methods are algorithmic, much like the state-space design methods, and the issue of efficient numerical design procedures is of central importance.

3.3.2 Issues in the Implementation of Filters and the Choice of Filter Structure

Once an IIR or FIR filter has been determined, there still remains the major problem of implementation—the determination of a filter structure (algorithm) that realizes the given transfer function. One factor in this design question is the number of storage elements (delays) in the filter structure. Structures that contain the minimal number of delays are called canonic, clearly the same as the concept of minimal realization. Of course, in dealing with single-input, single-output transfer functions, one can read off the order of a canonic structure and construct several minimal realizations quite easily by simple inspection of the specified transfer function [1, ch. 4]. In addition, as memory becomes cheaper, the importance of minimality in digital filter design steadily diminishes.

Determining the order of a canonic realization and constructing several minimal realizations without much difficulty barely scratches the surface of the structures problem. The question of minimizing storage, essentially what the state space-realization problem considers, is just one of several problems in digital filter implementation. While the filter structures available may be equivalent from an input-output viewpoint, they may have very different characteristics with respect to computation time, the complexity of the digital architecture or algorithm required to implement a given structure, the effect of finite precision in representing filter coefficients, or the effects of overflow and quantization [1]. It is these issues that motivate much of the study of filter structures. It is not our intention to explore all the filter structures and their analytical considerations. We mention a few, however, to illustrate several key points. See [1, 28, 34] and the many papers in the *IEEE Transactions on Circuits and Systems*.

For FIR filters a number of methods exist for the implementation of the finite convolution

$$y(n) = \sum_{k=0}^{N-1} h(k)x(n-k) \tag{39}$$

(here h is the FIR). Clearly one can directly implement the product by keeping the last N values of the input in storage. This is the so-called direct form realization [1] and requires N multiplications per stage. If one is designing a linear phase network, this number can be cut in half by using the symmetry properties of the impulse response [1]. The convolution (39) can be implemented using fast Fourier transform (FFT) techniques. This is particularly useful when N is large, in which case one might use a sectioning algorithm [1, 32, 101] (also see [86, 87] for recent techniques that are faster than the FFT). In using FFT techniques, one often sacrifices storage in order to gain computational efficiency; for example, we may take N to be a power of 2 or may use overlap sectioning methods [1] for efficient operation when the length of x is long.

For IIR filters a number of filter structures have been developed. In this case we are attempting to realize the transfer function

$$H(z) = \sum_{k=0}^{M} b_k z^{-k} / 1 - \sum_{k=1}^{N} a_k z^{-k}, \tag{40}$$

which is equivalent to the difference equation

$$y(n) = \sum_{k=1}^{N} a_k y(n-k) + \sum_{k=0}^{M} b_k x(n-k). \tag{41}$$

The direct implementation of (41), called the *direct form I realization*, requires storage of the last N values of y and the last M values of u. This structure is far from minimal; the minimal number of delays is

$\max{(N,\ M)}$. However, a slight modification of direct from I yields the canonic realization *direct form II* [1, p. 150].

By examining the transfer function (40), we can obtain a number of other canonic structures. For example, if $H(z)$ is expanded in partial fraction form, we can obtain parallel form structures; if we factor $H(z)$ as the product of simpler transfer functions, we can obtain series or cascade structures. Let us give an example of the cascade structure. Suppose we have

$$H(z) = \frac{z^2 + (b + d)\, z + bd}{z^2 - (a + c)\, z + ac} = \frac{(1 + bz^{-1})\, (1 + dz^{-1})}{(1 - az^{-1})\, (1 - cz^{-1})}. \tag{42}$$

In figure 3.3 we have realized this filter as the cascade of two first-order filters in direct form II. Note that the overall filter is canonic.

The major questions surrounding the choice of filter structure include the consideration of computational efficiency, the effects of finite word length on filter stability and performance, and the effect of finite precision in representing filter parameters. For further discussion of computational efficiency see the references; in particular, [1, 32] provide detailed discussions and further references on the use of the FFT algorithm.[7] In addition, in chapter 1 we considered the effects of quantization and overflow on system stability. An alternative, approximate method for evaluating the effect of finite word length on system performance is to model each quantization as if it introduced noise (representing, for example, roundoff or truncation) into the system [1, 33–37, 105, 106].[8] The basic idea is that whenever a quantization occurs, one replaces it by an equivalent noise source. Then by assuming independence of these sources—a strong and

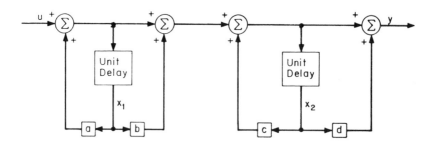

3.3
A second-order cascade filter structure.

often unjustified assumption, as the existence of periodic effects (limit cycles) indicates—one can in principle evaluate the overall noise power at the output and thus obtain a measure of the size of quantization effects.[9] For example, consider the case [1] of fixed-point arithmetic and roundoff quantization (figure 1.5) in which the quantization interval q is 2^{-b} (the number of bits used to represent fractions is b).[10] In this case the quantization error e introduced by a single multiplication falls in the bound

$$-2^{-(b+1)} < e < 2^{-(b+1)}. \tag{43}$$

If e is uniformly distributed, it has zero mean and variance

$$\sigma_e^2 = 2^{-2b}/12. \tag{44}$$

Using these assumptions, we can add independent noise sources to filter representations to account for quantization effects. For example, in the cascade example of figure 3.3 we could add one noise source following each of the four multiplications (fewer noise sources might result from a different quantization procedure, for example if we add the products bx_1 and cx_2 before quantizing).

Another important issue in filter design is the sensitivity of filter performance to variation in coefficients. This issue is central, since coefficients can be represented only to a finite degree of accuracy; hence filters with arbitrary pole and zero locations cannot be obtained. The allowable poles and zeros and the sensitivity to variations in parameters depend significantly on the structure under consideration [1, ch. 4; 28, 31]. For example, parallel and cascade structures are often used because of their sensitivity properties, since the perturbations in the poles are isolated from one another [1].

A great deal of work [1, 28–31, 33–37] has gone into developing methods for answering questions on filter structures, including (1) the number of bits needed in a given filter structure to obtain required accuracy in overall performance, both from the point of view of parameter sensitivity and quantization noise and (2) rules of thumb [33, 37] for the pairing and ordering of poles and zeros in a cascade structure to minimize the effects of quantization noise. The study of questions such as these for large interconnected networks is a complex problem, and efficient algorithms are needed to evaluate overall sensitivities, effects of noise, and so on. One such large-scale package involves the use of techniques for the manipulation of signal flow graphs [1, 28, 31]. A detailed description of a computer package to analyze digital networks is contained in [28].

3.3.3 Relationships between State-Space Techniques and Questions in Digital Filter Design

In this section we wish to examine the relationship of state-space techniques and concepts to some of the questions in digital filter design. This discussion is a first attempt to study such relationships, and a great deal more work is needed before the issues can be thoroughly understood. We first examine the use of state-space techniques to determine filter structures. Realization techniques can be used to obtain minimal realizations, that is, certain canonic algorithms. Consider the transfer function (42). In this case state-space techniques yield a variety of minimal-dimensional (in this case two-dimensional) realizations of the form

$$x(k + 1) = Fx(k) + gu(k), \qquad y(k) = h'x(k) + u(k), \tag{45}$$

where

$$h'(zI - F)^{-1}g + 1 = \frac{z^2 + (b + d) z + bd}{z^2 - (a + c) z + ac}, \tag{46}$$

$$F = \begin{bmatrix} f_{11} & f_{12} \\ f_{21} & f_{22} \end{bmatrix}, \qquad g = \begin{bmatrix} g_1 \\ g_2 \end{bmatrix}, \qquad h = \begin{bmatrix} h_1 \\ h_2 \end{bmatrix}. \tag{47}$$

Now we interpret (45) as an algorithm. Assume that we have computed $x(k)$ and receive the new input $u(k)$.

Part 1
(a) Multiply h_1 and $x_1(k)$.
(b) Multiply h_2 and $x_2(k)$.
(c) Add these, together with $u(k)$, to yield $y(k)$.

Part 2
(a) Multiply f_{11} and $x_1(k)$.
(b) Multiply f_{21} and $x_1(k)$.
(c) Multiply f_{12} and $x_2(k)$.
(d) Multiply f_{22} and $x_2(k)$.
(e) Multiply g_1 and $u(k)$.
(f) Multiply g_2 and $u(k)$.
(g) Add (a), (c), and (e) to yield $x_1(k + 1)$.
(h) Add (b), (d), and (f) to yield $x_2(k + 1)$.

Clearly a number of these steps can be done in different orders, but the steps indicate the basic algorithm implied by (45). Note that in general eight multiplications and six additions are required.

Now let us examine the cascade structure of figure 3.3, and let us interpret it as an algorithm.

(a) Multiply a and $x_1(k)$.
(b) Multiply b and $x_1(k)$.
(c) Multiply c and $x_2(k)$.
(d) Multiply d and $x_2(k)$.
(e) Add (a) and $u(k)$.
(f) Add (b) and (e).
(g) Add (c) and (f).
(h) Add (d) and (g).

Then

$$(e) = x_1(k + 1), \qquad (g) = x_2(k + 1), \qquad h = y(k).$$

This algorithm requires four multiplications and four additions, but this is not the most crucial difference between the two algorithms, since it is possible to obtain realizations (45) with some zero elements in (F, g, h). However, the crucial difference is the following: *If one interprets a state-space realization as determining an algorithm of the type indicated, then the cascade algorithm cannot be of this type.* This is not to say that one cannot find a state-space description of the cascade realization. In fact,

$$x(k + 1) = \begin{bmatrix} a & 0 \\ a + b & c \end{bmatrix} x(k) + \begin{bmatrix} 1 \\ 1 \end{bmatrix} u(k),$$

$$y(k) = [(a + b), (c + d)]x(k) + u(k) \tag{48}$$

is such a realization. Because it is not necessary to multiply by 1 and because one multiplication is used twice, (48) requires only four multiplications—$ax_1(k)$, $(a + b)x_1(k)$, $ex_2(k)$, $(c + d)x_2(k)$—and five additions.

The fact that all algorithms are not state-space algorithms may seem trivial, but it is not. It points out that although any (infinite-precision) algorithm can be described dynamically in state-space terms, direct interpretation of a state-space description as an algorithm does not allow one to consider all possible algorithms. That is, it is relatively easy to go from an algorithm to a state-space description such as (48), but it is not at all natural or clear how to go the other way and hindsight is needed to interpret the realization

$$x(k + 1) = \begin{bmatrix} f_{11} & 0 \\ f_{21} & f_{22} \end{bmatrix} x(k) + \begin{bmatrix} 1 \\ 1 \end{bmatrix} u(k),$$

$$y(k) = [f_{21}, h_2] x(k) + u(k)$$

(49)

as a cascade structure with

$$a = f_{11}, \qquad b = f_{21} - f_{11}, \qquad c = f_{22}, \qquad d = h_2 - f_{22}.$$

(50)

Recently Chan [107] defined a unified framework for the consideration of all one-dimensional structures. Chan noted that if (45) is viewed as a map from present state and input to next state and present output

$$\begin{bmatrix} x(k + 1) \\ y(k) \end{bmatrix} = \Phi \begin{bmatrix} x(k) \\ u(k) \end{bmatrix},$$

then any filter structure can be viewed as a factorization of Φ and a change of basis on x. Consider the example (46), with the realization (48), which yields

$$\Phi = \begin{bmatrix} a & 0 & 1 \\ a + b & c & 1 \\ a\cdot + b & c + d & 1 \end{bmatrix}$$

Let us write $\Phi = \Phi_2 \Phi_1$, where

$$\Phi_1 = \begin{bmatrix} a & 0 & 1 \\ b & c & 0 \\ 0 & d & 0 \end{bmatrix}, \qquad \Phi_2 = \begin{bmatrix} 1 & 0 & 0 \\ 1 & 1 & 0 \\ 1 & 1 & 1 \end{bmatrix}.$$

Then if we interpret this factorization as an algorithm (first perform the operations indicated by Φ_1 and then those specified by Φ_2), it is clear that we essentially have the cascade algorithm depicted in figure 3.3. Thus Chan's technique provides a conceptual framework for considering structures from a state point of view. As Chan points out, it is not yet clear how one can use this factorization technique in an algorithmic fashion to determine useful new structures. At the very least it provides a unified framework for the consideration of questions related to realization and structures.

Thus we see that there are potential limitations to the state-space framework for determining new filter structures, although the ideas of Chan may provide a conceptual unification of these subject areas. In addition to Chan's work there appear to be several other structure-related areas in which state-space concepts may play a role. Recall that state-space-realization techniques allow us to determine minimal realizations for systems with multiple inputs and outputs. This fact, combined with a thorough understanding of the relationship between state-space realizations and digital system structures, may lead to the development of useful filter structures (possessing desirable storage, computational, sensitivity, and quantization characteristics) for multivariable systems. This treatment of a simple cascade example may help expose some of the issues that need to be understood.

The state-space framework is particularly useful for the analysis of the properties of dynamical systems. Thus it seems natural to ask whether these techniques might be useful in the analysis of filter structures. We have already discussed this question in chapter 1 with respect to stability analysis techniques. State-space sensitivity techniques [23] may also be useful in the study of the sensitivity of digital filter structures.

Finally let us examine the utility of state-space techniques in the analysis of the effect of quantization noise on filter performance. We do this by example, although it should be clear that this approach extends to arbitrary structures. Consider the cascade structure in figure 3.4. Here we have included quantization noise after each multiplication. A state-space representation of this filter can be written by inspection:

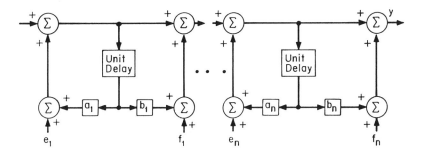

3.4
An nth-order cascade filter including quantization noise.

$$x(k + 1) = Ax(k) + bu(k) + \Gamma e(k) + \Delta f(k),$$
$$y(k) = c'x(k) + u(k) + \Theta e(k) + \Psi f(k), \tag{51}$$

where

$$x(k) = \begin{bmatrix} x_1(k) \\ \vdots \\ x_n(k) \end{bmatrix}, \quad b = \begin{bmatrix} 1 \\ \vdots \\ 1 \end{bmatrix}, \quad c = \begin{bmatrix} a_1 + b_1 \\ \vdots \\ a_n + b_n \end{bmatrix},$$

$$\Theta = \Psi = (1, \ldots, 1),$$

$$A = \begin{bmatrix} a_1 & 0 & \cdots & 0 \\ a_1 + b_1 & a_2 & & 0 \\ & & & \\ a_1 + b_1 & a_2 + b_2 & & a_n \end{bmatrix} \tag{52}$$

$$\Gamma = \begin{bmatrix} 1 & 0 & \cdots & 0 \\ 1 & 1 & & 0 \\ \vdots & & & \\ 1 & 1 & & 1 \end{bmatrix}, \quad \Delta = \begin{bmatrix} 0 & 0 & & 0 & 0 \\ 1 & 0 & & 0 & 0 \\ \vdots & & & \\ 1 & 1 & & 1 & 0 \end{bmatrix},$$

$$e(k) = \begin{bmatrix} e_1(k) \\ \vdots \\ e_n(k) \end{bmatrix}, \quad f(k) = \begin{bmatrix} f_1(k) \\ \vdots \\ f_n(k) \end{bmatrix}.$$

The noises $e_1, \ldots, e_n, f_1, \ldots, f_n$ are assumed independent, identically distributed, zero-mean white processes with variance (44). Then assuming that A is a stable matrix and using the covariance analysis procedure described in section 3.1, we can compute the steady-state covariance[11] Σ of y

$$\Sigma = c'Pc + n2^{-2b}/6, \tag{53}$$

where P, the covariance of x, is the solution of the Lyapunov equation

$$P = APA' + 2^{-2b} [\Gamma\Gamma' + \Delta\Delta']/12. \tag{54}$$

Equations (54) and (53) are perfectly suited to computer implementation. Note that the solution of (54) yields the effect of noise throughout the network. The utility of such an approach for digital network analysis needs to be examined more carefully, but it may be computationally superior to other methods such as those that require computing partial transfer functions from each noise source to the output [5]. If the noise sources are correlated [55], one can adapt the preceding procedure by augmenting the filter-state equations with a shaping filter that yields the correct correlation in the error sources. Parker and Girard [55] used Lyapunov-type equations and analysis quite similar to our development for the evaluation of output noise power due to correlated quantization errors. In addition, similar analyses have been undertaken by Hwang [64, 81], Mullis and Roberts [65, 80], and Sripad and Snyder [66, 67]. Hwang uses Lyapunov state-space equations to study the effects of possible structural transformations and state-amplitude scalings. Mullis and Roberts have obtained some significant results for digital filter design using a framework similar to Hwang's to study what they call minimal noise realizations. Their results indicate the potential of the use of state-space formulations to study digital filter structures. Further results along these lines, including the use of a state-space formulation to study the coefficient sensitivity of different filter structures, are reported by Jackson et al. [79]. Sripad and Snyder develop conditions under which quantization errors are in fact white, and they also use Lyapunov-type analysis to compare the performance of two different realizations.

Within this framework one can pose a number of other questions. For example one can perform a similar noise analysis if random rounding is used.[12] Schüssler [51] has proposed a figure of merit for structures—the required number of bits to meet given noise specifications. In terms of (53) and (54) this would mean determining b so that the resulting Σ is less than some prescribed limit. Can we devise algorithms for the solution of such problems for this and for more general structures? In the case of floating point arithmetic, the quantization error depends on the size of the signal. Can state-space procedures for analyzing state-dependent noise [57, 58] be of value here? Questions such as these await future investigation.

3.4 Questions in the Design of Digital Control Systems

Design procedures in both disciplines consist of several parts: determining the desired input-output behavior to be synthesized and designing an algorithm that approximates this behavior given the constraints of digital implementation. The procedures described so far treat these issues separately, but it would be of value to consider overall design methods that take the discrete nature of the computer into account during the process of developing design specifications and allow the study of trade-offs such as performance versus number of bits used [101]. The development of full-fledged design procedures is clearly a long way off; however, in recent years some research in control and estimation theory has been aimed at developing designs that reflect the interaction of system specification and the limitations and structure of the digital system to be used to implement the system. We will briefly describe several of these; see [38–46, 70–78, 108–114] for details and discussions of other related issues.

Consider the continuous-time linear system

$$\dot{x}(t) = Ax(t) + Bu(t), \tag{55}$$

where $x \in R^n$ and $u \in R^m$. Suppose we wish to control the system with a digital control system. Specifically, suppose we can observe $x(k) \triangleq x(k\varDelta)$, $k = 1, 2, \ldots$; based on these observations we feed back a control

$$u(t) = u(k), \qquad k\varDelta < t \le (k + 1)\varDelta. \tag{56}$$

In addition, suppose we wish to design the control law to minimize

$$J = \int_0^\infty [x'(t)Qx(t) + u'(t)Ru(t)] \, dt. \tag{57}$$

For a fixed value of $\varDelta$ this problem leads to an optimal discrete-time control problem [39] with the feedback law

$$u(k) = Gx(k). \tag{58}$$

Suppose this law is to be implemented in a digital system that takes τ_m seconds to perform a multiplication. Then (if add time is negligible) in general the control law requires

$$\varDelta \ge nm\tau_m. \tag{59}$$

Thus each control algorithm requires a minimum time $\varDelta_{min}$ between successive samples, and the following question arises. Suppose we consider a suboptimal control algorithm that can be implemented at a faster sampling rate than the bound for the optimal law in (59). Can such a law outperform the slower, optimal law? This question is answered in the affirmative in [38], in which a simple example indicates that one can improve performance for a class of large-scale, loosely coupled systems. One can also interpret these results as providing a method for determining the value of a faster computer, as measured by the accompanying decrease in J; that is, for a given control law and two possible multiplication times τ_1, $\tau_2(\tau_1 < \tau_2)$ the cost difference $J(\tau_2) - J(\tau_1)$ can be interpreted as the amount one would be willing to pay for the faster machine. This can provide a basis for a trade-off analysis—the cost of a faster computer versus achievable performance improvement.

The question of devising control and estimation designs and digital architectures that are especially natural for particular applications is receiving more and more attention as digital systems are being improved and made less expensive. Specifically, the development of microprocessor technology has led to a great increase in the design of control and estimation systems involving a number of identical modules, parallel structures, and distributed processing [40–46, 115, 116]. In decentralized control [108–114] one often has an extremely large and distributed system with many inputs and outputs, and one wishes to design a set of local controllers—a set of several control laws, each using only some of the inputs and some of the outputs and perhaps implemented on a dedicated processor. Clearly the architecture of such a system (who gets to know what) is a major design variable. Again one can interpret the difference in performance of two architectures as a measure of how much more one would be willing to pay for one system than another. Clearly a totally centralized system would perform best, as it would have all available system information at its disposal, but the cost of relaying all information to and from one central location may be prohibitive.

3.5 Concluding Remarks

The study of problems such as the interaction of implementation and architecture issues (parallelism, decentralization) and the design of control and signal processing algorithms is still in its infancy, and it appears to offer a promising avenue for research and for applications to problems in fields such as aircraft control [40, 42–44] and nonlinear stochastic filtering [45, 46, 90]. Architectural issues have received a great deal of attention in digital signal processing [28, 31, 47, 48], and this appears to be a promising direction for future interaction and collaboration. In addition, truly efficient digital systems often involve sampling at several different rates, and researchers in both fields [89, 117, 118] have addressed some of the issues in multirate system design, Collaboration in this area appears to be particularly natural.

There has been work [68, 69] in digital filter design aimed at developing structures and design techniques that take the constraints of finite arithmetic into account at the start. In addition, the restrictions of finite arithmetic have in part motivated the study of linear systems in which the vectors and scalars are all integer-valued, that is, linear systems over rings [119, 122]. The work so far has been quite theoretical, and its value in allowing one to design digital controllers or filters has yet to be established.

Both disciplines are interested in the development of fast on-line algorithms. In digital signal processing fast Fourier transform algorithms [1, 59, 60] have been widely used (for example, in the implementation of FIR filters). The FFT has also been used in control theory, for example in implementing matched filters for detection of failures in dynamic systems [61] and in designing efficient optimal controllers for certain large interconnected systems that possess some symmetry in their structure [123]. Willsky [62], motivated by the algebraic treatment of Nicholson [60], has developed fast algorithms for several types of "noncommutative convolution" that occur in certain nonlinear filtering problems [63]. Also all the fast Kalman-gain algorithms discussed in chapter 2 are potentially useful in the design of efficient adaptive control systems. The implementation of systems along these lines and the development of new efficient on- and off-line procedures remains an active area of research in both disciplines.

Perhaps the most important point we can make about control system design and its relationship to digital filtering is that a great deal of work remains to be done before many modern control designs can be turned into usable digital control systems. Researchers in digital signal processing have devoted much effort to the analysis of digital filter structures, and this expertise seems a useful starting point for the investigation of digital controller structures. This is not to say that the digital filter design methods will completely solve the problems of digital control system implementations. Indeed, the existence of a closed loop around a digital filter creates new and important problems concerning limit cycle and roundoff noise analysis. Some results on problems such as the effect of roundoff noise and input quantizations on the performance of optimal linear regulators and estimators are reported in [70–78], but a great deal of work remains to be done.

3.6 Notes

1. As mentioned in [10, 93], if K is real analytic in t and τ (as it is if A, B, C are constant), then (4) and (5) are equivalent, since H has a unique extension to $\tau < t$. Otherwise there can be nonunique extensions [10]

2. For time-varying systems, the intervals over which one can control or observe the system may vary with time [91, 93, 2, 10].

3. It is easy to allow deg (denom) = deg (num) by including a feedthrough term: $y(t) = C(t)x(t) + D(t)u(t)$. This is readily taken care of and leads to minor modifications of these results.

4. Note that (A, C) is observable if and only if (A', C') is controllable (see (11), (12)), and that the eigenvalues of $A - HC$ are the same as for $A' - C'H'$. Thus we can use the same algorithms for finding H as that used to find K in (20).

5. The problem of computer design algorithms is a very important one at present. Difficulties with ill conditioning are present in many of these, and the design of "robust" algorithms is a crucial research question in control theory [22].

6. As mentioned in chapter 1, this equation appears in several problems in state-space system analysis.

7. An interesting question in the area of computational efficiency is the determination of filter structures that require the smallest number of delays and multiplies. For second-order transfer functions Lueder [50] has shown that there are precisely 32 such structures. An intriguing related question in the state-space area is the determination of a realization in which A, B, and C have as few elements as possible that are not 0, 1, or -1. As far as I am aware, no work exists on this problem.

8. See also [88] for a statistical analysis of roundoff errors in FFT calculations.

9. Parker and Girard [55] have shown how one can take the correlation in these noise sources into account. Quantization noises due to multiplication of the same signal by two different coefficients are correlated, and the correlation can be approximated by a function that depends on the coefficients. In addition, Parker and Girard point out that correlation increases as the number of bits decreases. See also the work of Eckhardt and Schüssler [56] on evaluating quantization error variances.

10. Here we follow the standard fixed-point procedure in which all numbers are represented as fractions. One can also consider noise analysis for floating point [1, 33]. See also the work of Fettweis [52, 53, 54] in which noise analysis is performed with the aid of certain system sensitivity functions.

11. Here we have assumed $u = 0$. The analysis of the deviation of y from the desired value when $u \neq 0$ is identical to the above (if e and f are independent of u).

12. As Schüssler [51] points out, one often designs filters with limit cycles, since filters without limit cycles often have poor noise behavior, and one can over-

come the limit cycle problem by using randomized rounding, hence adding a bit more noise to the system [84, 85].

3.7 References

1. A. V. Oppenheim and R. W. Schafer, *Digital Signal Processing*, Prentice-Hall, Englewood Cliffs, N. J., 1975.

2. C.-T. Chen, *Introduction to Linear System Theory*, Holt, Rinehart and Winston, New York, 1970.

3. R. W. Brockett and R. A. Skoog, "A New Perturbation Theory for the Synthesis of Nonlinear Networks," in *Mathematical Aspects of Electrical Network Analysis, SIAM-AMS Proc.*, Vol. 3, American Mathematical Society, Providence, R. I. (1971), pp. 17–33.

4. S. I. Marcus and J. C. Willems, "Nonstationary Network Synthesis via State-Space Techniques," *IEEE Trans. Circ. and Sys.* CAS-22 (1975), pp. 713–720.

5. R. Yarlagadda, "Network Synthesis—A State-Space Approach," *IEEE Trans. Circ. Th.* CT-19 (1972), pp. 227–232.

6. B. D. O. Anderson and S. Vongpanitlerd, *Network Analysis and Synthesis*, Prentice-Hall, Englewood Cliffs, N. J., 1973.

7. D. Youla and P. Tissi, "*n*-Port Synthesis via Reactance Extraction. I," in *IEEE Int. Conv. Rec.*, part 7, 1966, pp. 183–208.

8. B. D. O. Anderson and R. W. Newcomb, "Impedance Synthesis via State-Space Techniques," *Proc. Inst. Elec. Eng.* 115(1968), pp. 928–936.

9. P. Dewilde, L. M. Silverman, and R. W. Newcomb, "A Passive Synthesis for Time-Invariant Transfer Functions," *IEEE Trans. Circ. Th* CT-17 (1970), pp. 333–338.

10. L. Weiss and R. E. Kalman, "Contributions to Linear System Theory," *Int. J. Eng. Sci.* 3(1965), pp. 141–171.

11. E. G. Gilbert, "Controllability and Observability in Multivariable Control Systems," *SIAM J. Contr.* 1 (1963), pp. 128–151.

12. R. E. Kalman, "Mathematical Description of Linear Dynamical Systems," *SIAM J. Contr.* 1 (1963), pp. 152–192.

13. L. M. Silverman and H. E. Meadows, "Equivalence and Synthesis of Time-Variable Linear Systems," in *Proc. 4th Allerton Conf. on Circuit and System*

Theory, sponsored by the Dept. of Elec. Eng. and the Coordinated Science Laboratory of the University of Illinois, Urbana-Champaign, 1966, pp. 776–784.

14. J. C. Willems and S. K. Mitter, "Controllability, Observability, Pole Allocation, and State Reconstruction," *IEEE Trans. Aut. Contr.* AC-16 (1971), pp. 582–595.

15. D. G. Luenberger, "An Introduction to Observers," *IEEE Trans. Aut. Contr.* AC-16 (1971), pp. 596–602.

16. A. S. Morse and W. M. Wonham, "Status of Noninteracting Control," *IEEE Trans. Aut. Contr.* AC-16 (1971), pp. 568–581.

17. M. L. Sain and J. L. Massey, "Invertibility of Linear Time-Invariant Dynamical Systems," *IEEE Trans. Aut. Cont.* AC-14 (1969), pp. 141–149.

18. I. B. Rhodes, "A Tutorial Introduction to Estimation and Filtering," *IEEE Trans. Aut. Contr.* AC–16 (1971), pp. 688–706.

19. G. C. Newton, Jr., L. A. Gould, and J. F. Kaiser, *Analytical Design of Linear Feedback Controls,* Wiley, New York, 1967.

20. W. B. Davenport and W. L. Root, *An Introduction to the Theory of Random Signals and Noise*, McGraw-Hill, New York, 1958.

21. J. H. Laning and R. H. Battin, *Random Processes in Automatic Control*, Wiley, New York, 1961.

22. J. M. Mendel and D. L. Gieseking, "Bibliography on the Linear-Quadratic-Gaussian Problem," *IEEE Trans. Aut. Contr.* AC-16 (1971), pp. 847–869.

23. J. B. Cruz, Jr., ed., *Feedback Systems*, McGraw-Hill, New York, 1972.

24. B. Francis, O. A. Sebakhy, and W. M. Wonham, "Synthesis of Multivariable Regulators: The Internal Model Principle," *J. Appl. Math and Opt.* (1974), pp. 64–86.

25. J. B. Pearson, R. W. Shields, and P. W. Staats, Jr., "Robust Solutions to Linear Multivariable Control Problems," *IEEE Trans. Aut. Contr.* AC-19 (1974), pp. 508–517.

26. A. S. Willsky and S. I. Marcus, "Analysis of Bilinear Noise Models in Circuits and Devices," *J. Franklin Inst.*, 301 (1976), pp. 103–122.

27. A. Gelb and R. S. Warren, "Direct Statistical Analysis of Nonlinear Systems: CADET," *AIAA Journal* 11 (1973), pp. 689–694.

28. R. E. Crochière, "Digital Network Theory and Its Application to the An-

alysis and Design of Digital Filters," Ph. D. dissertation, Massachusetts Institute of Technology, 1974.

29. B. Gold and C. M. Rader, *Digital Processing of Signals*, McGraw-Hill, New York, 1969.

30. L. R. Rabiner and B. Gold, *Theory and Application of Digital Signal Processing*, Prentice–Hall, Englewood Cliffs, N. J., 1975.

31. R. E. Crochiere and A. V. Oppenheim, "Analysis of Linear Digital Networks," *Proc. IEEE* 63 (1975), pp. 581–595.

32. R. C. Agarwal and C. S. Burrus, "Number Theoretic Transforms to Implement Fast Digital Convolution," *Proc. IEEE* 63 (1975), pp. 550–560.

33. C. Weinstein and A. V. Oppenheim, "A Comparison of Roundoff Noise in Floating Point and Fixed Point Digital Filter Realizations," *Proc. IEEE* 57 (1969), pp. 1181–1183; correction, p. 1466.

34. R. C. Agarwal and C. S. Burrus, "New Recursive Digital Filter Structures Having Very Low Sensitivity and Roundoff Noise," *IEEE Trans. Circ. and Sys.* CAS–22 (1975), pp. 921–927.

35. S. K. Mitra, K. Hirano, and H. Sakaguchi, "A Simple Method of Computing the Input Quantization and Multiplication Roundoff Errors in Digital Filters," *IEEE Trans. Acoust., Speech, and Sig. Proc.* ASSP-22 (1974), pp. 326–329.

36. L. B. Jackson, "On the Interaction of Roundoff Noise and Dynamic Range in Digital Filters," *Bell Sys. Tech. J.* 49 (1970), pp. 159–184.

37. L. B. Jackson, "Roundoff-Noise Analysis for Fixed-Point Digital Filters Realized in Cascade or Parallel Form," *IEEE Trans. Audio Electroacoust.* AU-18 (1970), pp. 107–122.

38. G. K. Roberts, "Consideration of Computer Limitations in Implementing On-Line Controls," MIT ESL Rept. ESL-R-665, Cambridge, Mass., June 1976.

39. A. H. Levis, "On the Optimal Sampled-Data Control of Linear Processes," Sc. D. thesis, Massachusetts Institute of Technology, 1968.

40. M. Athans, K.-P. Dunn, C. S. Greene, W. H. Lee, N. R. Sandell, I. Segall, and A. S. Willsky, "The Stochastic Control of the F-8C Aircraft Using the Multiple Model Adaptive Control (MMAC) Method," *Proc. 1975 IEEE Conf. Dec. and Contr.*, Catalog No. 75CH1016–5CS, IEEE, New York, 1975, pp. 217–228.

41. D. G. Lainiotis and S. K. Park, "On Joint Detection, Estimation and System Identification: Discrete Data Case," *Int. J, Contr.* 17 (1973), pp. 609–633.

42. M. Johnson, "Architectural Study for Microprocessors," presented at NASA Langley Workshop on Realizing the Potentials of Microprocessors for Aircraft Avionics Systems, NASA Langley Research Center, Hampton, Va., January 22, 1976.

43. J. Deyst, A. Hopkins, B. Smith, and K. Daly, "Internally Funded Research in Microprocessor-Based Fault-Tolerant Flight Control Systems at the Draper Laboratory," presented at NASA Langley Workshop on Realizing the Potentials of Microprocessors for Aircraft Avionics Systems, NASA Langley Research Center, Hampton, Va., January 22, 1976.

44. R. C. Montgomery and P. Lee, "Distributed Microprocessor-Based Control Systems at Langley Research Center," presented at NASA Langley Workshop on Realizing the Potentials of Microprocessors for Aircraft Avionics Systems, NASA Langley Research Center, Hampton, Va., January 22, 1976.

45. H. Kaufman and J. Modistino, "On-Line Digital Flight Control and Estimation Using Parallel Arrays of Microprocessors," presented at NASA Langley Workshop on Realizing the Potentials of Microprocessors for Aircraft Avionics Systems, NASA Langley Research Center, Hampton, Va., January 22, 1976.

46. Private communication with Dr. F. Levieux (Institut de Recherche en Informatique et Automatique, Domain de Voluceau, Rocquencourt, 78150, Le Chesnay, France) concerning ongoing research at IRIA on parallel nonlinear filtering algorithms.

47. J. Allen, "Computer Architecture for Signal Processing," *Proc.* IEEE 63 (1975), pp. 624–633.

48. S. L. Freeny, "Special-Purpose Hardware for Digital Filtering," *Proc. IEEE* 63 (1975), pp. 633–648.

49. J. F. Kaiser, "Some Practical Considerations in the Realization of Linear Digital Filters," in *Proc. 3rd Allerton Conf. on Circuit and System Theory*, sponsored by the Dept. of Elec. Eng. and the Coordinated Science Laboratory of the University of Illinois, Urbana-Champaign, 1965, pp. 621–633.

50. E. Lueder, "Design and Properties of Equivalent and Digital Two-Ports," presented at 1976 IEEE Arden House Workshop on Digital Signal Processing, Harriman, N. Y., February 1976.

51. H. W. Schüssler, "On the Required Wordlength inside a Recursive Digital Filter," presented at 1976 IEEE Arden House Workshop on Digital Signal Processing, Harriman, N. Y. February 1976.

52. A. Fettweis, "On the Connection between Multiplier Word Length Limita-

tion and Roundoff Noise in Digital Filters," *IEEE Trans. Circ. Th.* CT–19 (1972), pp. 486–491.

53. A. Fettweis, "Roundoff Noise and Attenuation Sensitivity in Digital Filters with Fixed-Point Arithmetic," *IEEE Trans. Circ. Th.* CT-20 (1973), pp. 174–175.

54. A. Fettweis, "On Sensitivity and Roundoff Noise in Wave Digital Filters," *IEEE Trans. Acoustics, Speech, and Sig. Proc.* ASSP-22 (1974), pp. 383–384.

55. S. R. Parker and P. E. Girard, "Correlated Noise due to Roundoff in Fixed Point Digital Filters," *IEEE Trans. Circ. and Sys.* CAS-23 (1976), pp. 204–211.

56. B. Eckhardt and H.W. Schüssler, "On the Quantization Error of a Multiplier," in *Proc. IEEE Internat. Symp. on Circ. and Sys.*, Catalog No. CH1074–4CAS, IEEE, New York (1976), pp. 634–637.

57. W. M. Wonham, "Random Differential Equations in Control Theory," in *Probabilistic Methods in Applied Mathematics*, vol. 2., edited by A. T. Bharucha-Reid, Academic Press, New York, 1968.

58. D. L. Kleinman, "On the Stability of Linear Stochastic Systems," *IEEE Trans. Aut. Contr.* AC-14 (1969), pp. 429–430.

59. R. C. Agarwal and J. W. Cooley, "Some New Algorithms for Fast Convolution by Multidimensional Techniques," presented at 1976 IEEE Arden House Workshop on Digital Signal Processing, Harriman, N. Y., February 1976.

60. P. J. Nicholson, "Algebraic Theory of Finite Fourier Transforms," *J. Comp. and Sys. Sci.* 5 (1971), pp. 524–547.

61. R. Bueno, E. Y. Chow, K.-P. Dunn, S. B. Gershwin, and A. S. Willsky, "Some Insights into the Performance Characteristics of the GLR Method for Failure Detection," *Proc. 1976 IEEE Conf. on Dec. and Contr.*, Catalog No. 76CH1150–2CS, IEEE, New York (1976), pp. 38–47.

62. A. S. Willsky, "Filtering for Random Finite Group Homomorphic Sequential Systems," in *Proc. Symp. on Alg. Sys. Th.*, edited by G. Marchesini and S. K. Mitter, Springer-Verlag, New York, to appear.

63. M. Loui, "Complexity of Convolutions in Semigroup Algebras," S. M. thesis, Massachusetts Institute of Technology, 1976.

64. S. Y. Hwang, "Roundoff Noise in State-Space Digital Filtering: A General Analysis," *IEEE Trans. Acous., Speech, and Sig. Proc.* ASSP–24 (1976), pp. 256–262.

65. C. T. Mullis and R. A. Roberts, "Synthesis of Minimum Roundoff Noise

Fixed Point Digital Filters," *IEEE Trans. Circ. and Sys.* CAS–23 (1976), pp. 551–562.

66. A. Sripad and D. L. Snyder, "Steady-State, Roundoff-Error Analysis in Digital Filters Realized with Fixed-Point Arithmetic," in *Proc. 14th Allerton Conf. on Circuit and System Theory*, sponsored by the Dept. of Elec. Eng. and the Coordinated Science Laboratory of the University of Illinois, Urbana-Champaign, IEEE, New York (1976).

67. A. Sripad and D. L. Snyder, "A Necessary and Sufficient Condition for Quantization Errors to be Uniform and White," *IEEE Trans. Acoust., Speech, and Sig. Proc.* ASSP–25 (1977), pp. 442–448.

68. C. Charalambous and M. J. Best, "Optimization of Recursive Digital Filters with Finite Word Lengths," *IEEE Trans. Acoustics, Speech, Sig. Proc.* ASSP–22 (1974), pp. 424–431.

69. E. Avenhaus, "A Proposal to Find Suitable Canonical Structures for the Implementation of Digital Filters with Small Coefficient Wordlength," *Nachrichtentech. Z.* 25 (1972), pp. 377–382.

70. R. E. Rink and H. Y. Chong, "Performance of State Regulator Systems with Floating-Point Computation," submitted to *IEEE Trans. Aut. Control.*

71. R. E. Rink, "Optimal. Utilization of Fixed-Capacity Channels in Feedback Control," *Automatica* 9 (1973), pp. 251–255.

72. R. E. Rink, "Coded Data Control of Linear Systems," in *Proc. 8th Princeton Conf. on Inf. and Sys.*, Dept. of Elec. Eng., Princeton University, Princeton, N.J. (1974), pp. 86–89.

73. J. B. Knowles and R. Edwards, "Effect of a Finite-Word-Length Computer in a Sampled-Data Feedback System," *Proc. IEEE* 112 (1965), pp. 1197–1207.

74. J. B. Slaughter, "Quantization Errors in Digital Control Systems," *IEEE Trans. Aut. Control* AC–9 (1964), pp. 70–74.

75. B. Widrow, "Statistical Analysis of Amplitude-Quantized Sampled-Data Systems," *Trans. AIEE* 79, pt. II (1961), pp. 555–567.

76. A. A. Kosyakin, "Taking the Effect of Quantization by Level into Account in the Statistical Analysis of Closed-Loop Digital Automatic Systems," *Automation and Remote Control* 27 (1966), pp. 799–805.

77. R. Curry et al., "State Estimation with Coarsely Quantized, High-Data-Rate Measurements," *IEEE Trans. Aerospace and Elec. Sys.* AES–11 (1975), pp. 613–620.

78. R. Curry, *Estimation and Control with Quantized Measurements*, MIT Press, Cambridge, Mass., 1970.

79. L. B. Jackson, A. G. Lindgren, and Y. Kim, "Synthesis of State-Space Digital Filters with Low Roundoff Noise and Coefficient Sensitivity," in *Proc. IEEE Internat. Symp. Circ. and Sys.*, Catalog No. CH11882, IEEE, New York (1977).

80. C. T. Mullis, and R. A. Roberts, "Roundoff Noise in Digital Filters: Frequency Transformations and Invariants," *IEEE Trans. Acoust., Speech, and Sig. Proc.* ASSP–24 (1976), pp. 538–550.

81. S. Y. Hwang, "Minimum Uncorrelated Unit Noise in State-Space Digital Filtering," *IEEE Trans. Acoust., Speech, and Sig. Proc.* ASSP–25 (1977), pp. 273–281.

82. L. M. Silverman, "Inversion of Multivariable Linear Systems," *IEEE Trans. Aut. Cont.* AC–14 (1969), pp. 270–276.

83. M. Morf and T. Kailath, "Recent Results in Least-Squares Estimation Theory," *Ann. of Econometrics*, to appear.

84. R. B. Kieburtz, V. B. Lawrence, and K. V. Mina, "Control of Limit Cycles in Recursive Digital Filters by Randomized Quantization," *IEEE Trans. Circ. and Sys.* CAS–24 (1977), pp. 291–299.

85. M. Büttner, "Elimination of Limit Cycles in Digital Filters with Very Low Increase in the Quantization Noise," *IEEE Trans. Circ. and Sys.* CAS–24 (1977), pp. 300–304.

86. S. Winograd, "On Computing the Discrete Fourier Transform," *Proc. Nat. Acad. Sci. USA* 73 (1976), pp. 1005–1006.

87. J. McClellan and C. M. Rader, *Number Theory Concepts in Digital Signal Processing* (tentative title), Prentice-Hall, Englewood Cliffs, N. J., to appear 1978.

88. T. Thong and B. Liu, "Accumulation of Roundoff Errors in Floating Point FFT," *IEEE Trans. Circ. and Sys.* CAS–24 (1977), pp. 132–143.

89. A. F. Konar and J. K. Makesh, "Digital Flight Control Systems Analysis Workshop," Rept. No. F0510–TR1, Systems and Research Div., Honeywell, Minneapolis, Minn., 1977.

90. R. S. Bucy, "Nonlinear Filtering with Pipeline and Array Processors," in *Proc. 1977 IEEE Conf. on Dec. and Contr.*, Catalog No. 77CH1269–OCS, IEEE, New York (1977), pp. 626–629.

91. R. W. Brockett, *Finite Dimensional Linear Systems*, John Wiley and Sons, New York, 1970.

92. M. Athans, ed., "Special Issue on Linear-Quadratic-Gaussian Problem," *IEEE Trans. Aut. Contr.* AC–16, December 1971.

93. L. Silverman, "Realization of Linear Dynamical Systems," *IEEE Trans. Aut. Contr.* AC–16 (1971), pp. 554–567.

94. B. L. Ho and R. E. Kalman, "Effective Construction of Linear State Variable Models from Input-Output Functions," *Regelungstechnik* 14 (1966), pp. 545–548.

95. R. E. Kalman, P. L. Falb, and M. A. Arbib, *Topics in Mathematical System Theory*, McGraw-Hill, New York, 1969.

96. B. C. Kuo, *Analysis and Synthesis of Sampled-Data Control Systems*, Prentice-Hall, Englewood Cliffs, N. J., 1963.

97. W. A. Wolovich, *Linear Multivariable Systems*, Springer-Verlag, New York, 1974.

98. H. H. Rosenbrock, *State-Space and Multivariable Theory*, J. Wiley, New York, 1970.

99. B. W. Dickinson, T. Kailath, and M. Morf, "Canonical Matrix Fraction and State-Space Descriptions for Deterministic and Stochastic Linear Systems," *IEEE Trans. Aut. Contr.* AC–19 (1974), pp. 656–667.

100. A. H. Jazwinski, *Stochastic Processes and Filtering Theory*, Academic Press, New York, 1970.

101. L. R. Rabiner, J. H. McClellan, and T. W. Parks, "FIR Digital Filter Design Techniques Using Weighted Chebyshev Approximation," *Proc. IEEE* 63 (1975), pp. 595–610.

102. B. W. Dickinson, M. Morf, and T. Kailath, "A Minimal Realization Algorithm for Matrix Sequences," *IEEE Trans. Aut. Contr.* AC–19 (1974), pp. 31–38.

103. J. L. Massey, "Shift Register Synthesis and BCH Decoding," *IEEE Trans. Inf. Th.* IT–15 (1969), pp. 122–127.

104. J. Rissanen, "Recursive Identification of Linear Systems," *SIAM J. Contr.* 9 (1971), pp. 420–430.

105. T. A. C. M. Claasen, W. F. G. Mecklenbräuker, and J. B. H. Peek, "Effects

of Quantization and Overflow in Recursive Digital Filters," *IEEE Trans. Acoust., Speech, and Sig. Proc.* ASSP–24 (1976), pp. 517–529.

106. A. V. Oppenheim and C. J. Weinstein, "Effects of Finite Register Length in Digital Filtering and the Fast Fourier Transform," *Proc. IEEE* 60 (1972), pp. 957–976.

107. D. S. K. Chan, "Theory and Implementation of Multidimensional Discrete Systems for Signal Processing," Ph.D. dissertation, Massachusetts Institute of Technology, 1978.

108. N. R. Sandell, "Information Flow in Decentralized Systems," in *Directions in Large Scale Systems*, edited by Y.-C. Ho and S. K. Mitter, Plenum Press, New York, 1976.

109. N. R. Sandell, P. Varaiya, and M. Athans, "A Survey of Decentralized Control Methods for Large-Scale Systems," presented at Engineering Foundation Conference on System Engineering for Power: Status and Prospects, Henniker, N. H., August 1975.

110. Y. C. Ho and K. C. Chu, "Team Decision Theory and Information Structures in Optimal Control Problems, I," *IEEE Trans. Aut. Contr.* AC–17 (1972), pp. 15–22.

111. K. C. Chu, "Team Decision Theory and Information Structures in Optimal Control Problems, II," *IEEE Trans. Aut. Contr.* AC–17 (1972), pp. 22–28.

112. R. Muralidharan, "Memory Considerations in Stochastic Control Problems", Tech. Rept. 626, Div. Eng. Appl. Phys., Harvard Univ., Cambridge, Mass., October 1971.

113. D. Teneketzis, "Peturbation Methods in Decentralized Stochastic Control," MIT Elec. Sys. Lab. Rept. ESL–R–664, Cambridge, Mass., June 1976.

114. T. M. Athay, "Numerical Analysis of the Lyapunov Equation with Application to Interconnected Power Systems," MIT Elec. Sys. Lab. Rept. ESL–R–663, Cambridge, Mass., June 1976.

115. A. S. Willsky, "A Survey of Failure Detection Methods in Linear Dynamic Systems," *Automatica* 12 (1976), pp. 601–611.

116. D. L. Gustafson, A. S. Willsky, J.-Y. Wang, M. C. Lancaster, and J. H. Triebwasser, "A Statistical Approach to Rhythm Diagnosis of Cardiograms," *Proc. IEEE*, 65 (1977), pp. 802–804.

117. R. A. Meyer and C. S. Burrus, "A Unified Analysis of Multirate and Period-

ically Time-Varying Digital Filters," *IEEE Trans. Circ. and Sys.* CAS–22 (1975), pp. 162–168.

118. R. A. Meyer and C. S. Burrus, "Design and Implementation of Multirate Digital Filters," *IEEE Trans. Acoust., Speech, and Sig. Proc.,* to appear.

119. Y. Rouchaleau, B. F. Wyman, and R. E. Kalman, "Algebraic Structure of Linear Dynamical Systems. III: Realization Theory over a Commutative Ring," *Proc. Nat. Acad. Sci.* 69 (1972), pp. 3404–3406.

120. E. D. Sontag, "Linear Systems Over Commutative Rings: A Survey," *Ricerche di Automatica* 7 (1976), pp. 1–34.

121. E. W. Kamen, "On an Operator Theory of Linear Systems with Pure and Distributed Delays," in *Proc. 1975 IEEE Conf. on Dec. and Contr.,* Catalog No. 75CH1016–5CS, IEEE, New York (1975), pp. 77–80.

122. R. Johnston, "Linear Systems over Various Rings," Ph. D. dissertation, Massachusetts Institute of Technology, 1973.

123. H. S. Witsenhausen, "Some Remarks on the Concept of State," in *Directions in Large-Scale Systems,* edited by Y.-C. Ho and S. K. Mitter, Plenum Press, New York, 1976.

4

Multiparameter Systems, Distributed Processes, and Random Fields

4.1. Introduction

A growing interest has developed over the past few years in problems involving signals and systems that depend on more than one independent variable. In some cases one of these variables is time and the others represent spatial dimensions, as in the study of distributed parameter systems [157–159] or decentralized control [87, 88, 93, 94]. For other problems, such as image processing [4, 6, 7, 20, 21], none of the independent variables can be thought of as time.

This area is rich in both potential applications and challenging theoretical problems. Among the applications are image processing, seismic signal processing, meteorology, gravity field mapping, pollution monitoring and control, and inertial navigation. On the theoretical side are a number of basic conceptual questions. How does one process distributed data efficiently? What properties do recursive techniques have when the recursion is in more than one dimension? Do causality and state make any sense here? What about stability? What are the tools for analyzing stochastic processes? How do we "predict" when time is not the independent variable? What role do recursive estimation techniques play? What are recursive estimation techniques? Which concepts concerning signals and systems in one independent variable carry over to the multiparameter case? Which do not, and why don't they?

In this chapter we consider several problems involving multiparameter signals and systems in order to discuss some of these issues in more detail. For an up-to-date view of some of the research in this area, see the recent special issue of the *Proceedings of the IEEE* [248].

4.2 Two-Dimensional Systems and Filters

4.2.1 Shift-Invariant Linear Systems

Over the past few years a great deal of work has been done in attempting to extend one-dimensional filtering concepts to the design and analysis of systems that process data distributed in two-dimensional arrays. The consideration of two-dimensional systems has raised an entirely new set of questions, and in this section we want to explore some of these design and analysis issues. For an excellent and thorough overview of two-dimensional digital filtering see [3].

As in one dimension, we can define a linear shift-invariant (LSI) system that processes two-dimensional input arrays $x(m, n)$ to produce two-dimensional output arrays in a linear fashion and so that a shift in the "time" origin for the input merely induces an analogous shift in the output. Such a system has a convolutional representation, much as in one dimension.

$$y(m, n) = \sum_{k, l=-\infty}^{+\infty} h(m - k, n - l)x(k, l) = h(m, n) * x(m, n)$$
$$= x(m, n) * h(m, n)$$
(1)

Here $h(j, k)$ is the unit sample response, that is, the response of the system to the input

$$x(k, l) = \delta_{k0}\delta_{l0}.$$
(2)

The Kronecker delta δ_{ij} is nonzero and equals 1 only if $i = j$. The unit sample response is sometimes referred to as the *point-spread function* [4], a term used in image processing, where $h(j, k)$ is the observed image when the input illumination is a point source at the origin.

Again as in the one-dimensional case we can take z-transforms. For example, the *system function* of (1) is

$$H(z_1, z_2) = \sum_{k, l=-\infty}^{+\infty} h(k, l) z_1^{-k} z_2^{-l},$$
(3)

and a simple calculation transforms (1) into

$$Y(z_1, z_2) = H(z_1, z_2)X(z_1, z_2). \tag{4}$$

An important class of LSI systems arises from rational system functions

$$H(z_1, z_2) = \frac{A(z_1, z_2)}{B(z_1, z_2)}, \tag{5}$$

$$A(z_1, z_2) = \sum_{(k, l) \in I_1} a(k, l) z_1^{-k} z_2^{-l},$$
$$B(z_1, z_2) = \sum_{(k, l) \in I_2} b(k, l) z_1^{-k} z_2^{-l}, \tag{6}$$

where I_1 and I_2 are finite sets of pairs of integers. As a straightforward consequence of (4)–(6), we obtain a two-dimensional (partial) difference equation relating y and x:

$$\sum_{(k, l) \in I_2} b(k, l)y(m - k, n - l) = \sum_{(k, l) \in I_1} a(k, l)x(m - k, n - l). \tag{7}$$

4.2.2 Recursion, Causality, and Partial Orders

The mathematical steps taken so far follow the one-dimensional steps very closely, but now we begin to see some of the conceptual as well as mathematical difficulties that arise in the two-dimensional case. Let us first discuss the problem of recursion. We want to use (7) to calculate the next output, given previous outputs and the input. Embedded in this statement is the heart of one of the problems. In the one-dimensional case the index n has the interpretation of time, but in the two dimensioned case it is not in general clear what "next" or "previous" means.[1] In fact, if we are given just (7), it is not clear that there is any definition of next or previous that allows us to recursively compute $y(m, n)$. Dudgeon [3, 5, 33], Pistor [42], and Ekstrom and Woods [103, 119] have studied this problem in great detail, and we now briefly examine their work.

In the nonrecursive (FIR) case (when $B = 1$) there is no problem computing (7) output point by output point. There is, however, a question concerning the part of the input that must be stored at any one time. In one dimension we just keep the most recent input points (assuming we compute $y(n)$ sequentially), but the situation is more complex in two dimensions. For example, suppose we have the "nearest-neighbor" filter [31]

$$I_1 = \{(-1, 0), (0, 0), (1, 0), (0 - 1), (0, 1)\}. \tag{8}$$

Then to compute $y(m, n)$ we need $x(m + 1, n)$, $x(m, n)$, $x(m - 1, n)$, $x(m, n + 1)$, $x(m, n - 1)$. Conversely we must hold $x(m, n)$ until we have computed $y(m - 1, n)$, $y(m, n)$, $y(m + 1, n)$, $y(m, n - 1)$, $y(m, n + 1)$. Thus, depending on the order in which we compute the y's, we can have very different requirements for storing the x's. We can begin to see that the required storage depends not only on the degree of the filter but also on the sequencing of computations. For FIR filters, as in the one-dimensional case, we can process inputs in blocks, using a two-dimensional FFT algorithm together with an appropriate method for taking care of the overlaps in the blocks. Methods along these lines exactly parallel the one-dimensional methods [3].

Thus the right-hand side of (7) does not raise any insurmountable obstacles for the sequential processing of inputs (although there are several interesting questions). The situation is far different in the recursive case ($B \neq$ constant). Since the right-hand side of (7) causes no difficulties, we assume that it is trivial ($A = 1$) for convenience. Let us consider one of the most widely used special cases of (7):

$$\sum_{k=0}^{M} \sum_{l=0}^{N} b(k, l)y(m - k, n - l) = x(m, n). \tag{9}$$

Assuming that $b(0, 0) \neq 0$, we have

$$y(m, n) = - \frac{1}{b(0, 0)} \sum_{k=0}^{M} \sum_{l=0}^{N} b(k, l)y(m - k, n - l)$$
$$+ \frac{1}{b(0, 0)} x(m, n), \qquad (k, l) \neq (0, 0), \tag{10}$$

and we immediately see that to calculate $y(m, n)$, we need only the values of outputs to the "southwest".[2] Figures 4.1–4.4 illustrate the situation. In figure 4.1 we see that the support of the function $b(k, l)$ is in the first quadrant. We call such a function a northeast (NE) function, for reasons that will become clear shortly. In figure 4.2 we see the set of data points to the southwest must be stored in order to enable us to calculate $y(m, n)$. A consequence of this is seen in figure 4.3. If we are interested in calculating $y(m, n)$ in the NE quadrant, we must specify initial or boundary conditions as shown. As we calculate and store some of the output points, we can discard some of the old values. But it is clear that the amount of storage needed depends not only on M and N in (9) but also on the range of values

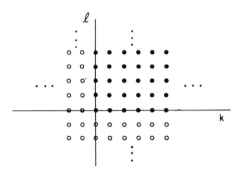

4.1
Support of a first-quadrant or Northeast (NE) function (possible nonzero locations are indicated by solid dots).

of m and n for which we want to calculate y. If either of these ranges is infinite, the storage needed is infinite.

The storage requirements also depend on the sequencing of the recursion, as in the FIR case. Several directions of recursion are indicated in figure 4.4. Here (a) depicts the north recursion, (b) is the east recursion, and (c) is a NE recursion. We can generate other directions of recursion as long as they remain within the NE quadrant. Each recursion calls for its own sequence of data accessing and discarding. The N and E recursions appear to have particularly simple sequencing rules, but the data must be processed serially. On the other hand, the NE recursion has a more com-

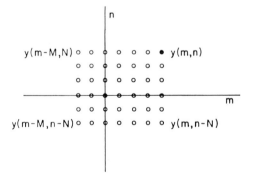

4.2
Required output points (open dots) to calculate $y(m, n)$ for the system given by (9).

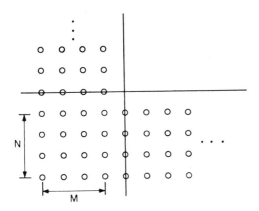

4.3
Required boundary conditions for (9) to calculate NE quadrant of y.

plex sequencing but leads to the possibility of parallel computation, since points 4, 5, and 6, for example, can be calculated simultaneously. The possible directions for recursion and potential uses of parallel computation can be determined with the aid of a conceptual device—the precedence relation, which partially orders points with the rule

$(m, n) \prec (l, k)$ if $y(m, n)$ has to be calculated first in order to be able to calculate $y(l, k)$.   (11)

Thus $(m, n) \prec (l, k)$ if $y(m, n)$ is directly needed to calculate $y(l, k)$ or if it is used to calculate some $y(r, s)$ that is used directly to calculate $y(l, k)$, and so on. This topic has been discussed by Chan [107, 152].

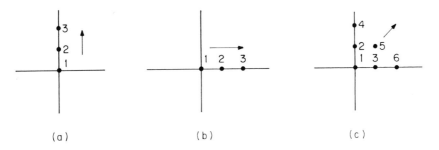

     (a)   (b)   (c)

4.4
Several possible directions of recursion for (9).

Let us now return to the question of recursibility. Clearly the picture is symmetric; we can have NW, SE, and SW recursions, with $b(k, l)$ restricted to be a function on the corresponding quadrant. However, as Dudgeon [5, 33] shows, this by no means exhausts the possibilities for recursion. In addition to the one-quadrant functions, we can obtain recursive difference equations with $b(k, l)$'s that are one-sided [5]. To illustrate, consider the equation

$$y(m, n) = -\frac{1}{b(0, 0)} \sum_{k=1}^{M} \sum_{l=-N}^{N} b(k, l)y(m - k, n - l)$$

$$-\frac{1}{b(0, 0)} \sum_{l=1}^{N} b(0, l)y(m, n - l) + \frac{1}{b(0, 0)} x(m, n).$$

(12)

Figure 4.5 illustrates the support of such a function, while figure 4.6 indicates the direction of recursion and the required initial conditions. Here we calculate the data points column by column, using data points to the south and the west (not just the southwest). Hence the directions of recursion are far more limited than in the single-quadrant case, since we cannot move east until all the data points required in the present column have been calculated. For more details see [5, 33, 100]; these works discuss related issues such as the rotation of the support of one-sided or one-quadrant functions to obtain recursions at various angles.

Thus the two-dimensional case is more complex than the one-dimensional one in the notion of recursibility and some of its geometric in-

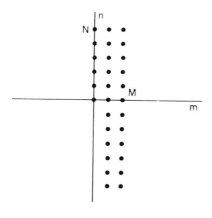

4.5
Support of a one-sided function.

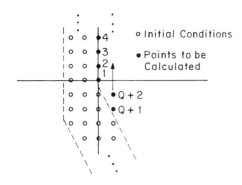

4.6
Required initial conditions and the direction of recursion for the filter of (4.12).

terpretations. One can avoid many of these difficulties by sticking to nonrecursive designs, but recursive techniques offer enough potential advantages in computation time and storage to warrant further detailed study.

Let us make another connection with one-dimensional processing. Suppose that one of the two index, say m, is interpreted as time. Then one might think of $y(m, n)$ and $x(m, n)$ as (one-dimensional) spatially distributed processes that evolve in time. Temporal causality might then correspond to modifying the support of b in figure 4.5 by deleting the points on the positive n axis, yielding a "strictly" one-sided function. In this case one could define the state of the system, and it is clear that this state is finite dimensional only if the range of n is bounded, which is precisely when the required storage for the two-dimensional recursion is finite. This clearly shows why the order of a two-dimensional filter does not itself specify the storage requirements; one must also know the range of m and n. Hence we see that two-dimensional digital filtering of scalar (or perhaps vector) variables bears some resemblance to the one-dimensional state-space framework for multi- and possibly infinite-dimensional systems that arise in multivariable and distributed system and control theory.

An intriguing question is, Can this interrelationship be exploited to yield useful insights and results for either one- or two-dimensional problems? The answer is, of course, yes. Such problems arise in seismic signal processing, in which the data to be processed $x(m, n)$ vary in time (m) and also in array sensor location (n). This successful exploitation of the two-dimensional, multivariable one-dimensional interrelationship raises a number of speculative questions. In large-scale system theory a number of subsystems are often coupled, and we are interested in efficient processing of data and control of such systems. If we view the variables as functions of two independent parameters, time and subsystem index, can we obtain any insights into the control and processing of large systems with the aid of two-dimensional digital filtering concepts? Note that this would involve the consideration of feedback for two-dimensional systems,[3] a topic that to our knowledge has never been addressed in the digital filtering context (with good reason—it is irrelevant for usual two-dimensional processing problems). We have been somewhat vague about this topic, but we shall return to this large-system, two-dimensional filter idea several times in this chapter, since some interesting insights and questions arise. Another possible use of two-dimensional concepts for one-dimensional problems is for the analysis of time-varying one-dimensional systems, in which one can define a system function in two variables—a transform variable and time. Such concepts may also have value in developing time-varying linear prediction algorithms. On the other side, to study questions such as stability or roundoff noise behavior for two-dimensional filters, is there any benefit in viewing the two-dimensional filter as a multivariable one-dimensional system [90]? The answers to all of these questions require further study.

The ability to solve a two-dimensional difference equation recursively leads directly to the definition of a partial order (11) on the part of the two-dimensional grid over which we wish to solve the equation [107, 152]. Given this partial order (the precedence relation), we then have some freedom in deciding how to sequence the calculations. If we think of a sequence of calculations as determining a total order (denoted by $\leq$) on the part of the two-dimensional grid of interest, all we require is that this total order be compatible with the precedence relation. That is, (m, n) is calculated before (l, k), written $(m, n) \leq (l, k)$, if $(m, n) \prec (l, k)$. Manry and Aggarwal [56] have studied such order relations for NE recursive filters. One of their first observations is the following. Given a compatible total order $\leq$, the first quadrant can be put into a one-to-one, order-preserving correspondence with the nonnegative integers:

$Q(m, n) = r \Leftrightarrow$ there are precisely $(r + 1)$ points in the NE
quadrant $\leq (m, n)$.   (13)

Given the function Q, we can think of (10) as determining a one-dimensional filter, with (m, n) replaced by $Q(m, n)$, and so on. Alternatively, given the ordering (13), we can think of processing the input $x(m, n)$ with a linear time-invariant one-dimensional filter. In general neither of these filters—the one-dimensional filter obtained from (10) and (13) or the two-dimensional filter obtained from a given LTI one-dimensional filter and (13)—is shift-invariant; of course, both are still linear (see also Mersereau and Dudgeon [3, 55]).

Let us examine several orders. Manry and Aggarwal suggest the order of figure 4.4c, since every point in the NE quadrant is mapped by (13) into a finite integer. The orders suggested by figure 4.4a, b are well-posed only if the desired range of one of the variables m or n is finite. In this case we obtain several possible orders, as given in figure 4.7. In both cases the range of values is limited in the n direction. Manry and Aggarwal suggest the section scan of figure 4.7b. They then show that except for effects near the bottom line or at the junction of two sections, the one-dimensional difference equation from (10) and (13) looks shift-invariant. Assuming this shift-invariance holds throughout the entire region, they then obtain a one-dimensional stable filter and show that sections can be overlapped to reduce the errors at section junctions, leaving substantial errors only at the far left and along the bottom. Despite these errors, this is a promising method for using one-dimensional techniques to design filters to process two-dimensional data.

The scan order of figure 4.7a has been widely used in processing images using line-by-line scans [3, 21, 55, 58]. Nahi [21, 58] has used this to develop stochastic models for image processing, and the shift variance introduced by doing one-dimensional processing on the scan-ordered data points causes errors along the bottom. Mersereau and Dudgeon [3, 55] point this out, noting that only periodic unit sample responses of the form $h(m, n) = h(m + 1, n - N)$ can be realized exactly by a one-dimensional shift-invariant filter working on the scan-ordered data. They also study this order when the data array is finite in both directions, such as it is for a two-dimensional finite impulse-response function. As they point out, the Fourier transform of the one-dimensional scan signal in this case is a slice of the two-dimensional Fourier transform of the original data array.

(a)

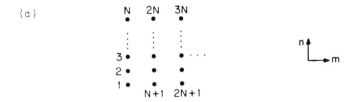

(b)

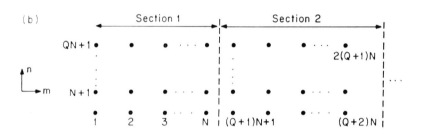

4.7
Two orders for one-dimensional processing of two-dimensional signals: (a) The
scan order of Dudgeon-Mersereau [3, 55] and Nahi et al. [21, 58]. (b) The section-scan order of Manry-Aggarwal [56].

Since the order is invertible, we can completely recover the two-dimensional transform from this slice (which they term a *critical slice* because of this property). Consequently, with the aid of one-dimensional design methods we can use this scan ordering for two-dimensional FIR filter design. Given the Fourier transform of the ideal two-dimensional filter, we take a critical slice, hence obtaining an ideal one-dimensional filter. We use one-dimensional design methods to determine an approximation to this ideal transfer function. We then either use this one-dimensional filter to process the scanned data[4] or invert the one-dimensional filter, regarded as a critical slice, to find a two-dimensional filter that can operate directly on the two-dimensional array [3, 55]. A closely related result involves the recovery of two-dimensional images from one-dimensional projections of the array. Such a technique is of great interest in biomedical applications such as tomography. A detailed survey of the theory and available algorithms related to this subject can be found in [29].

Two-dimensional orders and precedence relations arise naturally in certain feedback control problems. Ho and Chu [87, 88] consider optimal control problems in which a set of decision makers base their decisions on certain observed data, which may be affected by the decisions of others. These decisions may be made at different points in time and/or by distinct decision makers at the same points in time. Ho and Chu define a precedence relation among decisions,

$$j \prec i \text{ if the decision of } j \text{ affects the observation of } i, \tag{14}$$

and they assume that this is a partial order; that is, if $j \prec i$ we cannot have $i \prec j$ (this is precisely the condition needed for recursibility of two-dimensional filters). Then under a "partially nested information condition"—if $j \prec i$, then i's observation includes knowledge of j's observation—they solve an optimal control problem.[5] When the partial order is a total order, for example when $\prec$ is really just time ordering, this is the usual optimal control problem. When the order is not total, one can have simultaneous (incomparable) decision makers who do not affect the others' observations.

Witsenhausen [93, 94] has also studied this partial order and has raised issues analogous to those of Chan [107, 152]. Witsenhausen points out that the amount of parallelism in the control system is essentially a measure of the number of incomparable decision makers (this number may vary with time). In addition, if one totally orders the set of decision makers in a way compatible with (14), one can then define the state evolution of the system. Hence we see that there may be many possible sets of state descriptions corresponding to different compatible total orders (just as storage requirements vary with the choice of recursion). In fact, using a generalization of the Nerode notion of state, Witsenhausen shows that the set of possible states forms a lattice. All this is developed with certain decentralized control problems (involving incomparable decision makers) in mind, and Witsenhausen points out that it is not clear whether his notion of state will be useful in solving such problems (as it is in the classical totally ordered case). He mentions that the a priori partial-order restriction does not hold in some game-theory problems, in which the sequence in which future decision makers act can be affected by prior decisions. The difficulties here, as with those of nonrecursible two-dimensional filters, are substantial.[6]

4.2.3 Stability

An important problem in the study or design of two-dimensional recursive filters is stability. See [297] for a thorough survey of results for this problem. We define stability as the absolute summability of the unit impulse response [3, 16, 49, 264]

$$\sum_{m, n=-\infty}^{+\infty} |h(m, n)| < \infty. \tag{15}$$

This condition is equivalent to bounded-input, bounded-output stability. As one might expect from knowledge of the one-dimensional case, the stability of a filter might depend on the direction of recursion. That is, the equation

$$y(m + 1, n) = 2y(m, n) + x(m + 1, n) \tag{16}$$

is unstable if solved to the east, but it is stable

$$y(m, n) = \tfrac{1}{2}y(m + 1, n) - \tfrac{1}{2}x(m + 1, n) \tag{17}$$

if solved to the west.

Shanks, Treitel, and Justice [49] considered the stability of two-dimensional systems with rational transfer functions as in (5), (6), with b a NE function, as in (9). They also explicitly considered stability of the recursion in the NE direction only; that is, they used (10) to compute $y(m, n)$ from

inputs plus outputs to the SW. In this case they obtained a direct analog
of the one-dimensional stability result:

A rational transfer function $H(z_1, z_2)$ as in (5) with b a
NE function is recursively stable in the NE direction if and
only if no zero of the denominator $B(z_1, z_2)$ lies in the
region $\{|z_1| \geq 1\} \cap \{|z_2| \geq 1\}$. (18)

As in the one-dimensional case, we can use a NE b to define a SW recursion; instead of going from (9) to (10), remove $y(m - M, n - N)$ from
the sum in (9). We can then recursively compute this quantity using outputs to the NE. Similarly we can pull out the other two "corner" elements
to obtain NW and SE recursions. Hence we have four possibilities as opposed to the two in one dimension (16), (17). As in the one-dimensional
case, we obtain different stability conditions for those four cases, which
Huang [50] has derived. For example, for the SW recursion we have
stability if and only if no zeros of $B(z_1, z_2)$ lie in $\{|z_1| \leq 1\} \cap \{|z_2| \leq 1\}$.
Huang showed that at most one of the four directions of recursion can
lead to a stable filter. Justice and Shanks [16] extended these ideas to recursions in different directions for N-dimensional filters in which B does
not necessarily have finite degree in $z_1, \ldots, z_N$ and $z_1^{-1}, \ldots, z_N^{-1}$. We
refer the interested reader to [16] for a detailed statement and proof of
these results.

We now turn to the problem of checking conditions such as (18). The
problem is complicated by the fact that the zeros of $B(z_1, z_2)$ are not
isolated points but surfaces [3]. This makes the direct checking of (18) quite
difficult. We must map $|z_1| \geq 1$ into the z_2-plane via the implicit relation
$B(z_1, z_2) = 0$; we then have stability if and only if the image lies within
$|z_2| \leq 1$. Fortunately a number of simplifications of the criterion (18)
have been made. Huang [50] showed that (18) holds if and only if

$$B(z_1, \infty) \neq 0, \qquad |z_1| \geq 1, \tag{19}$$

$$B(z_1, z_2) \neq 0, \qquad |z_1| = 1, |z_2| \geq 1. \tag{20}$$

This type of criterion has been generalized to N dimensions by Anderson
and Jury [45].

Let us consider the computations in (19) and (20). The test of condition
(19) is essentially a one-dimensional stability test, since $B(z_1, \infty)$ is a polynomial in z_1^{-1}. On the surface, however, it appears that (20) requires an

infinite amount of computation (again we must map $|z_1| = 1$ into the z_2-plane via $B(z_1, z_2) = 0$). There are several finite algorithms for testing for conditions such as (20). Huang used a two-dimensional bilinear transformation to modify condition (20) so that the continuous two-dimensional parameter results of Ansell [64] could be used. Ansell used a Hermite test, which checks for the positivity of the principal minors of a symmetric matrix of polynomials in one variable (this is a positive-real test). The positivity tests in turn can performed using Sturm tests [50, 54, 64].

Anderson and Jury [54] suggested another method for checking (20). Instead of using the bilinear transform plus the Hermite test, one can work directly with condition (20), using a Schur-Cohn test [125] that replaces (20) with a check for the positivity of all the minors of a certain Hermitian matrix of polynomials in one variable. Again one can use Sturm tests on the individual minors. An alternative to this approach was proposed by Maria and Fahmy [130], who used a modified version of the Jury table [125] to obtain a finite check of (20).

Recently an algorithm far simpler than these and better suited for computer implementation was developed by Siljak [27]. The key to this algorithm is a powerful result [122] on the positivity of polynomial matrices. This result was developed with the applications of multivariable positive real functions to networks in mind [131]; it replaces the sequence of tests of positivity of principal minors with two tests, independent of the dimension of the matrix. One need test only for positivity of the matrix at a single value of the independent variable and for the positivity of the determinant. We refer the reader to [27] for details and for further remarks on the relationship of these stability results to multivariable techniques arising in network synthesis. See also the recent work of Strintzis [254, 255, 262], who has devised alternative stability criteria for multidimensional filters. In [254] he develops a test that in the two-dimensional case is simpler than that of Anderson and Jury [54], while in [255, 262] he considers stability conditions for NE causal and certain noncausal systems. (Essentially these have impulse responses that are nonzero in a full half-plane, as in figure 4.5 but with support including the negative part of the n axis.) Strintzis applies these results to determine conditions guaranteeing the stability of minimum mean-square estimators of random processes in the plane. Given observations $y(m, n)$ and a process to be estimated $x(m, n)$, Strintzis derives conditions on the power spectral density of y (plus a technical condition that is almost always satisfied) that guarantee the stability of certain estimators having either a NE causal structure or the half-plane structure.

Much work has been done to extend tests for stability and positivity to the N-dimensional case. Anderson and Jury [45] extended their use of the Schur-Cohn test to higher dimensions, but they did not directly propose a finite algorithm for the positivity tests that must be performed on polynomials in N-1 variables (which arise as principal minors from the Schur-Cohn test). Bose and Jury [57] developed such an algorithm in the three-dimensional case, in which the two-dimensional positivity tests reduce to tests for sign variations of single-variable polynomials defined on the unit circle in the complex plane. They also developed an extremely efficient method for computing multidimensional bilinear transformations, which allows them to develop a stability test algorithm for three-dimensional continuous systems. With the aid of results from decision algebra, Bose and Kamat [124] devised an algorithm for implementing Jury table calculations for an N-dimensional stability test that involves a finite number of multivariable polynomial multiplications and a finite number of single-variable polynomial factorizations (a nontrivial numerical problem). In addition Bose [147, 148] and Bose and Modarressi [118, 150] have used concepts from Jury's theory of inners [123] to develop tests for positivity, nonnegativity, and greatest common factors of multivariable polynomials. Such tests are useful not only in multivariable stability and positivity tests, but also in applying Lyapunov's direct method to test for the stability of multi-state-variable, one-dimensional systems.

4.2.4 Stabilization, Spectral Factorization, and Least-Squares Inverses

Stability is clearly important in filter design, but Mersereau and Dudgeon [3] point out that it is not enough to have a stability test. Rather, one wants a procedure for taking given frequency response characteristics and generating stable, recursive filters that possess these characteristics. One approach is to take a given transfer function and stabilize it by finding a stable system function that has the same magnitude function for its frequency response. In one dimension this process can easily be accomplished by replacing poles outside the unit circle with poles at conjugate reciprocal locations. An algebraic approach to this problem does not work in two dimensions, since in general we cannot factor two-dimensional polynomials. This is often referred to as the "absence of the fundamental theorem of algebra" for multivariable polynomials [3]. However, another one-dimensional approach to performing this stabilization, which involves the use of the discrete Hilbert transform techniques, has been extended to the two-dimensional case by Read and Treitel [53]. In this approach one takes the denominator polynomial of a given rational response and calculates its log-magnitude function. Then the two dimensional discrete Hilbert transform can be used to determine the minimum-phase function associated with the log-magnitude function. One can then exponentiate to obtain the desired stable denominator. As Mersereau and Dedgeon [3] point out, one of the difficulties with this method is that the resulting denominator need not be of finite order. Read and Treitel point out that this also can be traced to the lack of a fundamental theorem of algebra.

Another approach to stabilization is to use spectral factorization to break a given system function into the product of several system functions, each stable with respect to a different direction of recursion. In one dimension the fundamental theorem of algebra allows us to write any rational $H(z)$ as

$$H(z) = H_E(z)H_W(z), \tag{21}$$

where H_E has all its poles inside the unit circle (and hence is stable if used to process inputs in the eastern direction) and H_W has all its poles outside the unit circle (stable to the west). Thus in two dimensions one is tempted to seek one of several such factorizations. All these involve the use of two-dimensional cepstral analysis to perform the factorization [33, 42, 61, 63, 100, 119]. Given a two-dimensional signal $s(m, n)$ and its transform $S(z_1, z_2)$, the complex cepstrum (if it exists) $\hat{s}(m, n)$ is the inverse transform of $\ln [S(z_1, z_2)]$. Thus suppose that we are given a rational system function $H(z_1, z_2)$ and wish to break it up into the cascade of four stable quadrant filters [42][7]

$$H(z_1, z_2) = H_{NE}(z_1, z_2)H_{NW}(z_1, z_2)H_{SW}(z_1, z_2)H_{SE}(z_1, z_2) \tag{22}$$

or two stable half-plane filters, using Dudgeon's one-sided functions [5, 33],

$$H(z_1, z_2) = H_E(z_1, z_2)H_W(z_1, z_2). \tag{23}$$

We can do this by additively decomposing $\hat{h}(m, n)$ into the corresponding pieces. Thus we will in principle have developed the desired spectral factorization algorithm once we determine the properties of cepstra of signals that are minimum phase, where we define minimum phase analogously to the definition in one dimension [100]. Specifically $s(m, n)$ is minimum phase with respect to a given quadrant (NE, NW, SW, SE) or half-plane (E, W) if the signal and its inverse $\breve{s}(m, n)$ (under convolution) are zero outside the given sector and if $s(m, n)$ and $\breve{s}(m, n)$ are the impulse responses of stable filters that are recursively implemented in the direction associated with the given sector. The factorizations of interest in (22) and (23) have the property that the impulse response for each piece is minimum phase. For example, $H_{NE}(z_1, z_2)$ has no poles or zeros in $\{|z_1| \geq 1\} \cap \{|z_2| \geq 1\}$ and $h_{NE}(n, m)$, $\breve{h}_{NE}(n, m)$ are NE quadrant signals.

One then obtains the desired algorithm by using the following important property [100]: A signal is minimum phase with respect to a given sector *if and only if* its two-dimensional cepstrum is zero outside this sector. Using this property, we can derive the four-piece spectral factorization of Pistor [42] or the two-piece factorization of Dudgeon by the following algorithm: Given $h(m, n)$, calculate $\hat{h}(m, n)$. Consider the restrictions of $\hat{h}$ to the (four or two) sectors of interest; for example

$$\hat{h}(m, n) = \hat{h}_{NE}(m, n) + \hat{h}_{NW}(m, n) + \hat{h}_{SW}(m, n) + \hat{h}_{SE}(m, n). \tag{24}$$

The desired spectral factors are the complex exponentials of the transforms of these restrictions. This in principle solves the spectral factorization problem, but unfortunately the fundamental theorem of algebra gets in the way again. The factors in (22) and (23), unlike those in the one-dimensional case, need not be ratios of finite-order polynomials. Hence each piece in principle requires an infinite amount of storage (for a NE filter we must keep all data points to the SW). Approximations are clearly needed [33, 42].

An excellent treatment of the use of cepstra for spectral factorization is given in Ekstrom and Woods [119]. In addition to considering the two- and four-factor cases, they consider an eight-factor case—four factors corresponding to signals that are strictly in the four quadrants (they are zero along the coordinate axes) plus four factors for the four pieces of the axes ($m = 0$ and $n \geq 0$, $m = 0$ and $n \leq 0$, $m \geq 0$ and $n = 0$, $m \leq 0$ and $n = 0$). These last four pieces correspond to the separable part of the system function ($H(z_1, z_2)$ is separable if and only if it is of the form $H_1(z_1)H_2(z_2)$), while the other four pieces can be viewed as totally non-separable. Applying this factorization to a NE quadrant filter, Ekstrom and Woods obtain an interesting interpretation of the two conditions of

Huang's [50] stability test (19) and (20). Essentially we factor our system function as follows:

$$B_{NE}(z_1, z_2) = B_1(z_1)B_2(z_2)B_{SNE}(z_1, z_2), \tag{25}$$

where SNE means strictly NE. Then (19) implies that $b_1(m)$ is minimum phase, while (20) implies that $b_2(n) * b_{SNE}(z_1, z_2)$ is NE minimum phase.

Ekstrom and Woods also discuss the likelihood that the factors are not of finite order; in fact, that one factorization has finite-order factors does not imply that either of the other two factorizations does. They also discuss the numerical calculation of cepstra and of the spectral factors, and they propose this as an algorithm to test for stability (B satisfies (19) and (20) if and only if $\hat{b}$ is a NE quadrant function). Such a procedure in principle requires an infinite amount of computation (we must check $\hat{b} = 0$ over all three other quadrants), but we can obtain a fast approximate test by looking over a restricted part of the plane.

The question of stable filter design to approximate a given frequency magnitude-response function is considered in [119]. Ekstrom and Woods point out that to do this one needs two one-quadrant filters (NE and NW, NW and SW, SW and SE, or SE and NE), but one can make the approximation with a single half-plane filter.[8] They also consider the finite-order approximation of the infinite-degree rational functions that arise as factors in the spectral factorization. Intuitively we want to window the denominator power series to obtain a finite-order series that remains stable. In [119] they show that stability is preserved if we use an exponential window.

In chapter 2 we saw that state-space stochastic realization procedures can be devised to perform the desired spectral factorization. As one might expect, in two dimensions there are some difficulties with this type of procedure, but some results do exist. We will talk about this further when we discuss two-dimensional state-space methods.

A final stabilization procedure is based on the guaranteed stability of least-squares inverses in one-dimension. The least-squares inverse (LSI) is obtained using exactly the methodology for performing linear prediction of speech. Given the denominator B and its inverse transform b, one seeks a finite-extent impulse response p that approximates the convolutional inverse of b. One then seeks to choose the coefficients in p that minimize the sum of the squares of the difference between $b * p$ and the unit impulse. In one-dimension this leads to the fast algorithms described in chapter 2, in which one iterates on the extent of p. One also has the guarantee that p is minimum phase (that the all-pole model $1/p$ is stable). In [49] Shanks et al. conjectured that this minimum-phase property holds in two dimensions. Under this assumption they proposed the use of a double least-squares inverse to stabilize an unstable denominator. That is, given b we calculate its LSI p and then the LSI $\tilde{b}$ of p. By conjecture this is minimum phase, and we hope $\tilde{B}(z_1, z_2)$ is a good approximation of $B(z_1, z_2)$ (at least in magnitude on $|z_1| = |z_2| = 1$). This procedure has been used to design numerous two-dimensional filters [49]. Unfortunately Genin and Kamp [144, 145, 256] have recently shown that this conjecture is false in two dimensions if one is constrained to quarter-plane filters, although it is true in certain restricted cases [249]. This not only makes the design procedure suspect, but also hinders the extension of linear prediction concepts to two-dimensions. For example, if a quarter-plane filter is used, then unlike the one-dimensional solution [26], the linear prediction solution in the two-dimensional case does not match the first few correlation coefficients [66, 156]. On the other hand, Marzetta [66] has shown that the situation is much nicer if the least-squares inverse problem is posed in terms of half-plane filters. In this case the minimum-phase property does hold.

4.2.5 Extension and Use of One-Dimensional Design Techniques for Two-Dimensional Problems

Let us make a few final comments concerning two-dimensional design and structures questions. Again, certain one-dimensional concepts and techniques extend, while others do not. In one of the earliest design methods proposed, Treitel and Shanks [48] suggested approximating a desired impulse response $h(m, n)$ as sum of separable terms

$$h(m, n) = \sum_{i=1}^{N} f_i(m)g_i(n). \tag{26}$$

If h is of limited extent, one can in principle do this exactly by viewing h as a matrix and then finding its spectral representation. In general this leads to no efficiencies in implementation unless N is substantially less than the extent of h. Treitel and Shanks suggest a method for truncating (26), essentially keeping only the dominant terms, corresponding to the largest eigenvalues of $h'h$, and they perform an error analysis for such approximate filters. Having a decomposition such as (26) suggests several interesting structures. The summation can clearly be realized through a parallel arrangement of the separable terms, and each separable term is a cascade of two one-dimensional FIR filters—one operating vertically, the other horizontally. Thus each can be implemented with an FFT, or one might approximate each one-dimensional filter by a recursive filter that can be implemented even more efficiently. Thus we see that the separable and sum-of-separable cases can be handled using techniques and concepts that are essentially one-dimensional in nature. Such cases have special implications in the state-space framework.

Motivated by a similar desire to use one-dimensional design methods for two-dimensional problems, Shanks et al. [49] considered taking a one-dimensional continuous time filter $F(s)$, which can be viewed as either a horizontal or vertical two-dimensional filter, and rotating it by an angle β,

$$\tilde{F}(s_1, s_2) = F(s_1 \cos \beta + s_2 \sin \beta), \tag{27}$$

thus obtaining a one-dimensional filter that processes data along lines at an angle β with the s_1 axis. One can then apply the two-dimensional bilinear transformation to obtain a two-dimensional digital filter design. Several examples of such rotated designs are given in [49]. Costa and Venetsanopoulos [51] have considered this design technique in more detail. They note that F factors because it is one-dimensional; thus the stability test for the final two-dimensional filter can be reduced to very simple tests on the factors. They find that for given directions of recursion, there are constraints on the angle β for which the resulting filter is stable. In addition, they consider the design of filters with circular symmetry, obtained by cascading identical one-dimensional filters that have been rotated to be spaced evenly between $0°$ and $360°$. Such designs have the advantages of guaranteed stability, efficient computer design, and cascade implementation because the one-dimensional prototype filter can be factored.

The use of transformations to take one-dimensional designs into two-dimensional designs is conceptually appealing. In addition to these methods and the one-dimensional projections of Mersereau and Dudgeon [55] and Manry and Aggarwal [56], several other methods have been devised for utilizing one-dimensional filter designs. One of the most powerful methods of this type for designing two-dimensional FIR filters involves the so-called McClellan transformations [2, 36, 127, 128, 129]. The original algorithm developed in [2, 36] involves transforming a one-dimensional filter of the form

$$G(e^{j\omega}) = \sum_{n=0}^{M} b(n) \cos n\omega \qquad (28)$$

into a two-dimensional linear phase filter

$$H(e^{j\omega_1}, e^{j\omega_2}) = \exp\{-j(n_1\omega_1 + n_2\omega_2)\}\hat{H}(\omega_1, \omega_2), \qquad (29)$$

where

$$\hat{H}(e^{j\omega_1}, e^{j\omega_2}) = \sum_{k=0}^{n_1} \sum_{p=0}^{n_2} a(k, p) \cos k\omega_1 \cos p\omega_2. \qquad (30)$$

The specification of (30) is obtained from (28) by means of the transformation

$$\cos \omega = A \cos \omega_1 + B \cos \omega_2 + C \cos \omega_1 \cos \omega_2 + D, \qquad (31)$$

where choices of A, B, C, D determine the shape of contours along which ω is constant. Clearly $|H|$ is constant on such contours. For example, the choice $A = B = C = -D = \frac{1}{2}$ yields nearly circular contours, and hence one can map a low-pass filter G into a low-pass circularly symmetric filter H. Thus one can use one-dimensional FIR techniques to design two-dimensional FIR filters of high order in a reasonably efficient manner. In some cases one can show that transformations of one-dimensional optimal filters (in the Chebyshev sense of minimizing maximum deviation from a desired frequency response) are the optimal two-dimensional designs [36]. In [128] an extension of this design criterion was considered; (31) was replaced by

$$\cos \omega = \sum_{p=0}^{P} \sum_{q=0}^{Q} t(p, q) \cos p\omega_1 \cos q\omega_2 = H_p(e^{j\omega_1}, e^{j\omega_2}). \qquad (32)$$

Careful choice of the parameters $t(p, q)$ yields a variety of contour shapes in the two-dimensional frequency plane. Reference [128] contains details of algorithms for choosing these parameters to obtain best approximations to given desired contours. Having the desired contours, one can then turn to the problem of designing the one-dimensional FIR filter that is to be transformed. Numerous methods exist for this design problem [2].

An attractive feature of these transformation designs is that they lead directly to efficient structures. The development of these structures and a study of their relative merits based on number of multiplies, coefficient sensitivity, and roundoff noise is given in [127, 129]. We briefly illustrate the idea by following the development of Chan and McClellan in [127]. From (28) we note that

$$\cos n\omega = T_n[\cos \omega], \tag{33}$$

where T_n is the nth Chebyshev polynomial, which satisfies the recursion

$$T_0(x) = 1, \qquad T_1(x) = x, \qquad T_n(x) = 2x\, T_{n-1}(x) - T_{n-2}(x). \tag{34}$$

Rewriting (28) as

$$G(e^{j\omega}) = \sum_{n=0}^{M} b(n)T_n[\cos \omega] \tag{35}$$

and replacing $\cos \omega$ by (32), we can directly obtain a realization of $\hat{H}(e^{j\omega_1}, e^{j\omega_2})$ as an interconnection of M copies of $H_p(e^{j\omega_1}, e^{j\omega_2})$, where one uses the recursion (34) in interconnecting the copies of H_p to obtain realizations of each of the $T_n[H_p(e^{j\omega_1}, e^{j\omega_2})]$. See [127] for details.

Another two-dimensional design method adapted from one-dimension was proposed by Shanks et al. [49], who modified the time-domain design technique of Burrus and Parks (see p. 49). As in the one-dimensional case, given a desired impulse response $h(m, n)$, we want to find a rational transfer function $A(z_1, z_2)/B(z_1, z_2)$ that yields an impulse response "close" to h. We first solve for the denominator B by a method similar to that used in computing the least-squares inverse (and which evidently has the same stability problems). One can then solve for the numerator using the analog of the method described in [114] and in chapter 2.

One of the most widely used FIR design procedures in one dimension is the optimum Chebyshev design method, where the Remez exchange algorithm leads to an extremely efficient computer design technique [2]. Kamp and Thiran [74] have extended this algorithm to two dimensions but not without some severe complications. The Haar condition does not hold in the two-dimensional case, leading to degeneracies that can keep the algorithm from converging. In the ordered one-dimensional case errors between the optimal design and the desired response alternate between $\pm$ the maximum error (the Chebyshev norm) [2], but in the two-dimensional case one has no such alternation theorem. This makes the exchange algorithm far more complex and, together with several other factors, extremely slow. Hence it is limited to low-order impulse responses [74].

In the one-dimensional case, one can use the so-called differential correction method to find optimal Chebyshev rational frequency responses [52]; Bednar [13] extended this method to the two-dimensional case. This method requires a great deal of computation time [3], and the algorithm's output is an optimal rational magnitude-squared frequency response. Thus to obtain the actual filter specification one must perform a spectral factorization, which leads in general to infinite-order numerator and denominator.

A number of design methods in addition to these have been proposed: windowing [133], frequency sampling [134], transforming (z_1, z_2) to obtain new designs from old [149], and extending wave digital filters [151] to two dimensions, with all the pseudopassivity and stability properties of their one-dimensional counterparts.

The issue of two-dimensional filter structures and their effects on required storage, number of multiplies, coefficient sensitivity, and roundoff noise is clearly of great importance. The issue is complicated significantly by the fact that one cannot factor general two-dimensional polynomials. This immediately rules out cascade and parallel realizations unless one is dealing with one of the special classes of filters. Mitra et al. [26] show that one can write down the generalizations of one-dimensional direct-form realizations for NE recursions. In addition, for several special classes of NE rational filters they developed structures based on continued-fraction expansions.

As in the one-dimensional case, a critical question in the design of two-dimensional IIR filters is the existence of limit cycles and the effect of roundoff noise on filter output. Maria and Fahmy [28, 73] have considered the limit cycle problem for first-order two-dimensional recursive filters, both singly [73] and in cascade [28]; see also Chang [268]. The results in [28] on the existence of horizontal, vertical, and noninteracting diagonal limit cycles parallel the results of Jackson [280] quite closely, and their method for bounding the magnitude of limit cycles is similar to the one-dimensional result of Sandberg and Kaiser [281], although the bounds become far more complex as one looks at limit cycles on rows or columns other than the first ones. Open questions involve the extension of this type of result to higher-order filters. In addition, an intriguing question is whether one can extend any of the other techniques discussed in chapter 1. Do the positive real-frequency domain results of Claasen et al. [282] and others extend to the two-dimensional case? What about the Lyapunov techniques of Willson [283]? Of course in this case one would need two-dimensional state-space models and a two-dimensional Lyapunov theory.

The analysis of roundoff noise in two-dimensional filters can be carried out much as for one-dimensional filters; the references provide examples of this type of analysis. Another open question concerns the extension of the Lyapunov equation-state covariance noise analysis method described in chapter 3 for one-dimensional roundoff analysis. Again one would need a state-space model to consider this question.

Chan [107] has proposed a unified state-space framework for the study of one-dimensional and two-dimensional structures. In chapter 3 we discussed the one-dimensional aspects of this approach, in which all structures can be viewed as factorizations of the map that transforms the present state and next input into the next state and output. In the two-dimensional case one must process inputs sequentially according to any order function that is compatible with the recursion precedence relation (11). The resulting one-dimensional state-space realization is finite dimensional if and only if the data are defined on a domain bounded in one direction. Using the scan order described in section 4.2.2 (see figure 4.7), Chan develops a time-varying state realization. The time variations arise for precisely the same reason—we must consider the edge effects as we finish scanning one line and begin scanning the next. Chan develops a realization using the scan order for a general NE recursive filter. He conjectures that this realization is minimal in the recursive case but shows that it is not in the FIR case. On the other hand, in the FIR case one can realize the two-dimensional filter with the scan order and a time-invariant one-dimensional filter by padding the ends of each line with zeros, essentially what Mersereau and Dudgeon did [55]. Chan shows that he can do the same in his setting by finding a nonminimal (caused by padded zeros) time-invariant realization. This leads to an interesting trade-off— nonminimality of one realization versus the more complex control needed to implement the time-varying minimal one. The utility of such one-dimensional state-space models and the additional degree of freedom one has in choosing the order relation (and hence the state space, as Witsenhausen [93, 94] pointed out) makes this an interesting area for further research.

4.3 State-Space Models in Two Dimensions

4.3.1 Roesser's Model

In addition to these one-dimensional state-space descriptions for recursively ordered two-dimensional systems, some work has been done in the past few years on the definition and analysis of two-dimensional state-space models. Roesser [110] considers NE models of the form

$$v(i + 1, j) = A_1 v(i, j) + A_2 h(i, j) + B_1 x(i, j),$$
$$h(i, j + 1) = A_3 v(i, j) + A_4 h(i, j) + B_2 x(i, j), \qquad (36)$$
$$y(i, j) = C_1 v(i, j) + C_2 h(i, j) + D x(i, j).$$

Here x is the input, y is the output, and v and h together play the role of a state variable. Here v carries information vertically, and h conveys it horizontally. In addition, Roesser takes (36) to be a NE recursion $(i, j \geq 0)$.

Given this model, Roesser considers several issues. He solves (36), and the solution resembles the variation-of-constants formula for usual finite-dimensional one-dimensional linear systems. The main difference is that boundary conditions $v(0, j)$, $j \geq 0$, and $h(i, 0)$, $i \geq 0$, must be specified. Roesser also considers a two-dimensional version of the Cayley-Hamilton theorem. Taking the two-dimensional transform of (36), we obtain

$$\frac{Y(z_1, z_2)}{X(z_1, z_2)} = [C_1, C_2] \begin{bmatrix} z_1 I - A_1 & - A_2 \\ - A_3 & z_2 I - A_4 \end{bmatrix}^{-1} \begin{bmatrix} B_1 \\ B_2 \end{bmatrix} + D. \qquad (37)$$

Hence the role of the characteristic polynomial in this setting is played by

$$p(z_1, z_2) = \det \begin{bmatrix} z_1 I - A_1 & - A_2 \\ - A_3 & z_2 I - A_4 \end{bmatrix}.$$

Let

$$A = \begin{bmatrix} A_1 & A_2 \\ A_3 & A_4 \end{bmatrix} = A^{1,0} + A^{0,1}, \qquad (38)$$

where

$$A^{1,0} = \begin{bmatrix} A_1 & A_2 \\ 0 & 0 \end{bmatrix}, \quad A^{0,1} = \begin{bmatrix} 0 & 0 \\ A_3 & A_4 \end{bmatrix} \qquad (39)$$

represent the required dynamics to advance the system in the vertical and horizontal directions, respectively. We can then define the transition matrix over a number of vertical and horizontal steps

$$A^{0,0} = I, \qquad A^{i,j} = A^{1,0} A^{i-1,j} + A^{0,1} A^{i,j-1}. \qquad (40)$$

Then if we define

$$E^i F^j A = F^j E^i A = A^{i,j}, \qquad (41)$$

we have the two-dimensional Cayley-Hamilton theorem

$$p(E, F)A = 0. \tag{42}$$

Roesser uses this result to obtain an efficient method for computing the transition matrix. The result is also used to obtain finite-rank tests as in the one-dimensional case for controllability and observability, which are defined in analogy with one dimension. Specifically, a state (v, h) is observable if the zero-input response is not identically zero when the initial condition is $(v(0, 0), h(0, 0)) = (v, h)$, with all other boundary conditions zero. The state is controllable if there is some $(i, j) \geq (0, 0)$ and set of inputs so that $(v(i, j), h(i, j)) = (v, h)$ when the boundary conditions are all zero.

Several questions and issues arise in considering Roesser's model. First, not all NE quadrant rational transfer functions can be realized by systems of the form (36), although this can be remedied by modifying the output equations [164]; see [164] for more on realization theory and canonical forms for these systems. Also, in obtaining his algorithm for recursively computing the $A^{i,j}$ via the Cayley-Hamilton theorem, Roesser used the notion of two-dimensional eigenvalues in a crucial manner, and in the usual nonfactorable case the calculation of zeros of $p(z_1, z_2)$ is extremely difficult. This not only complicates his transition matrix algorithm, but also makes stability tests more difficult. One must use methods such as Siljak's [27] on $p(z_1, z_2)$ or the direct extension of Huang's stability test to model (36) [164]. An interesting open question is the development of Lyapunov stability methods for (36). Furthermore, the model (36) is limited to quadrant-causal systems. This is perfectly reasonable for the study of quadrant-recursive filters, but its value for the analysis of other two-dimensional signals is unclear. For example, Roesser mentions the possibility of a two-dimensional filtering theory based on (36). In this case one would want to model the observed signal z as

$$z(i, j) = y(i, j) + N(i, j), \tag{43}$$

where N is noise and y is generated by a model as in (36) with x a noise process. Thus (36) plays the role of a spatial shaping filter. As Ekstrom and Woods [119] point out, one cannot obtain arbitrary spectra from a NE shaping filter. Hence one may need two such filters, as well as a method for modeling the spectra of the signal field. The artificially imposed causality of model (36)—in fact, of any state-space model—may cause difficulties. For example, in an image one would not expect light intensity as a function of spatial location to have a NE causal structure. On the other hand, if a NE causal filter yields the proper shape for the intensity cor-relation function, there may be no difficulty in using such a model. Indeed, Andrews and Hunt [81] point out that the use of such models may be of value in leading to efficient recursive filtering methods for image pro-cessing. This remains an open area for further research.

Finally, Roesser's state $\left(v(i,j), h(i,j)\right)$ might better be termed a local state [97, 138]. The amount of storage required for recursively solving two-di-mensional equations depends in general on the size of the arrays of interest (see figures 4.3 and 4.6). If the array sizes are unbounded, the required memory is infinite. Thus v and h in Roesser's model do not represent the true state. Rather the model (36) can be viewed as arising by reducing a scalar, high-order two-dimensional difference equation to a vector, first-order equation. Thus the dimensions of v and h correspond to the order of the equations of interest.

4.3.2 The Models of Fornasini, Marchesini, and Attasi

The concept of state for two-dimensional systems has been considered in more depth by Fornasini and Marchesini [97, 138]. They consider im-pulse responses that lie strictly in the NE quadrant, and for such systems they define the notion of a global state using a direct generalization of the theory of Nerode. To define the global state as containing all relevant information concerning past inputs, one needs to define *past*. The defini-tion of past inputs at the point (i, j) is all $x(k, l)$ where either $k < i$ or $j < l$ (see figure 4.8). In this way the state must summarize all needed boundary conditions, and Fornasini and Marchesini point out that the state is us-ually infinite dimensional.

Attention in [97] then shifts to local NE state-space descriptions of the form

$$x(m + 1, n + 1) = A_0x(m, n) + A_1x(m + 1, n) + A_2x(m, n + 1)$$
$$+ Bu(m, n), \tag{44}$$
$$y(m, n) = Cx(m, n).$$

Note here that vertical and horizontal information is conveyed by a single state vector. With this model a NE IIR filter can be realized as in (44) if and only if the transform of the impulse response is rational. The "if" part of this result involves a procedure for constructing a realization in a form that is a generalization of the one-dimensional standard controllable form.

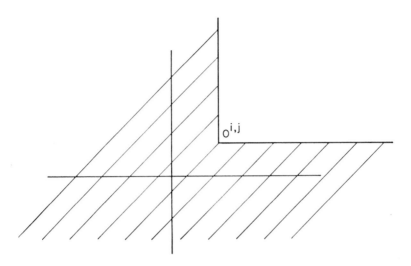

4.8
The "past" in the definition of Marchesini and Fornasini.

Such realizations naturally focus attention on minimality—obtaining a local state-space model (44) with as small a state space as possible. This leads directly to the notions of (local) controllability and observability, with finite-rank conditions for these properties developed in a manner analogous to that of Roesser. In fact, a simple proof of the two-dimensional Cayley-Hamilton result is given in [97] for systems as in (44). The main minimality result of Marchesini and Fornasini is that minimality implies local controllability and observability (an algorithm for reducing the dimension of uncontrollable and/or unobservable realizations is given) but that local controllability and observability do not imply minimality. They show this result by means of a counterexample.

The work in [97] is phrased in terms of the algebraic notion of formal power series (essentially (3) with no convergence properties attached to it). The most thorough treatments of the uses of this theory to study topics in formal language theory, automata theory, nonlinear systems analysis, and two-dimensional processes are the works of Fliess [98, 139, 140]. Fliess studies the properties of rational power series[9] in detail using a generalization of the Hankel matrix. He shows that the rank of this matrix equals the dimension of the minimal global state space. This is infinite dimensional in general, but Fliess notes [98] that the global state space is finite dimensional if and only if the formal power series is recognizable, which simply means that it has a separable denominator. Much analysis can be done for separable two-dimensional systems, since many one-dimensional concepts and results extend directly in this case.

Attasi [6, 35, 96] has studied such systems in great detail. His basic model is a special case of (44):

$$x(m + 1, n + 1) = F_1x(m, n + 1) + F_2x(m + 1, n) - F_1F_2x(m, n)$$
$$+ Gu(m, n), \qquad (45)$$
$$y(m, n) = Hx(m, n),$$

where it is assumed that

$$F_1F_2 = F_2F_1. \qquad (46)$$

With these assumptions the impulse response is strictly NE, and it and its transform are given by

$$h(i, j) = HF_1^{i-1}F_2^{j-1}G, \qquad i, j > 0, \qquad (47)$$

$$H(z_1, z_2) = H(z_1I - F_1)^{-1}(z_2I - F_2)^{-1}G. \qquad (48)$$

Clearly any FIR filter can be realized as in (45), and thus any stable impulse response can be approximated arbitrarily closely by a system of this form. This, of course, is neither startling nor necessarily very useful, since the dimension of the resulting state-space system may be extremely large.

With this framework Attasi defines dual notions of local controllability and observability and derives conditions somewhat simpler than in [97, 110] because of the special nature of (45). Attasi also considers minimal realizations of the form of (45), obtains a state-space decomposition result and minimal realization algorithm much like those in one dimension (here the two-dimensional Hankel matrix plays a crucial role), and shows that minimality implies controllability and observability. He also proves the converse of this last result, but this is true only if one looks for the minimal realization in the class of models given by (45). Consider the example constructed by Fornasini and Marchesini [97]:

$$H(z_1, z_2) = \frac{z_1^{-1}z_2^{-1}(1 + z_1^{-1} + z_2^{-1})}{1 + z_1^{-1} + z_2^{-1} + z_1^{-1}z_2^{-1}} = \frac{z_1^{-1}z_2^{-1}(1 + z_1^{-1} + z_2^{-1})}{(1 + z_1^{-1})(1 + z_2^{-1})}. \qquad (49)$$

The minimal realization of the form of (45) is of dimension ≥ 3, but one can find a realization of the form (44) of dimension 2. This clearly points out another of the many complications that arises in going from one to two-dimensions.

Undoubtedly the major contribution of Attasi's work is that he did something with his models.[10] He was able to develop a two-dimensional Lyapunov equation. More specifically, to show northern and eastern asymptotic stability, we simply need to check the one-dimensional systems along vertical or horizontal lines. This leads to one-dimensional Lyapunov equations and nothing new. However, Attasi did obtain an invariance principle type of result. If F_1 and F_2 are stable, then (45) is controllable if and only if the equation

$$P - F_1PF_1' - F_2PF_2' + F_1F_2PF_1'F_2' = GG^1 \tag{50}$$

has a unique positive definite solution P. The exact implication of this result for two-dimensional stability theory and its potential utility in such areas as limit cycle analysis are at present unclear and remain intriguing questions for further work.

Attasi also considers systems, as in (45), that are driven by white noise. Again he obtains a two-dimensional Lyapunov equation for the state covariance, and this result may be of some value in performing roundoff noise analysis for two-dimensional filters (see the analogous one-dimensional discussion in chapter 3). Attasi also shows that any two-dimensional stationary covariance function can be approximated arbitrarily closely by a system of this type, and he develops a stochastic realization theory that exactly parallels the one-dimensional case with one rather surprising exception. In the one-dimensional case there is in general a whole family of stochastic realizations; each essentially factors the spectral density $S(z)$ of the output process y. In the two-dimensional case, if one can factor the spectrum $S(z_1, z_2)$ of y, the stochastic realization is essentially unique. This is due primarily to the additional constraints on S imposed by the fact that we use a single-quadrant shaping filter (45). In addition to the constraints imposed by NE and SW correlations, another constraint arises in considering NW and SE correlations. This constraint leads to the uniqueness result.

This stochastic realization–spectral factorization result suffers from all the numerical problems mentioned in chapter 2 and from the difficulties of two-dimensional factorization. The one novel feature of Attasi's development is the use, in fact the necessity for using nonsquare factors. That is, to factor

$$S(z_1, z_2) = H(z_1, z_2)H'(z_1^{-1}, z_2^{-1}), \tag{51}$$

where H is NE causal and of the form (48), one must consider rectangular factors.[11] For example, if y is a scalar process, then H in general must be $1 \times m$; in fact, this uniqueness result fixes the value of m [6, 35, 96].

4.3.3 Fundamental Concepts in Two-Dimensional State-Space Analysis

Recently Morf et al. [162, 163] have made several noteworthy contributions to two-dimensional state-space theory. In [162] they consider the properties of polynomial and rational matrices in two variables. The motivation for this study, which leads naturally to multi-input, multi-output two-dimensional systems, is the generalization of the scalar two-dimensional polynomial results of Bose [147, 166] and the matrix one-dimensional polynomial results of Rosenbrock [168] and Wolovich [169]. Morf et al. generalize the scalar notion of primitive factorization to the matrix polynomial case, and they provide an existence and uniqueness proof for such a factorization. By regarding a two-dimensional polynomial $p(z_1, z_2)$ as one-dimensional polynomial (say in z_2) with coefficients that are rational functions in the other variable, and by introducing several notions from algebraic geometry, they are able to use many one-dimensional techniques to obtain two-dimensional generalizations of the Euclidean algorithm, Hermite and Smith forms, tests for relative coprimeness of polynomial matrices, matrix fraction descriptions of rational matrices, and the extraction of greatest common right divisors. In one dimension Rosenbrock and Wolovich utilize many of these properties to study multi-input, multi-output state-space models. In [163] the results of [162] are used to study two-dimensional state-space models. The models of Roesser, Fornasini-Marchesini, and Attasi are reviewed, and Morf et al. argue in favor of Roesser's model. They reason that (36) is a true first-order system, and hence v and h together make up a valid local state. The model (44), on the other hand, is not first order, and hence x is not a local state; the order of the system (44) may be larger than the dimension of x. The importance of this is not totally clear, since the required storage depends on more than the order of the system.

The concepts of local controllability and observability for the Roesser model are explored in [163]. The authors point out that these conditions neither imply nor follow from the minimality of the realization (this is done with several instructive examples). This difficulty can be partially overcome by redefining local controllability and observability for (36) by requiring these properties to hold separately in the horizontal and vertical directions (but not necessarily jointly). With this definition, minimality implies but is not implied by local controllability and observability.

To obtain notions of controllability and observability that are equivalent to minimality, Morf et al. generalize the approach of Rosenbrock in which coprimeness of polynomial matrices plays a crucial role. This leads to the notions of modal controllability and observability and a related concept of minimality; it also allows one to use the algebraic and geometric concepts developed in [162] to study the two-dimensional realization problem. In this setting the existence of minimal realizations becomes a difficult problem, and one may not even exist if we restrict ourselves to systems with real parameters (see [163] for an example). In related work Sontag [143, 154, 284] has also found realizations of lower dimension than those proposed by Fornasini and Marchesini, and he has shown that minimal realizations need not be unique up to a change of basis. All these facts indicate that the two-dimesional state-space model is complex and offers some difficult mathematical and conceptual problems. As with all other topics concerning two-dimensional systems, there are many ways to generalize one-dimensional concepts. It remains to be seen whether any of these state models and realization theories can provide a useful framework for solving two-dimensional analysis and synthesis problems.

4.3.4 Relationships with State-Space Models for Other Types of Systems

A number of authors have considered state-space and other dynamic models defined with very general independent variables. Motivated to a large degree by the partially ordered feedback structures of Ho and Chu [87, 88] and Witsenhausen [93, 94], Mullans and Elliott [95] and Wyman [143, 160, 161] have considered the development of an algebraic state-space theory on partially ordered sets. In addition, Seviora and Sablatash [114–116] have placed algebraic (specifically, abelian group) structures on the independent variable to consider a generalized transform and digital filter theory with the aid of tools from the theory of abstract harmonic analysis. Their framework is quite abstract and general, and it includes such possible time sets as the integers, the usual two-dimensional plane of integer pairs, and a variety of cylindrical time sets.

The issues arising in the analysis of two-dimensional discrete-time systems have many similarities to results in other areas. For example, Ansell [64] and Youla [77] studied continuoustime transfer functions in two variables that arise in the consideration of networks containing lumped and distributed elements. Along similar lines, Kamen (see p. 222) has developed an algebraic theory for considering continuous-time systems that contain time delays. In addition, Sontag [143, 154, 284] has considered a general algebraic framework of this type and has tied together some of the time-delay and two-dimensional results.

Other classes of systems have also been analyzed in a similar manner. Kamen [142] has developed a theory for time-varying one-dimensional systems that bears some resemblance to the two-dimensional theory. Fliess [98, 139, 140], Fornasini and Marchesini [138, 285], Bush [155], and Kamen [270] have taken advantage of some of the striking relationships among certain nonlinear and two-dimensional system results. To illustrate the basic idea, consider the following three systems:

Volterra (single input)

$$y(m) = \sum_{k,l} h(m - k, m - l)x(k)x(l), \tag{52}$$

Bilinear (two inputs)

$$y(m) = \sum_{k,l} h(m - k, m - l)x_1(k)x_2(l), \tag{53}$$

Two-dimensional (single input)

$$y(m, n) = \sum_{k,l} h(m - k, n - l)x(k, l). \tag{54}$$

One immediately sees the striking relationship among these three classes of systems, and it is not surprising that similar methods of analysis can be used on all of them. Indeed, Fliess' formal power series formulation leads directly to a methodology for analyzing algebraic properties of each kind of system. Fornasini and Marchesini were led to the study of two-dimensional systems by their earlier results on bilinear systems. In his work on bilinear systems Bush considered the two-dimensional transform $H(z_1, z_2)$ of the weighting function h that appears in (53). He showed that if one could write

$$H(z_1, z_2) = \frac{p(z_1^{-1}, z_2^{-1})}{q_1(z_1^{-1})q_2(z_2^{-1})q_3(z_1^{-1}z_2^{-1})}, \tag{55}$$

where p is a two-variable polynomial and the q_i are polynomials in a single variable, then the system could be realized by three finite-dimensional linear systems and a single multiplier (see Kamen [270] for some two-dimensional complements of these results). Again the fundamental theorem of algebra makes it difficult to find representations as in (55) (a condition slightly weaker than separability).

In this and the preceding section we have surveyed a large number of issues involving systems over a two-dimensional parameter space. We have seen that a number of one-dimensional concepts can be extended to the two-dimensional case (such as two-dimensional FIR implementation schemes using the FFT), while others cannot (for example, cascade structures). In many cases there are several possible extensions from one to two dimensions (as with the several notions of causality and the variety of directions of recursion), and in most situations the two-dimensional counterparts of one-dimensional results are far more complex (as with the two-dimensional stability tests). We have mentioned several of the reasons for difficulties in two dimensions—difficulties in defining notions of causality, recursibility, and state (local or global) in two dimensions, the absence of a two-dimensional factorization theorem, and the absence of the Haar condition. We have speculated on a wide range of open problems in such areas as filter design, filter structures, the accompanying issues of storage, sensitivity, and roundoff effects, and the development of useful state-space models and tools such as the two-dimensional Lyapunov equation. In the next section we raise several additional issues involving two-dimensional random processes.

4.4 Image Processing

4.4.1 The Image Formation Process

Digital processing of images for data compression, noise removal, or enhancement is one of the major areas of applications of two-dimensional digital signal-processing techniques. In addition, image processing has spurred a great deal of work in the analysis of spatially distributed stochastic variables—random fields. This section discusses some of the work concerning image processing and random fields and points out several particularly intriguing areas for further work. The reader who is interested in obtaining a detailed understanding of image formation and processing and of the response of the human visual system should consult the references. In particular, see the survey paper by Hunt [4], the book by Andrews and Hunt [81], the paper by Stockham [82], and the collection edited by

Huang [67]. We will refer to these references often as we sketch some of the issues involved in image processing.

Let $g(x, y)$ denote the image-radiant energy as a function of two spatial variables; for the time being we assume that the system is free of noise. The image results from an image formation process that transforms the original object-radiant energy $f(x, y)$ into the observed image. A general model often used for the image formation process is

$$g(x, y) = \int_{-\infty}^{+\infty} \int_{-\infty}^{+\infty} h(x, y, x_1, y_1, f(x_1, y_1))\, dx_1\, dy_1. \tag{56}$$

Although in some cases the formation process may be nonlinear [81], in many cases it is valid to assume a linear model

$$g(x, y) = \int_{-\infty}^{+\infty} \int_{-\infty}^{-\infty} h(x, y, x_1, y_1)f(x_1, y_1)\, dx_1\, dy_1. \tag{57}$$

Here $h(x, y, x_1, y_1)$ is called the *point-spread function* (PSF); it represents the image that results from a point source located at (x_1, y_1), that is, $f(x, y) = \delta(x - x_1)\, \delta(y - y_1)$.

This function models the smoothing and blur that take place in the image formation process. Sources of such blur abound [4, 19, 24, 65, 81]. Examples include blur due to motion, defocused systems, and the effects of atmospheric turbulence.

The model (57) represents a spatially varying two-dimensional linear system. In some cases one can take advantage of simplifying assumptions, such as shift invariance

$$h(x, y, x_1, y_1) = h(x - x_1, y - y_1), \tag{58}$$

separability

$$h(x, y, x_1, y_1) = h_1(x, x_1)h_2(y, y_1), \tag{59}$$

or both

$$h(x, y, x_1, y_1) = h_1(x - x_1)h_2(y - y_1). \tag{60}$$

As one might expect, these simplifications lead to gains in analytical tractability and computational efficiency.

It is clear that the continuous-space model of (57) is inappropriate for digital storage or processing of images, and one usually obtains a discrete model by sampling the left-hand side of (57) and by approximating the right-hand side using some type of quadrature formula (see [4, 23, 81] for discussions of the errors involved in this approximation). One then ends up with a model of the form

$$g(i, j) = \sum_{k, l} h(i, j, k, l) f(k, l),$$ (61)

where the $g(i, j)$ form the two-dimensional image array, the $f(k, l)$ form the object array, and the $h(i, j, k, l)$ form the discrete point-spread function. The simplifications (58)–(60) can also be imposed in the discrete domain. For example, shift invariance yields the two-dimensional convolution

$$g(i, j) = \sum_{k, l} h(i - k, j - l) f(k, l).$$ (62)

Most digital image-processing schemes involve the analysis of equations (61) or (62), and we will spend most of our time with them.[12] Since all images of interest are of finite extent, we assume that the range of $i, j, k,$ and l in (61) and (62) is $1, \ldots, N$.[13]

In addition to the image formation process, one must take into account the process of image recording and storing. Two well-developed image models for photographic images are the intensity and density images, which are related in an essentially logarithmic manner [4, 81, 82]. Let $g_i(x, y)$ be the intensity of light reflected from a photographic film on which is stored the image represented by the intensity function $g(x, y)$. Then [4] the *intensity image model* is

$$g_i(x, y) = N_i(x, y)[g(x, y)]^\gamma,$$ (63)

where γ is known for the given type of film (it essentially controls contrast), and $N(x, y)$ is *film grain noise* due to random fluctuations of silver density on the film. On the other hand, the *density image model* is essentially the logarithm of (63)

$$g_d(x, y) = \gamma \log [g(x, y)] + n_d(x, y).$$ (64)

The complexities of these models have been avoided in most cases [4, 81]. Equation (63) has been replaced by an additive model

$$g_i(x, y) = g(x, y) + n_i(x, y),$$ (65)

while the *low-contrast assumption* [4, 81] has been used to justify replacing (64) with

$$g_d(x, y) = \gamma g(x, y) + n_d(x, y). \tag{66}$$

It is not our purpose to justify these models and assumptions; see the references for more details for the modeling of imaging systems.

We now have the following mathematical model. A discretized object $f(i, j)$ and "noise-free" image $g(i, j)$, where $i, j = 1, \ldots , N$, are related by (61) or (62), and we observe the image

$$g(i, j) = g(i, j) + v(i, j) \tag{67}$$

where v is an additive noise process.[14] We now turn to the analysis of this model.

At some points in this development it will be more convenient to view f, g, q, and v as vectors by performing a scan (lexicographic) ordering. For example,

$$\begin{aligned} f' &= [f(1, 1), f(1, 2), \ldots, f(1, N), f(2, 1), \ldots, f(2, N), \ldots, f(N, N)] \\ &= [f_1, f_2, \ldots, f_N] \end{aligned} \tag{68}$$

where $f'_i = (f(i, 1), \ldots, f(i, N))$. In this case the relevant equation is

$$q = Hf + v, \tag{69}$$

where H is an $N^2 \times N^2$ matrix formed from the PSF. Examination of (61) and (68) yields the following form for H

$$H = \begin{bmatrix} H_{11} & H_{12} \ldots & H_{1N} \\ H_{21} & H_{22} & H_{2N} \\ \vdots & & \\ H_{N1} & H_{N2} & H_{NN} \end{bmatrix}, \tag{70}$$

where H_{ij} is $N \times N$ and its (m, n) element is $h(i, m, j, n)$. If the imaging system is shift invariant (if (62) holds), then H is block Toeplitz

$$H_{ij} = H_{i-j}; \tag{71}$$

in fact, each of the blocks is itself a Toeplitz matrix.[15] This fact will be extremely important when we discuss the computational aspects of certain processing algorithms. If H is separable, then

$$H = A_1 \otimes A_2 \tag{72}$$

where $\otimes$ denotes the tensor or Kronecker product, and A_1 and A_2 are $N \times N$ matrices given by

$$
A_i =
\begin{bmatrix}
h_i(1, 1) & h_i(1, 2) \ldots h_i(1, N) \\
h_i(2, 1) & h_i(2, 2) \quad h_i(2, N) \\
\vdots & \\
h_i(N, 1) & h_i(N, 2) \quad h_i(N, N)
\end{bmatrix},
\tag{73}
$$

where

$$
h(i, j, m, n) = h_1(i, m)h_2(j, n). \tag{74}
$$

Note that horizontal stationarity implies that A_1 is Toeplitz, while vertical stationarity implies that A_2 is Toeplitz.

4.4.2 Statistical Description of the Image and the Problem of Image Coding

It is evident from the preceding development that probabilistic and statistical methods must play some role in image processing. In this context f, g, v, and perhaps h are *random fields*. Such a random field $s(i, j)$ is characterized by some type of statistical description—the joint density of the values of the field at different points or perhaps a statistical model such as a two-dimensional ARMA model. We will consider some of these more complex descriptions later; all we use now is the mean and covariance

$$
\bar{s}(i, j) = E[s(i, j)], \tag{75}
$$

$$
r(i, j, m, n) = E\{[s(i, j) - \bar{s}(i, j)] [s(m, n) - \bar{s}(m, n)]\}. \tag{76}
$$

The field will be called (wide-sense) *stationary*[16] if

$$
r(i, j, m, n) = r(i - m, j - n). \tag{77}
$$

If s and $\bar{s}$ are ordered lexicographically, then

$$
E[(s - \bar{s}) (s - \bar{s})'] = R, \tag{78}
$$

where R is the $N^2 \times N^2$ matrix obtained from r in the same manner that H in (70) is obtained from the PSF h. We also observe that R is block Toeplitz if s is stationary in the horizontal direction, and each block is itself Toeplitz if we have vertical (and hence full) stationarity. In addition, if the covariance is separable

$$r(i, j, m, n) = r_1(i, m)r_2(j, n), \tag{79}$$

we can obtain a representation for R much as the one for H in (72). Note that in some sense (79) says that correlations in the data have horizontal and vertical as preferred directions. While this may be reasonable in some cases (perhaps for cases in which one variable is space and the other is time) and may be acceptable in others (because it leads to mathematical tractability and good results), in many cases the assumption of (79) may be totally inappropriate.

One important problem in image processing is the efficient representation of images for storage or transmission [4, 31, 37, 76, 241]. For such applications one wishes to represent the image with as few pieces of information as possible but with a reasonable level of accuracy. Intuitively one wants the redundancy in the pieces of information kept to a minimum. Suppose we are given an image[17] s with covariance R. The off-diagonal elements of R tell us how much correlation there is among the pixels (picture elements—components of s), and this correlation can be interpreted as a measure of the redundancy in the picture. One method for obtaining a less redundant representation is to transform s

$$\sigma = Ts \tag{80}$$

(where $T^{-1} = T'$) so that the covariance of σ

$$\Sigma = TRT' \tag{81}$$

is diagonal; that is, T is the matrix of eigenvectors of R and the components of σ are uncorrelated. This transformation is called the Karhunen-Loeve transform, and its use in efficient coding can be seen as follows [4]. Let us order the eigenvalues of R in order of decreasing magnitude. Then we store or transmit only those components of σ corresponding to the $M < N^2$ largest eigenvalues. We are guaranteed to have retained those coordinates of the image that contain the most information, and we can obtain an approximate image by inverting the transform

$$\hat{s} = T'\hat{\sigma}, \tag{82}$$

where $\hat{\sigma}$ is formed by setting to zero those components of σ that were discarded. We can decide how many terms to keep on the basis of the size of the reconstruction error

$$e = s - \hat{s}. \tag{83}$$

The Karhunen-Loeve transform leads to a very efficient coding scheme [4, 37]. However, in general, this transform involves exorbitant amounts of computation. We must find the eigenvectors and eigenvalues of R (usually just once off-line for a class of images with the same covariance), and then we must perform the transform coding (80) or decoding (82). This can involve a great deal of on-line computation [4, 37] since in general there is no fast method for performing this transform. There are, however, several special cases in which this transform can be calculated efficiently. One of these [241] involves the use of a more detailed model of the image as a random field; we defer discussion of it until we begin our treatment of more detailed models for fields and images. Another case, motivated by similar analysis performed by Hunt [4, 46] and Andrews and Hunt [81], is quite instructive. Since we will use this idea on several occasions, we will develop it here in detail (see Andrews' contribution in [67]).

Suppose that s is stationary. Then R is a block-Toeplitz matrix with Toeplitz blocks. Following [81], suppose further that a particular pixel is correlated with a number of surrounding pixels but is uncorrelated with ones some distance d away (Andrews and Hunt cite $d = 20$–30 pixels as a typical number). Then the block-Toeplitz covariance matrix takes the form

$$R = \begin{bmatrix} R_0 & \cdots & R_{d-1} & 0 & \cdots & 0 \\ \vdots & & & & & \vdots \\ R_{1-d} & & & & & 0 \\ 0 & & & & & R_{d-1} \\ \vdots & & & & & \vdots \\ 0 & \cdots & 0 & R_{1-d} & \cdots & R_0 \end{bmatrix}, \tag{84}$$

where each R_i is an $N \times N$ Toeplitz matrix

$$R_i = \begin{bmatrix} R_0^i & \cdots & R_{d-1}^i & 0 & \cdots & 0 \\ \vdots & & & & & \vdots \\ R_{1-d}^i & & & & & 0 \\ 0 & & & & & R_{d-1}^i \\ \vdots & & & & & \vdots \\ 0 & \cdots & 0 & R_{1-d}^i & \cdots & R_0^i \end{bmatrix}. \tag{85}$$

We now modify R and the R_i to make R block circulant and R_i circulant. A block-circulant matrix is block Toeplitz with each row a cyclic shift to the right of the preceding one, where the last block on the right of one row becomes the first block on the left in the next row. Examining (84) and (85), we see that this merely means replacing some of the zeros with non-zero entries.

The reasons for doing this and its interpretation can be found in the following observations:

1.   Let R_c denote the circulant approximation to R, and let T_c be the matrix of eigenvectors of R_c. Then the product $T_c s$ can be computed efficiently using the fast Fourier transform. This is shown in appendix 2 and is the reason for using this approximation.

2.   For N large compared to d, $\|R - R_c\|$ is small, where $\|\cdot\|$ is any matrix norm. In addition, this error can be made arbitrarily small by choosing N large enough [81].

3.   Let us see what the circulant approximation means. For R_c to be block circulant, we must have that

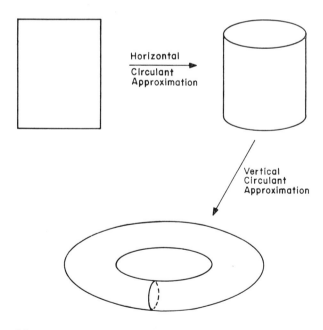

4.9
The circulant approximation.

$$r(i - j, m - n) = r[(i - j) \bmod N, m - n]. \tag{86}$$

Instead of thinking of the image as a flat array, think of it as a cylinder so that horizontal distance matters only modulo N. Furthermore, if each block is itself circulant, we should think of the image as the surface of a torus (connect the two ends of the cylinder).[18] See figure 4.9 for an illustration of this.

As discussed in [37] the Karhunen-Loeve expansion can also be performed quickly if the covariance is separable. In this case we perform the expansion separately in the horizontal and vertical directions, essentially one-dimensional transforms on data records of length N. Hence in the stationary or separable cases there appear to be relatively efficient methods to perform the transform. However, motivated by the complexity of the general Karhunen-Loeve expansion, researchers have applied other, more efficient transform techniques such as the FFT and the Hadamard transform to the problem of image compression and coding [4, 37, 81]. Many of these work nearly as well as Karhunen-Loeve [4]. This is not surprising given the discussion concerning circulant approximations.

4.4.3 Linear Prediction

One of the most widely used coding or compression schemes for one-dimensional time series, such as speech, is linear prediction, in which we design a one-step predictor or inverse-whitening filter (depending on point of view) for the time series. This method has several appealing features in one dimension. It is efficient (if one uses the Levinson algorithm), it leads to recursive coding and decoding algorithms, and it yields excellent performance. In two dimensions the situation is not nearly as clear. In what direction do we predict and what old data do we use? Answers to these questions are beginning to be found. Genin and Kamp [144, 145, 256] have shown that NE predictors need not be minimum phase, and Marzetta [66] has provided an argument showing why this is the case. Specifically, in one dimension we are guaranteed that the optimal predictor for $y(n)$, based on $y(n - 1)$, $y(n - 2)$, . . . , $y(n - r)$ is necessarily minimum phase; however, if we skip some points in the past, for example if we predict $y(n)$ based on $y(n - 1)$, $y(n - 2)$, and $y(n - 4)$, then the optimal predictor may not be minimum phase. Marzetta points out that NE predictors do skip points. For example, consider the predictor of $y(m, n)$

based on $y(m - 1, n)$, $y(m, n - 1)$ and $y(m - 1, n - 1)$. If we totally order the points in the plane to be compatible with the partial order for calculating points recursively to the NE, then $(m - 1, n)$, $(m, n - 1)$, and $(m - 1, n - 1)$ will never be the three immediate predecessors of (m, n). Thus, just as in one dimension, there is no reason to expect the optimal predictor to be minimum phase. Marzetta then points out that if we do not skip points—if we use a full half-plane causal predictor—we get the minimum-phase property and a Levinson-type algorithm involving reflection coefficients. This predictor is primarily of conceptual interest, since the predictor involves the incorporation of an entire, infinite-extent column before any points in the preceding columns may be included.[19] See [66] for details, for practical, suboptimal methods that also have the minimum-phase property, and for a generalization to two dimensions of Burg's maximum entropy spectral estimation algorithm [286].

For a particular ordering of the points in a two-dimensional array Habibi [76] and Habibi and Robinson [37] have obtained encouraging results using a predictive encoder. They found the predictive coding scheme to be superior to transform methods in terms of system complexity, time delay due to the coding operation, and coding performance at high-bit rates, but the transform methods were more robust to errors in the knowledge of the image covariance and required lower bit rates. In addition, Habibi and Robinson [37] suggest a hybrid scheme in which the data are transformed horizontally line by line and then one-dimensional linear prediction is performed on each column. They report that the performance of this system is excellent.

4.4.4 Nonrecursive Image-Processing Techniques

We now turn to the problem of restoring blurred and noise-corrupted images. Initially we will concentrate on the linear model (61), (62), (67), or equivalently (69). For details concerning these methods see the references, in particular the survey papers [4, 19, 38] and the text [81].

One of the first methods proposed for image restoration is aimed solely at removing the effects of blur and essentially ignores the presence of additive noise. This is the *inverse filter*

$$\hat{f} = H^{-1}q. \tag{87}$$

In the space-invariant case (62), we can take transforms

$$\hat{F}(z_1, z_2) = \frac{Q(z_1, z_2)}{H(z_1, z_2)}. \tag{88}$$

In addition, in this case H is block Toeplitz with Toeplitz blocks; hence we can make the circulant approximation (assuming that the extent of the PSF is much smaller than the size of the picture [81]) and take the DFT of (62), yielding

$$\hat{F}(m, n) = \frac{Q(m, n)}{H(m, n)}, \tag{89}$$

where, for example, with $W_N = \exp{(j2\pi/N)}$, we have

$$H(m, n) = \sum_{k, l=0}^{N-1} h(k, l) W_N^{-km-ln}. \tag{90}$$

As an alternative to making the circulant approximation, we can use the two-dimensional version of a standard one-dimensional idea. We embed the two-dimensional acyclic convolution (62) in a larger two-dimensional cyclic convolution by padding each row and column with a sufficient number of zeros. Equivalently, we intersperse zeros in the appropriate places in the lexicographically ordered vectors q, $\hat{f}$, and so on, and in the block matrix H [46]. The resulting matrix H is block circulant with circulant blocks (see appendix 2 for the correspondence between circulant matrices and cyclic convolution). Thus we can directly apply (89) with no approximation to this padded image.

Let us make several comments concerning the inverse filter. First, the image formation process (61), (62) may not be invertible, and thus we cannot even perform the calculation indicated by (87). One might consider using a pseudo-inverse, and we will discuss this in the context of another restoration methodology. In addition, examining the transformed versions (88), (89), we see the possibility of two further problems. The frequency response H usually falls off at high frequencies. Thus, assuming that high-frequency noise is present, we may observe extreme noise amplifications. In addition, the inverse filter transfer function blows up at the zeros of H, and this can cause severe difficulties. Looking at these equations in the space domain, Sondhi [19], Hunt [4], and Andrews and Hunt [81] argue that the difficulty arises from the severe problems encountered in attempting to invert integral equations such as (57). In the discrete domain this implies the ill conditioning of the matrix H; thus, even if its inverse exists, the solution suggested by (87)

$$\hat{f} = f + H^{-1}v \tag{91}$$

may be dominated by the noise.

To overcome difficulties such as these, one must explicitly take the presence of noise into account. This leads to the discrete Wiener filter formultion [4, 17, 19, 38, 40, 81]. Consider (69) with

$$E(ff') = P, \qquad E(vv') = R, \qquad E(fv') = 0, \tag{92}$$

and suppose we wish to choose our estimate $\hat{f}$ as the minimum mean square error (MMSE) estimate

$$\min_{\hat{f}} E[(f - \hat{f})'(f - \hat{f})]. \tag{93}$$

If we limit ourselves to linear transformations on the data or if we assume Gaussian statistics,[20] we obtain the optimal estimate

$$\hat{f} = PH'(HPH' + R)^{-1}q. \tag{94}$$

In the space-invariant, zero-mean,[21] stationary case, we can perform (94) in the frequency domain, obtaining an expression analogous to (88). In addition, in this case all the matrices are block Toeplitz, and we can use the same block-circulant approximation to obtain an expression analogous to (89)

$$\hat{F}(m, n) = \frac{H^*(m, n)Q(m, n)}{|H(m, n)|^2 + \Phi_v(m, n)/\Phi_f(m, n)}, \tag{95}$$

where $*$ denotes complex conjugate, Φ_v is the two-dimensional DFT of the noise covariance, and Φ_f is the DFT of the image covariance.

Note from (94) and (95) that the problem observed with the inverse filter has been removed; the inverse in (94) and the denominator in (95) will not blow up, since we have explicity included the effects of noise. The Wiener filter does, however, have some difficulties and limitations as an image-processing system, largely because the MMSE criterion is not particularly well-suited to the way the human visual system works (see Stockham [82] for a discussion of the visual system). In particular, the Wiener filter is overly concerned with noise suppression. In addition, in order to make the filter computationally feasible one often assumes stationarity. This in turn leads to a filter that is insensitive to abrupt changes; it tends to smooth edges and reduce contrast. On the other hand, in high-contrast regions the human visual system readily accepts more noise to obtain greater resolution. Thus the Wiener filter sacrifices too much in resolution in favor of noise suppression.

Another difficulty with the Wiener filter is the amount of a priori information that is required. For the inverse filter all we need is the PSF,[22] while for the Wiener filter we need the PSF and the second-order statistics of the original image and the noise. This is a great deal of information to assume, and a serious question concerns the robustness of the Wiener filter to errors in this a priori knowledge.

Several schemes that have been proposed are aimed at trading off between the potentially high-resolution, poor noise performance of the inverse filter and the lower-resolution, good noise performance of the Wiener filter. One of these is the *constrained least-squares filter*, suggested by Sondhi [19] and developed and discussed by Hunt [46] and Andrews and Hunt [81]. In this formulation we wish to choose $\hat{f}$ to minimize

$$J(\hat{f}) = \hat{f}'C'C\hat{f} \tag{96}$$

subject to the constraint

$$(H\hat{f} - q)'(Hf - q) = e. \tag{97}$$

The solution is

$$\hat{f} = (H'H + \gamma C'C)^{-1}H'q, \tag{98}$$

where γ is a Lagrange multiplier found by iteration in order to satisfy (97). Again one can obtain transform versions of (98) in the shift-invariant case.

Several comments are in order concerning this approach, which has been shown in several experiments to perform at a level superior to that of the Wiener and inverse filters [4, 81]. Note from (98) that we have eliminated the need for covariance information for f and v. In addition, by adjusting the size of e in (97) (or equivalently of γ in (98)), we can effectively control the amount of noise suppression. Also, we have some freedom in the choice of C; several possibilities and their interpretations are discussed in [81]. For example, choosing $C = I$ essentially leads to a pseudo-inverse filter; this filter resembles the inverse filter but avoids the ill conditioning by adding γI to $H'H$ before inverting. In addition, one can choose C as a finite-difference matrix, which leads to minimizing some measure of the rate of fluctuation in the estimated image. One can also choose C in order to match the characteristics of the human visual system [4], and the choice.

$$C = P^{-1/2}R^{1/2} \tag{99}$$

leads to a parametric Wiener filter, closely resembling (94) in structure.

Another approach, proposed by Stockham et al. [4, 81, 287], leads to a filter that is the geometric mean of the inverse and Wiener filters (hence it directly trades off between the properties of these systems):

$$\hat{F}(m, n) = \left[\frac{1}{|H(m, n)|^2 + \Phi_v(m, n)/\Phi_f(m, n)} \right]^{1/2} Q(m, n). \tag{100}$$

This filter, obtained by designing a system so that the output power spectral density equals that of the original image, has worked well in several experiments [4, 81, 287]. Equation (100) is not precisely correct, as it does not include the phase effect of the restoring filter. Since phase is important in image processing and viewing, one must take it into account. This has been done for several specific types of PSF [287]. In addition, from (100) it appears that we again require a great deal of a priori information; however, this filter is particularly well-suited to the use of on-line estimates of quantities such as the PSF.

At this point we want to make several observations concerning these processing systems. Note first that they are nonrecursive and in principle require the block processing of the entire image or substantial sections of the image [47]. Hence the computational burden of these schemes can be quite high. In the shift-invariant, stationary case this problem can be somewhat alleviated with the aid of FFT techniques, but the required amount of calculation is still substantial. The situation is even more complicated if the PSF is shift varying. Examples of such imaging systems are given by Sawchuk [65] and Robbins and Huang [20]. Sawchuk suggests breaking the PSF into shift-invariant pieces, and then using some of the techniques we have discussed. Sawchuk and Robbins and Huang also discuss the possibility of inverting nonlinear distortions in the imaging system and then using shift-invariant methods. Clearly the PSF must be of a special form for this to be possible.

4.4.5 Scan-Ordered Recursive Image Processing
The use of the FFT or the inversion of nonlinear distortions notwithstanding, it is clear that the processing methods described so far require

a great deal of on-line calculation. In one dimension one often finds recursive methods preferable to nonrecursive ones because of their computational advantages. Although the situation is not as clear in two dimensions, it certainly seems worthwhile to investigate resursive two-dimensional image-processing methods. The one-dimensional Kalman filter
offers great computational savings over nonrecursive methods [81], and
an appealing question is the extension of such filters to two dimensions.
Anyone familiar with one-dimensional Kalman filtering theory realizes
that the design of the filter relies heavily on a dynamic (recursive) representation of the received signal. Hence to develop such techniques in two
dimensions we need more complex models of images than that provided
by the mean and covariance. The need to use such models is an obvious
drawback to this approach, but the potential gains in computational
efficiency are a distinct advantage. We now describe several of the approaches taken in the application of recursive estimation techniques to
two-dimensional processing. This research topic is still in its early stages
of development, and many open questions remain.

One approach to recursive processing of images involves the one-
dimensional processing of the scan-ordered image. This work has been developed by Nahi, Silverman, and their colleagues [8, 18, 21, 24, 58, 174].
Suppose we have an image $f(m, n)$, assumed to be zero mean for convenience, with stationary covariance

$$r(k, l) = E[f(m, n)f(m + k, n + l)]. \qquad (101)$$

Suppose we observe

$$q(m, n) = f(m, n) + v(m, n), \qquad (102)$$

where the additive noise v is for simplicity assumed to be zero mean and
white, with

$$E[v(m' n)v(k, l)] = R\delta_{mk}\delta_{nl}. \qquad (103)$$

We now take the scan ordering of the $N \times N$ grid on which $q, f,$ and v
are defined. Let us use the same symbols to denote the resulting one-
dimensional processes. We then have

$$q(k) = f(k) + v(k), \qquad (104)$$

$$E[f(k)f(l)] = S(k, l), \qquad (105)$$

$$E[v(k)v(l)] = R\delta_{kl}, \tag{106}$$

where $S(k, l)$ can be calculated from $r(m, n)$.

Note that the scanned image $f(k)$ is not stationary, just as in section 4.2 we found that scanned two-dimensional systems do not become time-invariant one-dimensional systems. The problem is clearly due to the abrupt change that occurs when the scanner reaches the end of one line and begins the next. For example, it is clear that

$$S(i, i + 1) = S(i + 1, i + 2) = r(0, 1) \tag{107}$$

if and only if $i, i + 1$, and $i + 2$ come from the same line of the image. On the other hand, it is clear that two-dimensional stationarity plus the periodicity of the scanner should yield some structure for S, and, in fact, it is easily seen that

$$S(k, l) = S(k + N, l + N), \qquad \forall k, l. \tag{108}$$

A process with this property is called *cyclostationary*; many of its properties have been analyzed in detail [43, 80, 83].

Given the model (104)–(106), we want to use Kalman filtering techniques to suppress the noise. To do this we need a state-space model for f. That is, we have a stochastic realization problem. Find a finite-dimensional linear system driven by white noise that yields an output with correlation function given by (106). Unfortunately $S(k, l)$ does not have the required separability for such a realization to exist [21]. Hence some sort of approximation is needed, and several have been developed. The simplest of these involves finding a stationary approximation to (105), much as Manry and Aggarwal found shift-invariant approximations to the shift-varying scanned filters they studied in [56]. The basic idea here, due to Franks [43], is to use the stationary covariance

$$R(k) = \frac{1}{N} \sum_{m=1}^{N} S(m, m + k). \tag{109}$$

This is equivalent to randomizing the variable m over the scan of one line in the computation of $E[f(m)f(m + k)]$.

Having $R(k)$, one can then use some realization procedure to find a Markov model

$$x(k + 1) = Ax(k) + w(k), \tag{110}$$

$$f(k) = c'x(k), \tag{111}$$

$$E[w(k)w(j)] = Q\delta_{kj}, \tag{112}$$

that realizes or approximates the given correlation function. A method used by Nahi and Assefi is reported in [18].

We can now obtain an image restoration scheme by direct application of Kalman filtering to model (104), (106), (110)–(112). We first note that the filter has an artificial causality; only the points below and to the left on the same line affect the estimate of a given pixel. The effect produced by the causality of the filter can be partially removed by smoothing, that is, by estimating each $f(k)$ based on all the data. With the model we have developed the smoothing can be done efficiently with two Kalman filters scanning in opposite directions and starting at opposite ends of the image. The resulting estimate still has difficulties because the randomizing used to obtain (110)–(112) causes problems much like those caused by Manry-Aggarwal's shift-invariant approximation. In this case one can remove some of these difficulties by transposing the image and performing the same type of processing again (two more Kalman filters scanning in a direction orthogonal to the other two filters). This procedure is reminiscent of Pistor's four-quadrant decomposition [42]; we have NE, NW, SE, and SW Kalman filters.

A number of other comments can be made concerning this approach to image processing. First, like the Wiener filter, the Kalman filter is based on a MMSE criterion, and hence we can expect it to sacrifice resolution for noise suppression. In addition, this method relies heavily on a priori knowledge of the image covariance, and the robustness of the approach in the presence of modeling errors remains an open question. We have already commented on the problems inherent in the stationary approximation of the cyclostationary covariance of the scanned image. Nahi suggests using a piecewise stationary approximation over various sections of each scanned line [21]. This leads to a time-varying, piecewise-constant state variable description for the scanned process.

Several alternative methods exist for reducing the effect of the stationary approximation. Nahi and Franco [58] suggest the simultaneous scanning of a number of lines (vector scanning). One can then model correlations along both the scan and the components of the vector of the scan. If we scan all lines simultaneously, we can take all these correlations into account. In this case we have turned a two-dimensional, scalar signal into a one-dimensional, multivariable signal. Of course, this leads to problems with the dimensionality of the resulting processor. Thus Nahi and Franco suggest a section-scan scheme that is far more efficient than the scalar system. This sectioning approach is much like that of Manry and Aggarwal, in which a number of lines are processed together and different sections are processed independently. Manry and Aggarwal discussed the use of overlapping sections to avoid problems at the edges. A similar approach might work well in the framework developed by Nahi and Franco. However, the vector modeling in [58] requires the separability of the image covariance. In fact, Nahi and Franco [58] and Franks [43] argue that a good model is the exponential model

$$r(m, n) = \rho_1^{|m|} \rho_2^{|n|}. \tag{113}$$

The necessity for using separable covariances is clearly a limitation, but it does allow one to obtain detailed results. Powell and Silverman [8] used the separability assumption on $r(m, n)$ to develop exact dynamic models for each line of the scalar and vector scan processes. These models involve time delays in the output equation (due to the nonseparability of $S(k, l)$), and the dimension of the models increases in proportion to the width of the scan. This last fact is not surprising, since the dimension of the global state of a two-dimensional system grows in proportion to the extent of the plane on which the system is defined.

The recursive methods discussed so far have assumed that there is no blurring due to a nontrivial PSF. If there is such blurring, we must develop a one-dimensional dynamical model for the effect of the blur along the scan. The simplest example of this, motion blur along the direction of the scan, was considered by Aboutalib and Silverman [24]. In the absence of noise they design the line-by-line inverse system to remove the blur both in the space-invariant and space-variant cases. The inverse they propose is a recursive one and hence can be implemented with relatively small computational demands. If noise is present, one augments the scalar- or vector-scan dynamic models of Nahi, Assefi, and Franco with the dynamic model of the blur and uses the Kalman filter line by line (or section by section) to remove the blur and suppress the noise. Again this system offers computational advantages over nonrecursive schemes, but the inverse system may be very sensitive to errors in the knowledge of the PSF. The robustness properties of the Kalman filter in this case are not yet known. Aboutalib et al. [188] generalize the ideas of [24] to general motion blurs. The procedure for doing this involves some bookkeeping to define the appropriate state containing all the pixels of the unblurred image that affect a given pixel in the blurred image. The derivation in [188] is similar to our development in section 4.4.6 for the Woods-Radewan model. Having their model, Aboutalib et al. consider both noise-free inverse system deblurring and Kalman filtering in the noisy case in a manner very similar to that used in [24].

4.4.6 Two-Dimensional Optimal Kalman Filters

All the recursive scan techniques are basically one dimensional; no two-dimensional model for the image (beyond the usual covariance description) is used. Recently, however, a number of researchers [6, 22, 34, 35, 71, 96, 148, 173, 174, 229, 236] have considered two-dimensional recursive models for images. The first work along this line was that of Habibi [22], who considered the separable covariance function given in (113). Habibi noted that this covariance can be obtained from a two-dimensional, recursive, autoregressive shaping filter

$$x(k + 1, l + 1) = \rho_2 x(k + 1, l) + \rho_1 x(k, l + 1) \\ - \rho_1 \rho_2 x(k, l) + [(1 - \rho_1^2)(1 - \rho_2^2)]^{1/2} w(k, l), \tag{114}$$

where $w(k, l)$ is a white, zero-mean process with

$$E[w(k, l)w(m, n)] = \delta_{km}\delta_{ln}. \tag{115}$$

Assuming measurements of the form

$$y(k, l) = x(k, l) + v(k, l), \tag{116}$$

Habibi then developed an estimator for $x(k + 1, l + 1)$ based on $\{y(m, n)|m \le k, n \le l\}$; that is, this estimator is a one-step NE predictor. Habibi chose an estimator structure of the form

$$\hat{x}(k + 1, l + 1) = \rho_2 \hat{x}(k + 1, l) + \rho_1 \hat{x}(k, l + 1) - \rho_1 \rho_2 \hat{x}(k, l) \\ + F(k, l)[y(k, l) - \hat{x}(k, l)] \tag{117}$$

and determined a value for the gain $F(k, l)$. Unfortunately this estimator is suboptimal, as pointed out by Strintzis [165]. In one-dimensional Kalman filtering it is well-known that to obtain the optimal estimate recursively, one must estimate the entire state of the process. However, since the global state has dimension proportional to the extent of the two-dimensional domain under consideration, $x(k, l)$ is not the global state, and we cannot expect its estimate alone to suffice for recursive optimal estimation. In fact, as Morf et al. [162, 163] point out, $x(k, l)$ is not the complete local state; and this makes the meaning of (117) even more questionable. Still, as Strintzis mentions, the structure of this estimator is so simple and intuitively appealing that it would be worthwhile to determine just how suboptimal it is.

The most complete study of optimal two-dimensional Kalman filtering has been performed by Woods and Radewan [173, 229, 236]. We assume that we have a one-sided causal dynamic model (see figures 4.5, 4.6, equation (12)) for the random field

$$
\begin{aligned}
x(m, n) = & \sum_{k=1}^{M} \sum_{l=-M}^{+M} b(k, l)x(m - k, n - l) \\
& + \sum_{l=1}^{M} b(0, l)x(m, n - l) + w(m, n).
\end{aligned}
\tag{118}
$$

This model can be assumed to be given or can be obtained from the image power spectral density by means of two-dimensional spectral factorization [119]. This latter method in general leads to infinite-order factors that must be truncated. A third method for obtaining the model (118) is by direct parameter estimation using a method such as two-dimensional linear prediction [66].

Woods and Radewan consider the observation equation

$$
q(m, n) = x(m, n) + v(m, n),
\tag{119}
$$

where v is zero mean and white with variance R. Suppose we want to estimate $x(m, n)$ given all values of q in the past, where past is defined relative to the direction of recursion in (118); that is, $\{q(i, j) \mid i \leq m - 1,$ all $j\} \cup \{q(m, j) \mid j \leq n\}$. Woods and Radewan point out that this can be done optimally with an extremely high dimensional Kalman filter to estimate the global state of the system, which in this case has dimension on the order of MN (M = order of the filter, N = width of the image). In fact, a valid global state is (see figure 4.10).

$$
\begin{aligned}
s(m, n)' = & [x(m, n), x(m - 1, n), \ldots, x(1, m); x(N, n - 1), \ldots, \\
& x(1, n-1); \ldots; x(N, n - M), \ldots, x(m - M, n-M)].
\end{aligned}
\tag{120}
$$

By inspection of the state and the recursion (118), it is clear that we can write a one-dimensional equation for the scan-ordered process. Note that

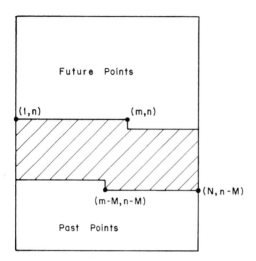

4.10
The global state of Woods-Radewan.

this model is time varying, since we must take into account the initiation
of a new line. We can also write a relation between q and s

$$q(m, n) = Hs(m, n) + v(m, n), \qquad (121)$$

where H merely picks off the first element of s. Given this development,
we can write a rather enormous Kalman filter. In addition, we can obtain
a more efficient optimal estimator by processing one line of data at a time
[229].

The filter developed in [173, 229, 236] does not correct for image blur.
However, it does appear that the development can be modified, in a manner similar to that employed in [188]. Suppose our observation is

$$t(m, n) = \sum_{j=-P}^{P} \sum_{k=-P}^{P} h(j, k)x(m - j, n - k) + \xi(n, m), \qquad (122)$$

where ξ is additive white noise. In terms of the ordering implied by the
recursion (118), $t(m, n)$ involves values of x that occur in the future. This
can be corrected by a time delay of the observations

$$q(m, n) = t(m - P, n - P). \qquad (123)$$

In this case, assuming $2P < M$, we may write a relation of the form of

(121), where v is a shifted version of ξ and H gives the proper blurring. If $2P > M$, we must increase the dimension of s (keep more data from the past) to make sure that s contains all the components of x that affect $q(m, n)$. Figure 4.11 illustrates these ideas. From the figure it is clear that H in (121) is not constant, since we must take end-of-line effects into account, when portions of the diagonally shaded region in figure 4.11 lie outside the range of the image. This clearly can be done, and as before we obtain a giant Kalman filter. Another method for optimal Kalman filtering in the presence of blurring has been developed by Hart et al. [71]. They also use a global state for the filter, but they assume that the different pixels are all independent, that is that all the $b(i, j)$ are zero in (118).

4.4.7 Attasi's Approach

Optimal line-by-line Kalman filtering for images has also been considered by Attasi and his colleagues [6, 34, 35, 96] using a stochastic version of the model discussed in section 4.2. Specifically, consider noisy observations of an image $f(i, j)$

$$q(i, j) = f(i, j) + v(i, j), \tag{124}$$

where the image is assumed to be generated by a separable vector analog of the model used by Habibi [22]

$$\begin{aligned} x(i, j) &= F_1 x(i - 1, j) + F_2 x(i, j - 1) - F_1 F_2 x(i - 1, j - 1) \\ &+ w(i - 1, j - 1), \\ f(i, j) &= H x(i, j). \end{aligned} \tag{125}$$

We wish to obtain the optimal estimate $\hat{x}(m, n)$ of $x(m, n)$ given $q(i, j)$ for $i \leq m$ and all j. The optimal estimate in this case consists essentially of two one-dimensional operations. Suppose we have $\hat{x}(m - 1, n)$ for all n. We first predict ahead one line to obtain

$$\bar{x}(m, n) = F_1 \hat{x}(m - 1, n), \qquad \forall n. \tag{126}$$

Note that each of these estimates is calculated independently. We now observe the new line of measurements $q(m, n)$ for all n, and we create the error process and the error measurement

$$e(m, n) = x(m, n) - \bar{x}(m, n), \tag{127}$$

$$y(m, n) = q(m, n) - H\bar{x}(m, n) = He(m, n) + v(m, n). \tag{128}$$

Thus we have a one-dimensional estimation problem: Estimate $e(m, n)$

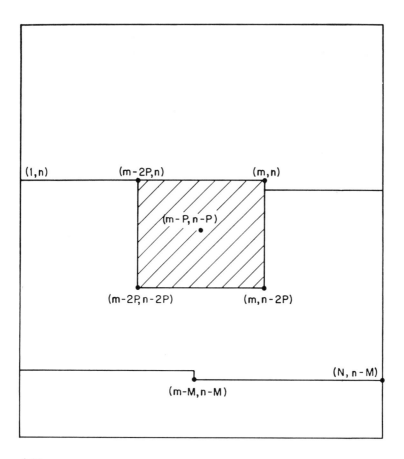

4.11
The adaptation of the Woods-Radewan model to allow blurring.

for all n, given $y(m, n)$ for all n. Attasi shows that one can obtain a finite-dimensional realization for $e(m, n)$ as a function of n. Hence this estimation problem reduces to the usual one-dimensional smoothing problem. The solution consists of two one-dimensional Kalman filters starting at opposite ends of the line. The estimates produced by these filters are then combined to produce $\hat{e}(m, n)$ and

$$\hat{x}(m, n) = \bar{x}(m, n) + \hat{e}(m, n). \tag{129}$$

For details see the references. The geometry of the estimator is illustrated in figure 4.12.

Let us make several comments concerning this estimator. First, we see that the decoupled structure of the estimator yields a far more efficient estimator than that of Woods and Radewan. This is apparently due to the separability of the underlying model (125). For this model it is not clear whether we can perform the same modifications to incorporate blurring. This and the separability restriction are obvious drawbacks, but the appealing structure of the filter is reason enough for further investigation, especially given the compatability of this algorithm with parallel processing techniques. Furthermore, the optimal smoother can again be implemented with two filters of the type devised by Attasi, one sweeping the columns in order of increasing m and the other in order of decreasing m. Again, this is reminiscent of the decomposition of zero-phase filters into two half-plane filters [42, 119].

The method of proof used by Attasi involves taking z-transforms along the n direction and treating m as a time variable. Essentially we are regarding the two-dimensional system as a high-dimensional (infinite if the domain of n is unbounded) one-dimensional system, where we can use a spatial transform "along" the one-dimensional state vector to simplify the calculations. The key step in Attasi's development is a derivation of a set of Riccati equations, parametrized by the transform variable z, for the power spectral density $S_m(z)$ of $e(m, n)$ considered as a function of n. One can then factor these spectra to obtain the one-dimensional realizations of the e's. As Attasi points out, the dimension of the realization for $e(m, n)$ is on the order of m times the dimension of x. One can avoid this difficulty by using reduced-order estimators. For example, we may choose to use the steady-state filter, in which case we can obtain a finite-dimensional system whose spectrum approximates $S_\infty(z)$.

Attasi's work brings out several crucial issues. Specifically we have seen

(a)

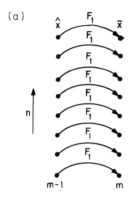

(b)

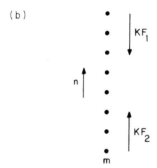

4.12
The structure of Attasi's estimator: (a) Predicting ahead one column. (b) Processing the new column of data with two Kalman filters.

the effective use of the equivalent representations of signals as multivariable one-dimensional and scalar two-dimensional. We have also seen that transforms along one of these variables can be useful in obtaining solutions (see [251] for a similar use of transforms for image processing). When we discuss the relation between two-dimensional processing and distributed and decentralized control, these issues will be of great importance again.

4.4.8 Suboptimal Recursive Processing
Since, optimal two-dimensional Kalman filtering algorithms require large amounts of storage and computation, a number of researchers [34, 148, 173, 174, 229, 236] have developed suboptimal estimators that require less computation. We will briefly describe several of these. Woods and Radewan [173, 229, 236] consider two types of suboptimal filters. The first involves breaking the picture up into strips of width $W < N$ and then processing across and up these strips individually, much as with the Manry-Aggarwal section scan. This reduces the dimension of the global state, as we replace N in (120) with W. Woods and Radewan also suggest overlapping the strips to avoid the edge effects caused by incorrect boundary conditions between strips.

The other suboptimal filter developed in [229] is the reduced-update Kalman filter. Examining the optimal filter of Woods and Radewan, we see that the predict cycle is computationally straightforward; one simply uses the recursion (118) assuming no noise and using preceding estimates. The measurement update part of the optimal filter, on the other hand, involves updating the estimates of all the components of the state. Assuming $N \gg M$, we expect that a given pixel is significantly correlated only with a small percentage of the elements of the state vector. Therefore, it seems reasonable to update the estimates of only the components of the state within a certain distance of the point being processed. This should greatly simplify the filter with minimal effect on performance. In other words, we are essentially designing a Kalman filter in which many of the gain elements are constrained to be zero and only "near-neighbor updates are allowed." A similar idea was proposed by Pratt [17] for the Wiener filter and by Murphy and Silverman [174] in the Kalman filtering context. Similar ideas have been proposed for large-scale systems in which measurements on a particular subsystem are used to update only subsystems "near" the subsystem in question, as determined by some measure of dynamic interaction (see, for example, [201, 205, 208] for related results for problems of freeway traffic control and estimation).

Motivated by the simplicity of the filter proposed by Habibi [22] and by the recursive local state-space model proposed by Roesser [110], Barry et al. [164] have developed a class of constrained filters. They consider a noisy version of Roesser's model (36)

$$\begin{bmatrix} v(i+1,j) \\ h(i,j+1) \end{bmatrix} = \begin{bmatrix} A_1 & A_2 \\ A_3 & A_4 \end{bmatrix} \begin{bmatrix} v(i,j) \\ h(i,j) \end{bmatrix} + w(i,j), \tag{130}$$

$$y(i,j) = C_1 v(i,j) + C_2 h(i,j) + \nu(i,j), \tag{131}$$

where w and ν are white noise processes. Their suboptimal estimator is then taken to be the optimum estimator of the form

$$\begin{bmatrix} \hat{v}(i+1,j) \\ \hat{h}(i,j+1) \end{bmatrix} = \begin{bmatrix} A_1 & A_2 \\ A_3 & A_4 \end{bmatrix} \begin{bmatrix} \hat{v}(i,j) \\ \hat{h}(i,j) \end{bmatrix} + \begin{bmatrix} K_1 \\ K_2 \end{bmatrix} \left(y(i,j) - [C_1, C_2] \begin{bmatrix} \hat{v}(i,j) \\ \hat{h}(i,j) \end{bmatrix} \right). \tag{132}$$

All the recursive estimators that we have examined so far have had two things in common: They have involved discrete two-dimensional space, and they have used recursive random field models. Recently Wong [172, 187] reported some work on two-dimensional continuous-space estimation. This theory involves the development of a stochastic calculus in two-dimensions, and this in turn has led to a number of interesting theoretical results (see section 4.5).

4.4.9 The Use of Nonrecursive Models and Transform Techniques in Recursive Processing

Some work has been performed on recursive processing of fields specified by nonrecursive models. Jain and Angel [32] have considered fields described by a nearest-neighbor, interpolative equation

$$x(m,n) = \alpha_1[x(m,n+1) + x(m,n-1)]$$
$$+ \alpha_2[x(m+1,n) + x(m-1,n)] + w(m,n). \tag{133}$$

Fields of this type have been studied by several authors and were proposed by Woods [9] as the prototype of discrete, two-dimensional Markov fields. We will have more to say about the properties and other uses of these fields. For now we concentrate on the estimation problem when we observe

$$y(m,n) = x(m,n) + v(m,n). \tag{134}$$

Following [32], let us consider the vector-scan process, in which we process an entire line of data at a time. Define the resulting one-dimensional vector processes x_m, y_m, w_m, and v_m; for example

$$x_m = \begin{bmatrix} x(m, 1) \\ \vdots \\ x(m, N) \end{bmatrix}. \tag{135}$$

Then one can write (134) and (135) as

$$x_{m+1} = Qx_m - x_{m-1} + w_m, \tag{136}$$

$$y_m = x_m + v_m, \tag{137}$$

where Q is a symmetric, tridiagonal, Toeplitz matrix

$$Q = \frac{1}{\alpha_2} \begin{bmatrix} 1 & -\alpha_1 & 0 & \cdots & 0 \\ -\alpha_1 & & & & \\ 0 & & & & \\ \vdots & & & & 0 \\ & & & & -\alpha_1 \\ 0 & \cdots & 0 & -\alpha_1 & 1 \end{bmatrix} \tag{138}$$

The structure of (138) tempts one to utilize the same type of circulant approximation used by Andrews and Hunt [81] to diagonalize the system efficiently with the aid of the FFT. However, as Jain and Angel point out, the diagonalization of Q

$$M'QM = \text{diag}(\lambda_1, \ldots, \lambda_N) \tag{139}$$

can be performed with the aid of the FFT without any approximation. Thus, if we define the transformed quantities $\bar{x}_m$, $\bar{y}_m$, where for example

$$\bar{x}_m = M'x_m, \tag{140}$$

we obtain a set of N decoupled estimation problems, indexed by j (which indexes the components of the transformed vectors):

$$\bar{x}_{m+1,j} = \lambda_j \bar{x}_{m,j} - \bar{x}_{m-1,j} + \bar{w}_{m,j}, \tag{141}$$

$$\bar{y}_{m,j} = \bar{x}_{m,j} + \bar{v}_{m,j}. \tag{142}$$

Each of these problems can be solved using a second-order Kalman filter (see [32] for an alternative method of derivation), and we obtain the efficient implementation illustrated in figure 4.13. Again, to utilize all the data to estimate each pixel, we can implement the smoother by including a second bank of filters that sweeps the lines in the opposite direction (m runs from N to 1). One can also implement a one-step smoother, which estimates x_m based on data through line $m + 1$. This requires only one bank of filters, as in figure 4.13. See [32] for details and [259] for a related study of smoothing of images using interpolative models.

The approach in [32] deserves some comment. As in Attasi's work, transforming variables in one dimension and processing in the other can lead to extremely efficient processing schemes.[23] Just as with the block-circulant approach of Andrews and Hunt, the spatial stationarity of the one-dimensional equation (136) is such that the FFT can be used to great advantage. This observation leads one to seek other formulations whose structures can be exploited in this manner. Jain and Angel mention several other random field models that lead to symmetric, tridiagonal, Toeplitz evolution equations when scanned line by line, and Jain [30] uses similar analysis for the efficient recursive filtering of one of these models, the so-called semicausal model

$$
\begin{aligned}
x(m, n) = {} & \alpha_1[x(m - 1, n) + x(m + 1, n)] \\
& - \rho\alpha_1[x(m + 1, n - 1) + x(m - 1, n - 1)] \qquad (143) \\
& + \rho x(m, n - 1) + w(m, n).
\end{aligned}
$$

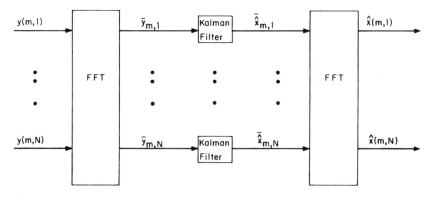

4.13
The optimal filter of Jain and Angel.

The model was given this name since $x(m, n)$ depends only on $x(i, j)$ with $j \leq n$ (note, however, that (143) is not recursive). Throughout the development in [30, 32] it is assumed that no blurring occurs. It is not clear whether the approach adopted in these references can be extended to include the effect of a PSF, but the efficiency of the algorithms developed by Jain and Angel indicates that it is certainly worth trying to find such an extension. As we shall see, the use of structure in this manner can be applied in a number of different settings.

4.4.10 A Critique of the Techniques and Key Questions for the Future

We have now surveyed a number of nonrecursive and recursive estimation methods. The recursive techniques are subject to many of the same criticisms made about nonrecursive filters. They require detailed models of the image statistics and image formation process, and they are essentially based on the MMSE criterion. Hence, in general they sacrifice resolution in favor of noise suppression. In addition, these recursive techniques necessarily affect the image because of the assumed model structure. The effect of this in some cases (such as in the Kalman filter based on a stationary approximation to the scanned image) may be to require additional processing (of the transposed image, for example); in other cases, such as the two-dimensional causal models of Woods-Radewan and Attasi or the noncausal models of Jain and Angel, the effects may not be so noticeable. Some of the recursive techniques allow the inclusion of image blur, while in other cases the extensions to include blur have yet to be developed. Optimal Kalman filtering in some cases is extremely complex, and suboptimal but intuitively appealing recursive filter structures must be used. In other cases, specifically in the work of Attasi and Angel and Jain, we have observed that the use of the structure of the assumed model can lead to extremely efficient optimal estimation algorithms (with the aid of transform techniques). Although work in this area has been limited [24, 174], the recursive techniques are directly amenable to the analysis of space-varying and nonstationary models. Thus, despite the many qualifications, we find enough positive attributes to warrant continued study of recursive techniques for image restoration.

Let us now comment and speculate on several aspects of image processing that we have previously mentioned only in passing. First, we have the problem of nonlinearities in image sensing. Consider the multiplicative noise model (63). As discussed in [82, 288] and in chapter 5, one can often filter signals corrupted by multiplicative noise by first taking the logarithm, then filtering with a linear system, and then exponentiating. This process, an example of *homomorphic filtering*, is described in chapter 5. This technique has been applied with great success [82, 288], and in [82] it is argued that this type of processing is extremely compatible with the response characteristics of the human visual system.

Equation (64) illustrates another kind of measurement nonlinearity, in which the noise is additive but the signal is distorted in a nonlinear fashion. Hunt [4, 81] has studied such image-processing problems in the context of nonrecursive restoration techniques. He has devised an iterative scheme for computing the maximum a posteriori image estimate given the observations. For linear measurements this reduces to the Wiener filter. The analog of this technique for the recursive methods is the extended Kalman filter (EKF), which essentially involves a continual relinearization about the present best estimate. This method can readily be derived for all the recursive methods discussed. See [21] for a discussion of this method in the context of the Nahi-Assefi scalar-scan recursive technique. There are, of course, many other nonlinear one-dimensional recursive estimation techniques besides the EKF, and most of these can be applied in this framework. For an example of one other such technique (again applied to the Nahi-Assefi method) see [75].

Another issue that we have mentioned several times is the incorporation of constraints, such as the positivity of the image estimate, into the estimation procedure. In many cases we do not have to worry about this constraint explicitly.[24] However, it is worth understanding the implications of such constraints. Andrews and Hunt [81] consider the constrained least-squares formulation together with the additional positivity constraint. In this case there is no closed-form solution, and iterative nonlinear programming methods must be used. Mascarenhas and Pratt [23] also consider the incorporation of upper bounds on pixel intensities to improve the conditioning of the restoration problem. Similar types of bound on the pixels and on the values of the PSF (assumed unknown in this case) were considered by MacAdam [39]. In the case of recursive techniques one can also include positivity constraints. In [239] Jain discusses a recursive, iterative method for incorporating this constraint into the Nahi-Assefi model. Thus we see that constraints such as these can be incorporated into the methods discussed previously. The cost is a great increase in computational complexity, and it is not clear that it is worth the trouble.

A third problem with many of the restoration techniques is their reliance on a priori information. One can often assume knowledge of the PSF or determine it by observing known test scenes through the imaging system. In other cases we may not have such information and must estimate the PSF as well as the image. Based on the assumption that the extent of the PSF is far less than that of the image, Stockham et al. [287] suggest a blind homomorphic deconvolution procedure, in which one breaks the received image into pieces, takes two-dimensional transforms and the logarithm of the transforms, and then averages over the pieces. Combined with the specification of a prototype transform (corresponding to the average of the logarithm of the transform of the original image), this procedure allows one to estimate the PSF and the other parameters needed for the geometric mean filter [287].

The question of parameter uncertainty is clearly of major importance for the recursive techniques, which all require a great deal of a priori information. Thus one important question concerns the robustness of these techniques in the face of modeling errors. Techniques exist for the sensitivity analysis of one-dimensional state-space models and one-dimensional Kalman filters [289, 290]. Can we extend these methods to the two-dimensional case, and how well do the two-dimensional algorithms perform? Is there any way to make them more robust? In addition, methods abound in one dimension for on-line parameter identification and adaptive estimation in the presence of unknown parameters. Can we apply these methods with any success to the two-dimensional problem? (See [260] for one such application for an interpolative image model.) The successes of such methods in one dimension and the several appealing features of two-dimensional recursive estimation techniques make these worthwhile questions for future research.

A final area of concern is the trade-off between resolution and noise suppression. The human visual system is willing to accept more noise in certain regions, such as edges, to improve resolution. Thus in relatively slowly varying regions of the image we would like to remove noise; where there are abrupt scene changes or other high-frequency fluctuations of interest, we would prefer to forego noise suppression in favor of resolution. Backus and Gilbert [78] (see also [19]) have devised a nonrecursive technique for taking this trade-off into account. They define a quantitative measure of the blur induced in the image by filtering. Then for any given value of this measure one can determine the restoration scheme that minimizes the effects of noise subject to this constraint [19, 78, 79]. Anderson and Netravali [99] have developed another nonrecursive approach involving a performance index that provides a trade-off between blur introduced by the filter and the level of noise suppression. Their criterion utilizes the results of certain psychovisual experiments designed to measure the relative importance of a unit of noise in high- and low-contrast conditions, but the evidence is still inconclusive as to whether a standard measure can be obtained for a large class of images. See [38, 44, 225, 272] for discussions of several other improved resolution, image enhancement techniques.

In the context of simultaneous image enhancement and noise suppression, an important problem is the detection of edges or boundaries between different regions in an image. Within each region one may be able to utilize one of the restoration techniques developed earlier, thus suppressing noise while preserving the resolution of the boundaries. In many applications the determination of the boundaries themselves may be the key issue [175]. In recent years a variety of techniques has been developed for detecting and recognizing boundaries in two-dimensional data. Many of these methods are based on pattern recognition techniques [243], and we will not discuss them here. See the references on this subject [15, 210, 240].

In one dimension recursive techniques have been developed for estimating and detecting abrupt changes in signals [291]. These techniques have been successfully used in a wide variety of applications, including automatic detection of cardiac arrhythmias [292] and the detection of sensor and actuator failures [291]. An important problem then is the extension of methods such as these to the detection of boundaries in images. To a large extent this remains an open problem, but there has been some work along these lines. Nahi and Habibi [25] considered the problem of the detection of an object superimposed on a background scheme. Their approach was to modify the methods of Nahi [18, 21, 58] and Habibi [22] to incorporate a binary variable that indicates whether a particular pixel is in the object or in the background. The scheme devised in [25] involves the recursive calculation of likelihood ratios for the existence of boundaries and incoporates the use of a bank of two filters (based on object and background statistics, respectively) for the suppression of noise once the boundaries have been determined. In [175] Nahi and Lopez-Mora were concerned primarily with the estimation of the boundary. Here the one-dimensional Markov scan model of [18, 21, 58] is augmented to include several states used to model the boundary. Because the resulting model is nonlinear, a nonlinear estimation scheme is employed, and some promising results are presented in [175]. A great deal of work remains to be done in the development of recrusive methods for the detection of boundaries in images. This may be one of the most important uses of two-dimensional recursive estimation techniques.

4.5 Random Fields

We now turn to the detailed analysis of statistical and probabilistic models for random fields. Applications of such techniques extend far beyond image processing into fields such as seismic signal processing [68, 70, 199, 209, 216, 227, 245], gravity mapping [1, 211, 212, 224], meteorology and atmospheric modeling [69, 214, 231], biomedical imagery and image reconstruction [11, 29, 213, 223, 279], modeling of scattering fields [222, 232–235], modeling of the distribution of earth resources [15, 61, 246], analysis and modeling of turbulence [217], and the modeling and analysis of random transport and wave propagation phenomena [170, 189, 193, 194, 215, 220, 226]. With such a variety of potential applications, there is clearly a need for a general methodology for the analysis of random fields. Much has been done in this direction, but as with all multidimensional topics much remains to be done. We will describe some of the work that has been done, touch on several of the applications, and speculate on some open questions.

4.5.1 Markov Models

Motivated to a great extent by the utility of Markov processes in one dimension, many researchers have investigated the extension of the concept to several dimensions. Perhaps the first of these was developed by Lévy for continuous parameter spaces [12, 197, 198, 230]. The situation in two dimensions is depicted in figure 4.14. Suppose we have a two-dimensional random field $f(x, y)$. Then f is called Markov of degree p if it essentially has the following property.[25] Let ∂G be any smooth closed curve encircling the origin and separating the plane into the past G_p, the present ∂G, and the future G_F. Given f and its first $p - 1$ derivatives at the present, the values of f in the future are independent of the values of f in the past. The field f is called Markov if it is Markov of degree one. This definition is

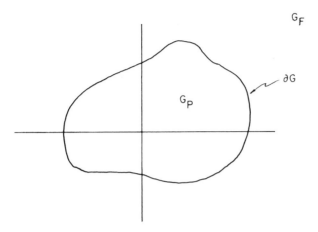

4.14
Lévy's two-dimensional Markov property.

quite intuitive, and one can imagine fields in a variety of physical situations that have this type of radial causality.

Lévy also defined a multidimensional Brownian motion process $x(t)$, $t = (t_1, \ldots, t_d)$, which is a Gaussian process with statistics

$$E[x(a)] = 0, \tag{144}$$

$$E[x(a)x(b)] = \tfrac{1}{2}(|a| + |b| - |b - a|). \tag{145}$$

Here $|\cdot|$ is the usual Euclidean distance. McKean [198] showed that for d odd $x(t)$ is Markovian of degree $(d + 1)/2$; for d even $x(t)$ has no Markovian property. Since Brownian motion and its Markovian properties are so useful in developing one-dimensional tools of stochastic analysis, this result is disappointing. The disappointment is compounded by the analysis of Wong [12], who showed that there are essentially no continuous Gaussian random fields in two or more dimensions that are simultaneously stationary, isotropic (the covariance function is invariant if we rotate the coordinates of the parameter space), and Markov (of degree one). Thus it is evident that this setting does not lead to a useful multidimensional stochastic calculus for the study of random fields. To obtain such a calculus, we must turn to a recursive formulation.

The analog of Lévy's notion for discrete space systems, as developed by Woods in [9], leads to far more useful results. Stationary Gaussian fields of this type can be generated by interpolative filters of the form[26]

$$x(n, m) = \sum_{D_p} h(k, l)x(n - k, m - l) + u(n, m), \tag{146}$$

where $u(n, m)$ is stationary and

$$D_p = \{(k, l)|k^2 + l^2 \leq p^2, k, l \text{ not both } 0\}, \tag{147}$$

$$E[x(n, m)u(k, l)] = c\delta_{nk}\delta_{ml}, \tag{148}$$

$$E[u(n, m)u(0, 0)] = \begin{cases} c, & m = n = 0, \\ -h(m, n)c, & (m, n) \in D_p, \\ 0, & \text{otherwise.} \end{cases} \tag{149}$$

Thus the driving noise in this case is not white but is finitely correlated.

The work of Jain and Angel [32] shows that interpolative models can be used for efficient recursive estimation of random fields. Such models also have several other uses. One possibility is in the area of spectral estimation. In [237] Woods proposes the fitting of observed correlation data to an interpolative Markov model. This technique again results in a set of normal equations for the coefficients of the model yielding the minimal interpolation error in a least-squares sense. Unfortunately, as Woods points out, these equations cannot be inverted efficiently as in the one-dimensional linear prediction case, and Woods proposes a complex algorithm for obtaining the desired spectral estimate.

Nearest-neighbor models have a great deal of structure that can be exploited to obtain efficient computational schemes [32]. Jain proposes a nearest-neighbor interpolative filter for image coding [32]. Basically Jain assumes a separable, stationary, isotropic model for the image

$$E[x(n, m)x(0, 0)] = \rho^{|n|+|m|} \tag{150}$$

and finds the optimum first-order ($p = 1$ in (147)) interpolative error filter. In this simple case the normal equations can be solved by inspection. With this filter we can consider a coding scheme in which we transmit only the interpolation error. Thus the decoder must essentially solve the interpolative and hence nonrecursive equation. In general this is a difficult task, but techniques analogous to those in [32] can be used to perform the reconstruction efficiently. That is, the image can be reconstructed line by line, and the resulting vector equations display the same type of tridiagonal structure exploited in the development of an efficient restoration scheme (see section 4.4.9). This structure can be exploited with the aid of FFT algorithms to produce an efficient image reconstruction technique. In addition, the use of interpolative models leads to efficient Karhunen-Loeve transform coding using the FFT [241, 242].

4.5.2 Spectral Estimation, Linear Prediction, and Statistical Analysis

Although interpolative models have a number of appealing properties, they also have their drawbacks, as in efficient spectral estimation,[27] and one is naturally led to seek other models and statistical methods for fitting two-dimensional data to parametric forms for such models. One immediate generalization from one dimension is the development of two-dimensional linear prediction techniques—the identification of two-dimensional, causal, autoregressive models by means of least-squares predictive error filter design. One problem that arises immediately is the choice of the direction of recursion for the AR model, that is, which elements of the field will be used to predict which other elements. Another problem is the stability of the resulting filter, which is guaranteed in one dimension but not in two for quarter-plane filters [145], although it is for half-plane filters [66]. The half-plane linear predictors derived in [66] lead to Levinson-type efficient algorithms for the solution of the normal equations. In addition, see [250, 263, 266, 267] for recent results on Levinson-type algorithms for quarter-plane filters.[28] As an example of what can be done, consider the algorithm described by Bednar and Farmer [266], Lévy et al. [263, 267], and Marzetta [66]. This algorithm uses one-dimensional techniques and the same two-dimensional, scalar/one-dimensional, vector interplay that we have seen before. Consider figure 4.15a. We have a stationary two-dimensional field $x(k, l)$, and we wish to predict $x(m, n)$ based on the array of $x(i, j)$ to the SW indicated in the figure. We do this in two steps. First, regarding each column as a one-dimensional vector, we use the preceding columns to predict the mth column. This can be done with standard fast algorithms for vector one-dimensional linear prediction. In fact, in this case we can effectively use the faster scalar one-dimensional algorithm since the block-Toeplitz matrix to be inverted is Toeplitz because of vertical stationarity. We then compute the prediction errors in the last column and use these to predict the error at (m, n) by performing a scalar one-dimensional prediction to the north. The algorithm of Lévy et al. allows one to increase either N or M in an efficient manner [267]. In addition, the algorithm we have described bears a striking resemblance to that of Attasi (see figure 4.12). The only difference is that Attasi uses two one-dimensional Kalman filters— one north, one south—to smooth along the last column. This observation

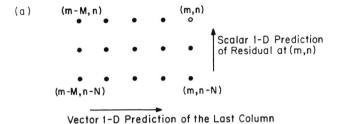

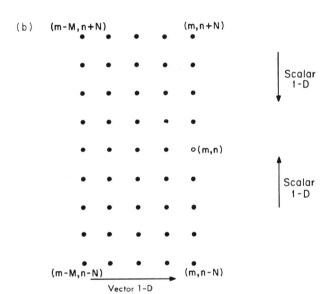

4.15
Known and conjectured fast algorithems for two-dimensional linear prediction and interpolation: (a) Marzetta's fast algorithm. (b) Does a fast algorithm like this exist?

leads us to speculate on the existence of a fast alogrithm for linear interpolation for the semicausal structure [30] illustrated in figure 15b. Similar
results are reported in [263, 267].

Identification of parametric two-dimensional models has attracted the
attention of several statisticians over the years [1, 59, 61], and several of
their results are definitely worth noting. Bartlett's recent book [273] provides an overview of some of the work in this area.

Whittle [61, 63] was one of the first researchers to consider the properties
of two-dimensional stationary processes. One of the topics he considered,
was the "unilateral" representation of a two-dimensional process, which is
simply a half-plane recursive representation of a given field. Using a
method exactly along the lines developed by Dudgeon [33, 102], Ekstrom
and Woods [119], and Marzetta [66], Whittle obtained an infinite-order
(in general) representation of this type by factoring the two-dimensional
power spectral density of the process. He also relates various recursive and
nonrecursive autoregressive discrete-space models to analogous stochastic
partial differential equations [61]. Such equations were considered by
Heine [60], who examined the properties of linear stochastic equations of
the parabolic, elliptic, and hyperbolic forms. Whittle noted that the
nearest-neighbor model corresponds to an elliptic equation for which
Heine showed that the correlation function takes the form of a modified
Bessel function of the second kind. Whittle then uses this fact to argue that
in the discrete-space case, such correlation function forms are preferable
to decaying exponentials.

Whittle also discussed the maximum likelihood and least-squares estimation of the parameters of a two-dimensional autoregressive model. This
subject is also considered in far greater detail by Larimore [1], whose
results reveal an important point. If Gaussian statistics are assumed,
finding the maximum likelihood parameter estimates in one dimension
is equivalent to finding the parameters of an inverse filter that yields
the least-squares prediction error; that is, the log-likelihood ratio is,
up to an additive constant, proportional to the negative of the sum of
squared estimation errors. In the two-dimensional problem this is not the
case, unless the field model is causal, because the Jacobean of the transformation from prediction errors to the field is not unity and is in general
a complicated function of the parameters. This greatly complicates parameter and spectral estimation, as we already noted in discussing the work
of Woods [237]. See [1] for details of the problem of two-dimensional

parametric model identification and for the consideration of other problems, such as the design of a one-dimensional shaping filter for the part of a two-dimensional field observed by a point tracing a path in the plane. These results are of great practical value in problems such as accurate inertial navigation and gravity field estimation [1, 193, 194].[29]

4.5.3 Two-Dimensional Martingale Theory

Since stochastic calculus facilitates the analysis of continuous-time random processes in one dimension, it seems natural to attempt to extend concepts such as the Markov property, Brownian motion, and stochastic calculus to two dimensions. We have seen, however, that the intuitively appealing approach of Lévy is not useful because of the lack of causality in this framework. In one dimension the basic tools of analysis—Brownian motion, Poisson processes, stochastic differential equations—are essentially based on the principles of martingale theory [247]. A martingale $M(t)$ is a one-dimensional random process such that for $t > s$ the best estimate $M(t)$ given $M(\tau)$, $\tau \leq s$, is $M(s)$:[30]

$$E[M(t)|M(\tau), \tau \leq s] = M(s). \tag{151}$$

To extend these notions to two dimensions, we immediately run into a problem: What does $t > s$ mean? We must be able to specify at least a partial order on the plane, and this can be done if we impose a causal structure on the processes considered.

In recent years two-dimensional martingales (and higher-dimensional generalizations) with a NE causal structure have been investigated by a number of authors [172, 176, 179–187, 191, 192, 196, 271]. We consider processes $M(z_1, z_2)$ defined on the NE quadrant, on which we place the partial order

$$(z_1, z_2) \succ (\xi_1, \xi_2) \Leftrightarrow z_i \geq \xi_i, \qquad i = 1, 2. \tag{152}$$

Then $M(z_1, z_2)$ is a (NE) martingale if, whenever $(z_1, z_2) \succ (\xi_1, \xi_2)$,

$$E[M(z_1, z_2)|M(s_1, s_2), (\xi_1, \xi_2) \succ (s_1, s_2)] = M(\xi_1, \xi_2). \tag{153}$$

The relevant geometry is depicted in figure 4.16. Here $\mathcal{F}(\xi_1, \xi_2)$ denotes the set of all $M(s_1, s_2)$ with $(s_1, s_2) \succ (\xi_1, \xi_2)$.

With this framework one can begin to develop all the tools for a usable two-dimensional stochastic calculus. The results obtained indicate that such a calculus can be developed, but it is not without its surprises and

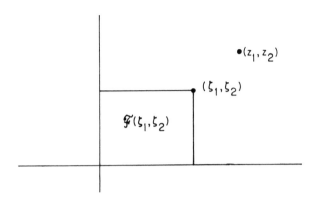

4.16
The structure of a NE martingale.

limitations. One of the major surprises is that given a NE martingale, the lack of a total order leads directly to the construction of a second martingale. This second martingale, which in some sense involves products of the original martingale at unordered points, is essential to the development of a full set of stochastic differentiation rules.[31] In addition, one of the major limitations of this approach appears to be the restriction to quadrant causality. But is this really a restriction? In one dimension one of the most important dynamic models represents a random process as the output of a causal stochastic differential equation driven by a martingale. Perhaps in two dimensions we must break the process into two parts, one driven by a NE martingale and one by a SE martingale. Since, as Ekstrom and Woods assert [119], any power spectral density can be created by using white noise to drive one half-plane or two quadrant filters, this idea may not be that far-fetched. In [182] a second type of martingale using a half-plane causal framework is considered. Its utility also remains to be assessed.

There certainly appear to be enough reasons for pursuing the utility of such a continuous-parameter two-dimensional stochastic calculus. In one dimension one often finds that the continuous-time solution is far simpler computationally and conceptually than the corresponding discrete-time solution; for digital systems one often solves the continuous problem and discretizes rather than discretizing the problem at the start. Examination of the recursive two-dimensional optimal estimation and detection results derived by Wong in the continuous case [172, 176, 179, 187, 265] and comparison of them to the analogous discrete-time results show that the same may be true here. In addition to applications such as these, a two-dimensional stochastic calculus may be useful in the analysis of processes that evolve in both space and time.

4.6 Space-Time Processes and Interconnected Systems

Throughout this chapter we have seen numerous examples of two-dimensional signal processing problems in which good use is made of the transformation of the signals obtained by considering them to be one-dimensional vector time signals, in which the other independent spatial variable is used to index components of the vectors. We now briefly examine several problems in which the processes are truly of this form—they are space-time processes—or from which one can benefit by viewing multivariable one-dimensional systems as systems with two independent variables.

4.6.1 Space-Time Signal-Processing Problems

One of the best examples of space-time processes arises in the consideration of seismic signal processing [68, 70, 199, 209, 215, 216, 227, 245], in which we observe the response of the earth to excitation through an array of sensors. In such a system the sensors receive signals due to reflections from different layers in the earth. In addition there is often coherent noise, resulting from various types of waves, and incoherent noise. Hence we obtain a two-dimensional signal $y(j, t)$, where t is time and j denotes the jth sensor (here j can be thought of as a measure of distance from the sensor to the location of the original excitation). If $S(t)$ denotes the response of the earth to the excitation, we can model $y(j, t)$ as follows [68]:

$$y(j, t) = S(t - \tau_j) + N(t - \delta_j) + w(j, t), \tag{154}$$

where τ_j and δ_j are the time delays incurred by the earth response and the coherent noise, respectively, in traveling to the jth sensor. Also $w(j, t)$ is the incoherent noise. Given this two-dimensional signal, we want to estimate $S(t)$ and the time delays τ_j (called moveouts).

A number of solutions have been developed for this problem. In the context of two-dimensional signal processing, if we assume constant but different speeds of propagation for S and N

$$\tau_j = d_j/v_S, \qquad \delta_j = d_j/v_N \tag{155}$$

where d_j is the distance to the jth sensor, we can use fan filters to discriminate between these signals. If we consider the two-dimensional Fourier transform of these space-time signals (let us assume for simplicity that we have a continuum of sensors)

$$Y(\omega_1, \omega_2) = \iint y(x, t) \exp^{(-j\omega_1 x - \omega_2 t)} \, dx \, dt, \tag{156}$$

then the point (ω_1, ω_2) corresponds to a plane wave traveling with velocity ω_2/ω_1, the slope of the line connecting this point to the origin. Hence all the velocities within a given range are obtained by points in a sector in (ω_1, ω_2)-space. Thus if we design a filter to pass only the frequencies in the appropriate sector, we can achieve the desired velocity discrimination (see figure 4.17).

Another approach is to consider the design of optimal filters for the estimation of S and the τ_j. Sengbush and Foster [68] derive the optimal

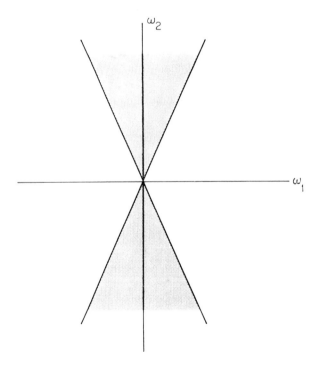

4.17
An ideal fan filter (passband is shaded).

nonrecursive Wiener filter for this problem and analyze its properties as a two-dimensional filtering system. The details of this development and a discussion of other two-dimensional nonrecursive techniques can be found in [68].

An interesting question concerns the development of recursive estimation techniques for problems such as these. Such algorithms may be particularly useful given the apparent need for using space-varying models [68]. We will discuss the problem of recursive techniques shortly.

Another class of space-time problems is essentially three-dimensional and involves the observation of a sequence of two-dimensional images to determine motion or scene changes. Such problems arise in meteorological problems such as the tracking of cloud motion [69, 231]. In addition, if one is processing a sequence of images, one might expect that the use of temporal as well as spatial correlations would improve overall processor performance [272]. The development of systematic recursive or nonrecursive approaches to problems such as these is an appealing area for future work.

A final area in which one finds space-time processes is the consideration of random vector (transport) or force fields that affect the motion of particles or waves. Applications for models such as these abound. How does the statistical description of a random gravitational field affect the motion of a satellite [224], and how can we obtain better estimates of the gravitational field from observations of the motion of the satellite? Given a statistical description of wind currents, predict the space-time distribution of pollutants coming from some source and determine the optimal locations for the placement of pollution sensors.

Techniques exist for all of these problems, but at this time there is no systematic theory for the probabilistic analysis and recursive estimation of general space-time stochastic processes; major steps have been taken in this direction for space-time point processes [11, 223], and some work has been done toward developing a calculus for isotropic random vector fields [226]. Mendel and his colleagues [274, 275], Bayliss and Brigham [276], Crump [277], and Ott and Meder [278] have developed state-space models and Kalman filtering techniques for deconvolution problems in seismic signal processing. Several of these applications have motivated Kam and Willsky [193–195] and Washburn [196] to utilize the tools of one-dimensional and two-dimensional stochastic calculus to develop recursive techniques for space-time processes.

The results in [193–195] are basically separable in that one-dimensional stochastic models are developed separately for the spatial and temporal variations. Time delay problems such as those that arise in seismic signal processing motivate the following problem. A source at spatial location $s = 0$ transmits a random signal $\phi(t)$, $t \geq 0$. This signal is modeled as the output of a possibly time-varying linear shaping filter

$$\dot{x}(t) = A(t)x(t) + w(t), \tag{157}$$

$$\phi(t) = C(t)x(t). \tag{158}$$

The signal is then propagated in the positive s direction by a random velocity field $v(s)$ with given statistics. At points $s_1, \ldots, s_n$ are sensors that measure delayed versions of the signal

$$y(i, t) = \phi(t - \tau_i) + \nu(i, t), \tag{159}$$

$$\tau_i = \int_0^{s_i} \frac{ds}{v(s)}. \tag{160}$$

Given this formulation we consider the recursive optimal estimation of ϕ and of the τ_i.[32] This is an extremely difficult problem, and implementable solutions have been found only in certain special cases. However, the work in [193, 194, 253] represents a useful first step in the development of such techniques, and the results obtained can be used to devise suboptimal recursive schemes. Work continues along these lines.

Another problem considered in [193, 195] has certain aspects in common with problems considered in [1, 24]. Specifically, we have a random field and a point sensor that traces a one-dimensional track along the field. Suppose as in [1] that we can model the spatial variations along this one-dimensional track by a spatial shaping filter

$$\dot{x}(s) = Ax(s) + w(s), \tag{161}$$

$$f(s) = Cx(s). \tag{162}$$

Let $v(t)$ denote the velocity and $s(t)$ the position of the point sensor as a function of time. The time history of the observations of the point sensor may then be modeled by

$$y(t) = f(s(t)) + \nu(t) \tag{163}$$

or, if we include the possibility of blurring, by

$$y(t) = \int_0^t h(t - \tau)f(s(\tau))\, d\tau + \nu(t). \tag{164}$$

Although only the case of (163) was considered in [193, 195], the analysis can readily be extended [258] to the case of (164). Extensions to allow for edges (abrupt changes in the field) can also be developed by combining the techniques in [258] and [291].

This formulation raises several questions. For example, one might wish to estimate the field f given these measurements. If the velocity history is known, this is not difficult; and this problem resembles that of [24] at least in spirit. If the velocity is unknown, if we have random motion blur, the problem is more complex. Methods are developed in [193, 195] for the suboptimal solution of this problem. In this case we have another difficulty, the mapping problem. At any time we do not know which point $s(t)$ we are looking at. Finally, the velocity $v(t)$ in all these problems must affect the accuracy of our observations; the faster we move, the less we observe. Thus an interesting problem is controlling the speed of the sensor to achieve certain performance specifications. An optimal control problem along these lines is considered in [193, 195].

A third class of separable space-time problems, motivated by the random force field problem, is being studied. We have a one-dimensional random acceleration field $a(s)$ that has a spatial shaping filter representation

$$\dot{x}(s) = Ax(s) + w(s), \tag{165}$$

$$a(s) = Cx(s). \tag{166}$$

Suppose a particle is subject to this field. The equations governing its motion are

$$\dot{s}(t) = v(t), \tag{167}$$

$$\dot{v}(t) = a(s(t)). \tag{168}$$

We wish to estimate the shape of the random field from noisy observations of the position of the particle

$$y(t) = s(t) + \nu(t). \tag{169}$$

Results for problems of this type are forthcoming.

Clearly all these problems are vast simplifications of real problems, but

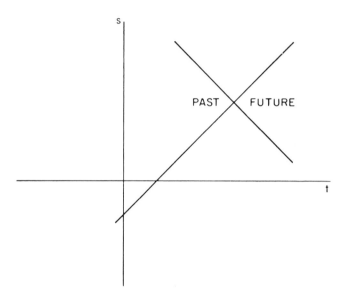

4.18
The two-dimensional causality structure for space-time processes.

they provide a start. One must now consider the extension of these ideas to several spatial dimensions and the use of nonseparable space-time stochastic models. The use of a multidimensional stochastic calculus such as that described in section 4.5.3 is clearly important. An observation of Washburn [196] indicates that in some cases the NE causal structure of this calculus may not be a problem and in fact may be natural. Suppose we consider a space-time system with one spatial dimension, and suppose that because of fundamental limitations (due, for example, to the finite speed of light) events at any given spatial point can affect those at another only with a certain time delay. This leads to the usual light-cone description of the future and past of a given space-time point. If we scale the axes appropriately, we can assume that this cone has an angle of 90°, as indicated in figure 4.18. Hence rotating the coordinates by 45° gives us a NE causal structure. The utility of this observation when combined with two-dimensional stochastic calculus and a variety of space-time analysis problems is reported in [196].

4.6.2 Interconnected Systems and Transform Techniques
In addition to systems that truly have a space-time character, any multi-

variable one-dimensional system can be viewed as a two-dimensional system by considering the space variable to be the index of the elements of the vector functions of time. Although in general, this may not be particularly natural, this philosophy appears to have some merit for large-scale systems consisting of a number of interconnected subsystems. In this case we let the spatial variable index subsystem variables, which may be vector quantities themselves. A general linear model for such a system is

$$x(k + 1, i) = \sum_j A_{ij}x(k, j) + \sum_j B_{ij}u(k, j) + w(k, j), \tag{170}$$

$$y(k, i) = \sum_j C_{ij}x(k, j) + v(k, j). \tag{171}$$

Clearly this is a recursive two-dimensional model. Examples of large-scale systems of this type abound in practice: power systems, communication networks, and freeway traffic systems.[33] See [84–89, 91–94, 190, 201, 203–208] for other examples and insight into the problems associated with such systems.

The problems with these systems are of two types. First, the analysis of these systems using tools such as the Lyapunov equation and the determination of optimal filter and controller designs is far too complex to be carried out using standard methods because of the high dimensionality of the overall system. Second, the implementation of standard controllers and estimators is out of the question, since these systems require totally centralized processing of all subsystem data to determine each subsystem control; what is needed is a decentralized scheme.

Similar problems arose in the study of recursive image-processing techniques. The full-state optimal Kalman filter of Woods and Radewan [173, 229, 236] was of enormous dimension, and one would never dream of attempting to solve the Riccati equation in this case. In addition, the on-line Kalman filter update is far too complex; Woods and Radewan suggested a nearest-neighbor constrained Kalman filter, in which only those pixels near the one presently being processed are themselves updated. This is clearly a decentralization of sorts, as are the techniques proposed by Murphy and Silverman [174] and Pratt [17]. What these methods have in common is the following. We specify some constraints on information transfer—we limit the extent of the update portion of the filter—and then we optimize the filter gains subject to these constraints. This same philosophy is precisely what is used in many decentralized control and estimation problems [86, 201, 205]. That is, we specify some constraints on the information pattern[34] (which data are available for each subsystem) and then we optimize the estimator and controller gains subject to these constraints.

Thus large-scale systems can be viewed as two-dimensional systems, and constrained optimization for efficient or decentralized processing is common in both settings. Can any other insight be gained or new results obtained by examination of large-scale systems as two-dimensional systems? The answer is perhaps, and some preliminary observations make us feel that the answer will ultimately be yes.

First suppose that the model (170), (171) falls into the class considered by Attasi [6, 35, 96]. Then the optimal centralized Kalman filter is nothing more than Attasi's line-by-line optimal processor. In this context let us reexamine the structure of this processor as pictured in figure 4.12. This processor may or may not be a good image restoration system, but it certainly is an extremely efficient centralized Kalman filter! The predict cycles for each subsystem are carried out in a totally decoupled fashion, and in the update stage each subsystem need only communicate with its nearest neighbors (two streams of information are flowing, corresponding to the two Kalman filters). The extension of this result to the design of estimation and control systems for a broader class of large-scale systems is reported in [261].

As a second example, consider the case in which (170) and (171) are spatially invariant[35]

$$x(k + 1, i) = \sum_j A_{i-j} x(k, j) + \sum_j B_{i-j} u(k, j) + w(k, j), \qquad (172)$$

$$y(k, i) = \sum_j C_{i-j} x(k, j) + v(k, j). \qquad (173)$$

In the case of an infinite string of subsystems, no noise, and a spatially invariant quadratic cost function, Melzer and Kuo [203] devised an efficient method for determining the optimal centralized controller, and Chu [205] used the same method to determine the optimal, constrained decentralized controller. The basic idea is identical to that used by Hunt [46], Andrews and Hunt [81], Jain and Angel [32], and Attasi [6, 35, 96]; take the z-transforms of (172) and (173) in the subsystem variable to obtain a system of decoupled optimal control problems (parametrized by z) of dimension equal to that of each x_i.

To clarify these ideas, let us consider the case in which we have a finite string of subsystems [190, 261], $i = 0, \ldots, N-1$. Then if we rewrite (172), (173) in terms of one giant state, input, and output vector, we find that the resulting A, B, and C matrices are block Toeplitz. As Andrews and Hunt [81] discuss, we then make the block circulant approximation to obtain[36]

$$x(k + 1, i) = \sum_{j=0}^{N-1} A_j x(k, i - j) + \sum_{j=0}^{N-1} B_j u(k, i - j) + w(k, i), \tag{174}$$

$$y(k, i) = \sum_{j=0}^{N-1} C_j x(k, i - j) + v(k, i), \tag{175}$$

with

$$E[w(k, i)w'(j, l)] = S_{i-j}\delta_{kl}, \tag{176}$$

$$E[v(k, i)v'(j, l)] = \Theta_{i-j}\delta_{kl}, \tag{177}$$

where all subsystem indexes are to be interpreted modulo N. Suppose we wish to design a controller to minimize the criterion

$$J = E\left\{\sum_{k=0}^{\infty} \sum_{i,j=0}^{N-1} [x'(k, i)\, Q_{i-j}x(k, j) + u'(k, i)R_{i-j}u(k, j)]\right\}. \tag{178}$$

Suppose we take subsystem transforms (see appendix 2). For example,

$$\bar{x}(k, l) = \sum_{i=0}^{N-1} x(k, i)W_N^{-il}. \tag{179}$$

We then obtain a set of decoupled problems, indexed by l:

$$\bar{x}(k + 1, l) = \bar{A}(l)\bar{x}(k, l) + \bar{B}(l)\bar{u}(k, l) + \bar{w}(k, l), \tag{180}$$

$$\bar{y}(k, l) = \bar{C}(l)\bar{x}(k, l) + \bar{v}(k, l), \tag{181}$$

$$E[\bar{w}(k, l)\bar{w}^*(j, m)'] = \bar{S}(l)\delta_{kj}\delta_{lm}, \tag{182}$$

$$E[\bar{v}(k, l)\bar{v}^*(j, m)'] = \bar{\Theta}(l)\delta_{kj}\delta_{lm}, \tag{183}$$

$$J_l = \frac{1}{N} E \sum_{k=0}^{\infty} [\bar{x}^*(k, l)'\bar{Q}(l)\bar{x}(k, l) + \bar{u}^*(k, l)'\bar{R}(l)\bar{u}(k, l)]. \tag{184}$$

Here * denotes complex conjugate. Since all original variables are real, we have $A(-l) = A^*(l)$, and so on. Thus we need only solve approximately half of these problems to obtain the optimal centralized controller that is efficiently implemented in figure 4.19. Compare this figure with Jain and

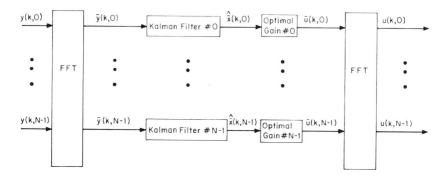

4.19
Optimal circulant feedback systems.

Angel's optimal image restoration scheme as depicted in figure 4.13. The similarity here is striking, as is the similarity in method and philosophy underlying both systems. Work involving the system (174), (175) is continuing [261]. We are examining such issues as the effects of the block-circulant approximation, the use of this method for fast algorithms for Lyapunov equations, Riccati equations, and pole placement, and for the design of decentralized controllers. One possible decentralization can be obtained by spatially windowing the optimal centralized filter and control gains. As the properties of various windows are well-known [293], it may be possible to obtain detailed performance evaluations for such schemes.

Thus there are points of contact between two-dimensional processing concepts and large-scale one-dimensional system analysis. Whether these points will lead to major new results or exciting concepts remains to be seen, but there certainly appear to be some intriguing possibilities.

4.7 Notes

1. Unless one of the two dimensions is time and we wish to process the input in real time.

2. This terminology appears to be due to Pistor [42]. It seems to be particularly appropriate for conveying the geometry of two-dimensional recursions and causality.

3. Of course, causality constraints would have to be built in. For example, the feedback from y to x would also have to involve a strictly one-sided recursion.

4. One must be careful here to pad the one-dimensional finite-impulse response and the scan signal with zeros. This is necessary because the extent of the convolution of two finite two-dimensional arrays is larger than the original arrays. To invert (unscan) the convolved one-dimensional signal to obtain the two-dimensional output, we must effectively scan enough zeros at the end of each of the original two-dimensional arrays. See [55] for details.

5. When this condition is not satisfied, the problem is more difficult; essentially information is forgotten. In this case Chu [88] discusses some examples in which the optimal solution can be found with the aid of the partially nested result, and he discusses some suboptimal methods. See [88] for details.

6. It is worth keeping the issue of causality—which carries certain implications about what effects what—separate from that of recursibility—which simply refers to our ability to implement a given system in a particularly efficient manner. These two issues often lead to related considerations, but there are important conceptual and philosophical differences. For example, one use for two-dimensional recursive filters is in image processing. Recently, several types of recursive image-processing systems have been devised based on Kalman filtering ideas, which require causal (scan-ordered, NE, or half-plane) models for the image being processed. Such causality clearly plays no intrinsic role in the description of an image, but its use may be justified as an intermediate step (obtained, perhaps, by spectral factorization [119]) if the recursive filter that results is useful for image processing.

7. Since it is only the denominator of $H(z_1, z_2) = A(z_1, z_2)/B(z_1, z_2)$ that affects the direction of recursibility and stability, one often considers applying this procedure to $1/B(z_1, z_2)$.

8. To implement a zero-phase filter by means of causal, recursive filters, one needs four identical quadrant filters (one for each direction) or two identical half-plane filters. This is the analog of the one-dimensional result, in which we realize a zero-phase filter as the cascade of a given filter, followed by an identical filter going backward in time [49].

9. In general the indeterminates in this theory are taken to be noncommuting. However in the two-dimensional case, the two shifts z_1 and z_2 do commute.

10. That may very well be because this is the one case in which one can readily see what to do.

11. Rectangular factors are considered in the general one-dimensional stochastic realization theory described in chapter 2, but they are not necessary in order to factor one-dimensional scalar spectra.

12. We refer the reader to [81] in which a mixed continuous-discrete digital scheme is discussed. The image g is sampled, but the continuous form of the right-hand side of (57) is left intact. Spline approximations are used to estimate the image between samples.

13. There is no loss of generality in assuming a square picture, as we can always pad a rectangular image array with zeros to make it square.

14. This noise may include more than film grain noise. Specifically, the effects of light from sources other than the object can be included in v.

15. All that is needed for (71) is horizontal stationarity—$h(i, m, j, n) = h(i - j, m, n)$. Vertical stationarity in turn implies that each block is Toeplitz.

16. This is not quite standard, since one usually also requires $s(i, j)$ = constant. Clearly any process stationary in our sense can be transformed into one in this stronger sense by subtracting out the mean.

17. Either an $N \times N$ array or an N^2 vector. We shall use these two forms interchangeably and without comment unless there is a chance of confusion.

18. Seviora [114] and Seviora and Sablatash [115] dealt with a general framework that included transforms on cylindrical and toroidal spaces for the purpose of digital signal processing.,

19. This is a problem with the ordering of points in the plane obtained by a half-plane recursion. Specifically, given two points in the plane, there is only a finite number of points between them (with respect to this order) if and only if they are in the same column. Otherwise, there is an infinite number of points between them.

20. The Gaussian assumption can be made only for convenience, since we know a priori that all components of f must be ≥ 0. Although this eliminates the Gaussian assumption in theory, in practice one often makes it anyway, since it leads to tractable problem formulations and acceptable system performance (see, for example, [292], where the same type of positivity assumption was encountered).

21. The zero-mean assumption is included to guarantee the block-Toeplitz structure of P and R. If we have nonzero means for f and v, we can subtract out their effects from (69) and proceed with the analysis. In this case the estimate produced by (95) is the estimate of the deviation of f from its a priori mean.

22. The PSF is usually assumed to be known [81], and for certain types of blur this is a reasonable assumption. However, in many cases either the entire PSF or several of its parameters are not known a priori and must be estimated.

23. Recall that the use of a transform in one direction followed by linear prediction in the other was proposed as an image-coding scheme by Habibi and Robinson [37].

24. For homomorphic techniques we have no reason to worry, since exponentiation at the end guarantees positivity. See chapter 5.

25. We say "essentially" here since f may not be differentiable. For the technically precise definition, see the references.

26. Such models have been considered by several authors, including Whittle [61] and Larimore [1].

27. See also [62] for another difficulty that arises with such discrete-time, nonrecursive, two-dimensional Markov models.

28. A related question, given the perspective of chapter 2, is the existence of fast algorithms for the calculation of the gains of recursive two-dimensional Kalman filters. There is a generalization [267] of the Berlekamp-Massey algorithm [294] for the efficient construction of partial two-dimensional realizations. Such algorithms may be useful in the design of two-dimensional recursive digital filters that match a specified impulse response out to a given point. Such a filter design problem is studied in [269].

29. The problem of modeling random perturbations in gravitational fields has been considered by a number of authors [211, 212, 224]. A common approach to this problem is the use of the spatial transform most appropriate for such problems—spherical harmonics. Wong [12, 230] has considered such transform methods in the general setting of isotropic random fields on spaces with constant curvature. The use of geometric concepts such as spherical harmonics greatly facilitates the analysis of random fields. Swerling [10] discusses many of the statistical properties of random contours.

30. The following discussion is greatly oversimplified; see the references for the full story.

31. In [184] it is argued that this second martingale arises naturally from the deterministic rules involving Stieltjes differentials on the plane.

32. We also allow the possibility that delayed versions of ϕ are transmitted from other locations. This can be used to model multiple reflections.

33. In this last case the subsystem index does represent a spatial variable, as each subsystem describes the aggregate behavior of traffic on a link of a freeway [208]. The choice of the size of each link is a type of sampling problem, and the issues of spatial sampling, such as those raised by Mascarenhas and Pratt [23] and Hunt [4] in the context of image processing, are clearly relevant here. See also [257] in which one-dimensional *space*-invariant and varying models are used to analyze the steady-state perturbations in the flow on sections of a freeway network caused by a traffic incident. Here is a good example of the use of one-dimensional control techniques to study spatial effects.

34. Choosing a good information pattern is an important and complex problem, but it is beyond the scope of this discussion. See the references, in particular [85].

35. Such models arise, for example, in the longitudinal control of a string of vehicles [204] such as one finds in personal rapid transit systems.

36. Approximations like these often arise in the discretization of partial differential equations such as the wave equation (see, for example, [295]); see also [296] for further discussions concerning approximation of matrices by circulant matrices.

4.8 References

1. W. E. Larimore, "Statistical Inference on Stationary Random Fields," *Proc. IEEE* 65 (1977), pp. 961–970.

2. L. R. Rabiner, J. H. McClellan, and T. W. Parks, "FIR Digital Filter Design Techniques Using Weighted Chebyshev Approximation," *Proc. IEEE* 63 (1975), pp. 595–610.

3. R. M. Mersereau and D. E. Dudgeon, "Two-Dimensional Digital Filtering," *Proc. IEEE* 63 (1975), pp. 610–623.

4. B. R. Hunt, "Digital Image Processing," *Proc. IEEE* 63 (1975), pp. 693–708.

5. D. E. Dudgeon, "Recursibility of Two-Dimensional Difference Equations," MIT Res. Lab. of Elec. Quarterly Prog. Rept. No. 113, April 15, 1974, pp. 151–158.

6. S. Attasi, "A Generalization of 'Kalman' Statistical Techniques to Image Processing," IRIA Report, Domaine de Voluceau, Rocquencourt, France, January 1975.

7. R. B. Asher, "Recursive Estimation in Image Enhancement: A Tutorial Review," Rept. from Frank J. Seiler Research Lab., U. S. Air Force Academy, Colorado Springs, to appear.

8. S. R. Powell and L. M. Silverman, "Modeling of Two-Dimensional Covariance Functions with Application to Image Restoration," *IEEE Trans. Aut. Contr.* AC-19 (1974), pp. 8–13.

9. J. W. Woods, "Two-Dimensional Discrete Markovian Fields," *IEEE Trans. Inf. Th.* IT-18 (1972), pp. 232–240.

10. P. Swerling, "Statistical Properties of the Contours of Random Surfaces," *IRE Trans. Inf. Th.* 8 (1962), pp. 315–321.

11. D. L. Snyder and P. M. Fishman, "How to Track a Swarm of Fireflies by Observing Their Flashes," *IEEE Trans. Inf. Th.* IT-21 (1975), pp. 692–695.

12. E. Wong, "Two-Dimensional Random Fields and Representation of Images," *SIAM J. Appl. Math.* 16 (1968), pp. 756–770.

13. J. B. Bednar, "Spatial Recursive Filter Design via Rational Chebyshev Approximation," *IEEE Trans. Circ. and Sys.* CAS-22 (1975), pp. 572–574.

14. C. M. Rader, "On the Application of the Number Theoretic Methods of High-Speed Convolution to Two-Dimensional Filtering," *IEEE Trans. Circ. and Sys.* CAS-22 (1975), p. 575.

15. A. S. Samulon, "Separation of Man-Made and Natural Patterns in High-Altitude Imagery of Agricultural Areas," *IEEE Trans. Circ. and Sys.* CAS-22 (1975), pp. 450–463.

16. J. H. Justice and J. L. Shanks, "Stability Criterion for N-Dimensional Digital Filters," *IEEE Trans. Aut. Contr.* AC-18 (1973), pp. 284–286.

17. W. K. Pratt, "Generalized Wiener Filtering Computation Techniques," *IEEE Trans. Comp.* C-21 (1972), pp. 636–641.

18. N. E. Nahi and T. Assefi, "Bayesian Recursive Image Estimation," *IEEE Trans. Comp* C-21 (1972), pp. 734–738.

19. M. M. Sondhi, "Image Restoration: The Removal of Spatially Invariant Degradations," *Proc. IEEE* 60 (1972), pp. 842–853.

20. G. M. Robbins and T. S. Huang, "Inverse Filtering for Linear Shift-Variant Imaging Systems," *Proc. IEEE* 60 (1972), pp. 862–872.

21. N. E. Nahi, "Role of Recursive Estimation in Statistical Image Enhancement," *Proc. IEEE* 60 (1972), pp. 872–877.

22. A. Habibi, "Two-Dimensional Bayesian Estimate of Images," *Proc. IEEE* 60 (1972), pp. 878–883.

23. N. D. A. Mascarenhas and W. K. Pratt, "Digital Image Restoration under a Regression Model," *IEEE Trans. Circ. and Sys.* CAS-22 (1975), pp. 252–266.

24. A. O. Aboutalib and L. M. Silverman, "Restoration of Motion Degraded Images," *IEEE Trans. Circ. and Sys.* CAS-22 (1975), pp. 278–286.

25. N. E. Nahi and A. Habibi, "Decision-Directed Recursive Image Enhancement," *IEEE Trans. Circ. and Sys.* CAS-22 (1975), pp. 286–293.

26. S. K. Mitra, A. D. Sagar, and N. A. Pendergrass, "Realizations of Two-Dimensional Recursive Digital Filters," *IEEE Trans. Circ. and Sys.* CAS-22 (1975), pp. 177–184.

27. D. D. Siljak, "Stability Criteria for Two-Variable Polynomials," *IEEE Trans. Circ. and Sys.* CAS–22 (1975), pp. 185–189.

28. G. A. Maria and M. M. Fahmy, "Limit Cycle Oscillations in a Cascade of Two-Dimensional Digital Filters," *IEEE Trans. Circ. and Sys.* CAS-22 (1975), pp. 826–830.

29. R. M. Mersereau and A. V. Oppenheim, "Digital Reconstruction of Multidimensional Signals from Their Projections," *Proc. IEEE* 62 (1974), pp. 1319–1338.

30. A. K. Jain, "A Semicausal Model for Recursive Filtering of Two-Dimensional Images," *IEEE Trans. Comp.*, to appear.

31. A. K. Jain, "Image Coding via a Nearest Neighbors Image Model," *IEEE Trans. Comm.* COM-23 (1975), pp. 318–331.

32. A. K. Jain and E. Angel, "Image Restoration, Modelling, and Reduction of Dimensionality," *IEEE Trans. Comp.* C-23 (1974), pp. 470–476.

33. D. E. Dudgeon, "Two-Dimensional Recursive Filtering," Sc. D. dissertation, Massachusetts Institute of Technology, 1974.

34. J. F. Abramatic, S. Attasi, J. P. Chieze, and N. Curie, "Modèles Statistiques 'Bidimensionnels' et Application au Traitement Numerique des Images," in *Proc. Colloque National sur le Traitement du Signal et Ses Applications*, Nice, France, June 16–21, 1975.

35. S. Attasi, "Modelisation et Traitement des Suites a Deux Indices," IRIA Rept., Domaine de Voluceau, Rocquencourt, 78150 Le Chesnay, B. P. 5, France, 1975.

36. J. H. McClellan, "The Design of Two-Dimensional Digital Filters by Transformations," in *Proc. 7th Annual Princeton Conf. Information Sciences and Systems*, Department of Elec. Eng., Princeton University, Princeton, N.J. (1973), pp. 247–251.

37. A. Habibi and G. S. Robinson, "A Survey of Digital Picture Coding," *Computer* 7 (1974), pp. 22–34.

38. H. C. Andrews, "Digital Image Restoration: A Survey," *Computer* 7 (1974), pp. 36–45.

39. D. P. MacAdam, "Digital Image Restoration by Constrained Deconvolution," *J. Opt. Soc. Amer.* 60 (1970), pp. 1617–1627.

40. C. K. Rushforth and R. W. Harris, "Restoration, Resolution, and Noise," *J. Opt. Soc. Amer.* 58 (1968), pp. 539–545.

41. W. H. Richardson, "Bayesian-Based Iterative Method of Image Restoration," *J. Opt. Soc. Amer.* 62 (1972), pp. 55–59.

42. P. Pistor, "Stability Criterion for Recursive Filters," *IBM J. Res. Devel.* 18 (1974), pp. 59–71.

43. L. E. Franks, "A Model for the Random Video Process," *Bell Sys. Tech. J.* 45 (1966), pp. 609–630.

44. E. L. Hall, "Almost Uniform Distributions for Computer Image Enhancement," *IEEE Trans. Comp.* C-23 (1974), pp. 207–208.

45. B. D. O. Anderson and E. I. Jury, "Stability of Multidimensional Digital Filters," *IEEE Trans. Circ. and Sys.* CAS-21 (1974), pp. 300–304.

46. B. R. Hunt, "The Application of Constrained Least Squares Estimation to Image Restoration by Digital Computer," *IEEE Trans. Comp.* C-22 (1973), pp. 805–812.

47. B. R. Hunt, "Minimizing the Computation Time for Using the Technique of Sectioning for Digital Filtering of Pictures," *IEEE Trans. Comp.* C-21 (1972), pp. 1219–1222.

48. S. Treitel and J. L. Shanks, "The Design of Multistage Separable Planar Filters," *IEEE Trans. Geo. Elec.* GE-9 (1971), pp. 10–22.

49. J. L. Shanks, S. Treitel, and J. H. Justice, "Stability and Synthesis of Two-Dimensional Recursive Filters," *IEEE Trans. Aud. Electr.* AU-20 (1972), pp. 115–128.

50. T. S. Huang, "Stability of Two-Dimensional Recursive Filters," *IEEE Trans. Aud. Electr.* AU-20 (1972), pp. 158–163.

51. J. M. Costa and A. N. Venetsanopoulos, "Design of Circularly Symmetric Two-Dimensional Recursive Filters," *IEEE Trans. Acous., Speech, and Sig. Proc.* ASSP-22 (1974), pp. 432–443.

52. D. E. Dudgeon, "Recursive Filter Design Using Differential Correction," *IEEE Trans. Acous., Speech, and Sig. Proc.* ASSP-22 (1974), pp. 443–448.

53. R. R. Read and S. Treitel, "The Stabilization of Two-Dimensional Recursive Filters via the Discrete Hilbert Transform," *IEEE Trans. Geo. Elec.* GE-11 (1973), pp. 153–160.

54. B. D. O. Anderson and E. I. Jury, "Stability Test for Two-Dimensional Recursive Filters," *IEEE Trans. Aud. and Electr.* AU-21 (1973), pp. 366–372.

55. R. M. Mersereau and D. E. Dudgeon, "The Representation of Two-Dimensional Sequences as One-Dimensional Sequences," *IEEE Trans. Acous., Speech, and Sig. Proc.* ASSP-22 (1974), pp. 320–325.

56. M. T. Manry and J. K. Aggarwal, "Picture Processing Using One-Dimensional Implementations of Discrete Planar Filters," *IEEE Trans. Acous., Speech, and Sig. Proc.* ASSP-22 (1974), pp. 164–173.

57. N. K. Bose and E. I. Jury, "Positivity and Stability Tests for Multidimen-

sional Filters (Discrete-Continuous)," *IEEE Trans. Acous., Speech, and Sig. Proc.* ASSP-22 (1974), pp. 174–180.

58. N. E. Nahi and C. A. Franco, "Recursive Image Enhancement—Vector Processing," *IEEE Trans. Comm.* 21 (1973), pp. 305–311.

59. D. R. Brillinger, "Fourier Analysis of Stationary Processes," *Proc. IEEE* 62 (1974), pp. 1628–1642.

60. V. Heine, "Models for Two-Dimensional Stationary Stochastic Processes," *Biometrika* 42 (1955), pp. 170–178.

61. P. Whittle, "On Stationary Processes in the Plane," *Biometrika* 41 (1954), pp. 434–449.

62. D. Brook, "On the Distinction between the Conditional Probability and the Joint Probability Approaches in the Specification of Nearest-Neighbour Systems," *Biometrika* 51 (1964), pp. 481–483.

63. P. Whittle, "Stochastic Processes in Several Dimensions," *Bull. Int. Stat. Inst.* 40 (1963), pp. 974–994.

64. H. G. Ansell, "On Certain Two-Variable Generalizations of Circuit Theory, with Applications to Networks of Transmission Lines and Lumped Reactances," *IEEE Trans. Circuit Th.* CT-11 (1964), pp. 214–223.

65. A. A. Sawchuk, "Space-Variant Image Motion Degradation and Restoration," *Proc. IEEE* 60 (1972), pp. 854–861.

66. T. L. Marzetta, "A Linear Prediction Approach to Two-Dimensional Spectral Factorizaton and Spectral Estimation," Ph.D. dissertation, Massachusetts Institute of Technology, 1978.

67. T. S. Huang, ed., *Picture Processing and Digital Filtering*, Topics in Applied Physics, vol. 6, Springer-Verlag, New York, 1975.

68. R. L. Sengbush and M. R. Foster, "Design and Application of Optimal Velocity Filters in Seismic Exploration," *IEEE Trans. Comp.* C-21 (1972), pp. 648–654.

69. E. A. Smith and D. R. Phillips, "Automated Cloud Tracking Using Precisely Aligned Digital ATS Pictures," *IEEE Trans. Comp.* (1972), pp. 715–729.

70. J. M. Davis, "Velocity Analysis: An Application of Deterministic Estimation to Reflection Seismology," *IEEE Trans. Comp.* C-21 (1972), pp. 730–734.

71. C. G. Hart, T. S. Durrani, and E. M. Stafford, "Digital Signal Processing for Image Deconvolution and Enhancement," in *New Directions in Signal Processing*

in Communication and Control, edited by J. K. Skwirzynski, NATO Advanced Study Institute, Noordhoff-Leyden, The Netherlands, 1975.

72. J. B. Bednar, "On the Stability of the Least Mean-Square Inverse Process in Two-Dimensional Digital Filters," *IEEE Trans. Acous., Speech, and Sig. Proc.* 23 (1975), pp. 583–585.

73. G. A. Maria and M. M. Fahmy, "Limit Cycle Oscillations in First-Order Two-Dimensional Digital Filters," *IEEE Trans. Circ. and Sys.* CAS-22 (1975), pp. 246–251.

74. Y. Kamp and J. P. Thiran, "Chebyshev Approximation for Two-Dimensional Nonrecursive Digital Filters," *IEEE Trans. Circ. and Sys.* CAS-22 (1975), pp. 208–218.

75. M. Naraghi, "An Algorithmic Image Estimation Method Applicable to Non-linear Observations," Rept. 580, Image Processing Institute, University of Southern California, Los Angeles, Calif., June 1975.

76. A. Habibi, "Comparison of nth-Order DPCM Encoder with Linear Transformations and Block Quantization Techniques," *IEEE Trans. Comm. Tech.* COM-19 (1971), pp. 948–956.

77. D. C. Youla, "The Synthesis of Networks Containing Lumped and Distributed Elements," presented at Symp. on Generalized Networks, Polytechnic Inst., Brooklyn, N. Y., April 1966.

78. G. Backus and F. Gilbert, "Uniqueness in the Inversion of Inaccurate Gross Earth Data," *Phil. Trans. Roy. Soc. Land. Ser. A*, 266 (1970), pp. 123–192.

79. H. A. Smith, "Improvement of the Resolution of a Linear Scanning Device," *SIAM J. Appl. Math.* 14 (1966), pp. 23–40.

80. W. R. Bennett, "Statistics of Regenerative Digital Transmission," *Bell Sys. Tech. J.* 37 (1958), pp. 1501–1542.

81. H. C. Andrews and B. R. Hunt, *Digital Image Restoration*, Prentice-Hall, Englewood Cliffs, N. J., 1977.

82. T. G. Stockham, "Image Processing in the Context of a Visual Model," *Proc. IEEE* 60 (1972), pp. 828–842.

83. W. A. Gardner and L. E. Franks, "Characterization of Cyclostationary Random Signal Processes," *IEEE Trans. Inf. Th.* IT-21 (1975), pp. 4–14.

84. N. R. Sandell and M. Athans, "Solution of Some Nonclassical LQG Stochastic Decision Problems," *IEEE Trans. Aut. Control* AC-19 (1974), pp. 108–116.

85. N. R. Sandell, "Information Flow in Decentralized Systems," in *Directions in Large Scale Systems*, edited by Y.-C. Ho and S. K. Mitter, Plenum Press, New York, 1976.

86. N. R. Sandell, P. Varaiya, and M. Athans, "A Survey of Decentralized Control Methods for Large-Scale Systems", presented at Engineering Foundation Conference on System Engineering for Power: Status and Prospects, Henniker, N. H., August 1975.

87. Y.-C. Ho and K. C. Chu, "Team Decision Theory and Information Structures in Optimal Control Problems. I," *IEEE Trans. Aut. Contr.* AC-17 (1972), pp. 15–22.

88. K. C. Chu, "Team Decision Theory and Information Structures in Optimal Control Problems. II," *IEEE Trans. Aut. Contr.* AC-17 (1972), pp. 22–28.

89. R. Muralidharan, "Memory Considerations in Stochastic Control Problems", Tech. Rept. 626, Div. Eng. Appl. Phys., Harvard University, Cambridge, Mass., October 1971.

90. J. Capetanakis, "Two-Dimensional Processing of Signals," 6.341 Term Paper, Massachusetts Institute of Technology, 1974.

91. D. Teneketzis, "Perturbation Methods in Decentralized Stochastic Control," Elec. Sys. Lab. ESL-R-664, Massachusetts Institute of Technology, 1976.

92. T. M. Athay, "Numerical Analysis of the Lyapunov Equation with Application to Interconnected Power Systems," MIT Elec. Sys. Lab. Rept. ESL-R-663, Cambridge, Mass., June 1976.

93. H. S. Witsenhausen, "Some Remarks on the Concept of State," in *Directions in Large Scale Systems*, edited by Y.-C. Ho and S. K. Mitter, Plenum Press, New York, 1976.

94. H. S. Witsenhausen, *The Intrinsic Model for Discrete Stochastic Control: Some Open Problems*, Lecture Notes in Econ. and Math. Systems, vol. 107, Springer-Verlag, 1975, pp. 322–335.

95. R. E. Mullans and D. L. Elliott, "Linear Systems on Partially Ordered Time Sets," in *Proc. 1973 Conf. on Dec. and Contr.*, Catalog No. 73CH0806–OSMC, IEEE, New York (1973), pp. 334–337.

96. S. Attasi, "Modelling and Recursive Estimation for Double Indexed Sequences," in *System Identification: Advances and Case Studies*, edited by R. K. Mehra and D. G. Lainiotis, Academic Press, New York, 1976.

97. E. Fornasini and G. Marchesini, "State-Space Realization Theory of Two-Dimensional Filters," *IEEE Trans. Aut. Contr.* AC-21 (1976), pp. 484–492.

98. M. Fliess, "Series Reconnaissables, Rationnelles et Algebriques," *Bull. Sci. Math.* 94 (1970), pp. 231–239.

99. G. L. Anderson and A. N. Netravali, "Image Restoration Based on a Subjective Criterion," Tech. Rept. 7521, Dept. of Elec. Eng., Rice University, Houston, Tex., December 1975.

100. D. E. Dudgeon, "The Computation of Two-Dimensional Cepstra," *IEEE Trans. Acoust., Speech, and Sig. Proc.* ASSP-25 (1977), pp. 476–484.

101. D. E. Dudgeon, "The Existence of Cepstra for Two-Dimensional Rational Polynomials," *IEEE Trans. Acous., Speech, and Sig. Proc.* ASSP-23 (1975), pp. 242–243.

102. D. E. Dudgeon, "Using a Two-Dimensional Discrete Hilbert Transform to Factor Two-Dimensional Polynomials," MIT Res. Lab. of Elec. Quarterly Prog. Rept. 113, April 1974, pp. 143–150.

103. J. W. Woods and M. P. Ekstrom, "Non-Symmetric Half-Plane Recursive Filters—Characterization, Stability Theorem, and Test," in *Proc. IEEE Internat. Symp. on Circ. and Sys.,* Catalog No. 75CH0937–3CAS, IEEE, New York (1975), pp. 447–449.

104. R. A. Meyer and R. S. Francis, "Implementation of Two-Dimensional Digital Filters for Spatial Interpolation or Reduction," presented at 1976 Arden House Workshop on Digital Signal Processing, Harriman. N. Y., February 1976.

105. R. A. Meyer and C. S. Burrus, "A Unified Analysis of Multirate and Periodically Time-Varying Digital Filters," *IEEE Trans. Circ. and Sys.* CAS-11 (1975), pp. 162–168.

106. R. A. Meyer and C. S. Burrus, "Design and Implementation of Multirate Digital Filters," *IEEE Trans. Acoust., Speech, and Sig. Proc.,* to appear.

107. D. S. K. Chan, "Theory and Implementation of Multidimensional Discrete Systems for Signal Processing," Ph.D. dissertation, Massachusetts Institute of Technology, 1978.

108. E. L. Hall, "A Comparison of Computations for Spatial Frequency Filtering", *Proc. IEEE* 60 (1972), pp. 887–891.

109. C. H. Farmer and D. S. Gooden, "Rotation and Stability of a Recursive

Digital Filter," in *Proc. Two-Dimensional Dig. Sig. Proc. Conf.,* Catalog No. 71 C69-C, IEEE, New York (1971), pp. 1-2-1-1-2-12.

110. R. P. Roesser, "A Discrete State-Space Model for Linear Image Processing," *IEEE Trans. Aut. Control* AC-20 (1975), pp. 1–10.

111. D. D. Givone and R. P. Roesser, "Multidimensional Linear Iterative Circuits—General Properties," *IEEE Trans. Computers* C-21 (1972), pp. 1067–1073.

112. D. D. Givone and R. P. Roesser, "Minimization of Multidimensional Linear Iterative Circuits," *IEEE Trans. Comput.* C-22 (1973), pp. 673–678.

113. B. Vilfan, "Another Proof of the Two-Dimensional Cayley-Hamilton Theorem," *IEEE Trans. Comput.* C-22 (1973), p. 1140.

114. R. E. Seviora, "Generalized Digital Filters," Ph.D. dissertation, University of Toronto, 1971.

115. R. E. Seviora and M. Sablatash, "Generalized Digital Filters," in *Proc. London 1971 IEEE Internat. Symp. on Elec. Network Th.,* Catalog No. 71C 53-CT, IEEE, New York (1971), pp. 72–73.

116. R. E. Seviora, "Causality and Stability in Two-Dimensional Digital Filtering," *Proc. 1973 Asilomar Conf.,* Monterey, Calif., 1973.

117. G. R. Redinbo, "Generalized Bandpass Filters for Decoding Block Codes", *IEEE Trans. Inf. Th.* IT-21 (1975), pp. 417–422.

118. N. K. Bose and A. R. Modarressi, "General Procedure for Multivariable Polynomial Positivity Test with Control Applications," *IEEE Trans. Aut. Contr.* AC-21 (1976), pp. 696–701.

119. M. P. Ekstrom and J. W. Woods, "Two-Dimensional Spectral Factorization with Applications in Recursive Digital Filtering," *IEEE Trans. Acoustics, Speech, and Sig. Proc.* ASSP-24 (1976), pp. 115–128.

120. A. Lavi and S. Narayanan, "Analysis of a Class of Nonlinear Discrete Systems Using Multidimensional Modified z-Transforms," *IEEE Trans. Aut. Cont.* AC-13 (1968), pp. 90–93.

121. M. B. Brilliant, "Theory of the Analysis of Nonlinear Systems," Res. Lab. of Elec. Tech. Rept. 345, Massachusetts Institute of Technology, Cambridge, Mass., 1958.

122. D. D. Siljak, "Algebraic Criteria for Positive Realness Relative to the Unit Circle," *J. Franklin Inst.* 29 (1973), pp. 469–476.

123. E. I. Jury, *Inners and Stability of Dynamic Systems*, Wiley, New York, 1974.

124. N. K. Bose and P. S. Kamat, "Algorithm for Stability Test of Multidimensional Digital Filters," *IEEE Trans. Acoust., Speech, and Sig. Proc.* 24 (1974), pp. 307–314.

125. E. I. Jury, *Theory and Application of the z-Transform Method*, Wiley, New York, 1964.

126. R. M. Mersereau, "Digital Reconstruction of Multi-Dimensional Signals from Their Projections," Sc.D. thesis, Massachusetts Institute of Technology, 1973.

127. J. H. McClellan and D. S. K. Chan, "A 2-D FIR Filter Structure Derived from the Chebyshev Recursion," *IEEE Trans. on Circ. and Sys.* CAS-24 (1977), pp. 372–378.

128. R. M. Mersereau, W. F. G. Mecklenbräuker and T. F. Quatieri, "McClellan Transformations for 2-D Digital Filtering. I: Design," *IEEE Trans. Circ. and Sys.* CAS–23 (1976), pp. 405–414.

129. W. F. G. Mecklenbräuker and R. M. Mersereau, "McClellan Transformations for 2-D Digital Filtering. II: Implementation," *IEEE Trans. Circ. and Sys.* CAS-23 (1976), pp. 414–422.

130. G. A. Maria and M. M. Fahmy, "On the Stability of Two-Dimensional Digital Filters," *IEEE Trans. Audio Electroacoust.* AU-21 (1973), pp. 470–472.

131. H. Ozaki and T. Kasami, "Positive Real Functions of Several Variables and Their Applications to Variable Networks," *IRE Trans. Circ. Th.* CT-7 (1960), pp. 251–260.

132. M. Marden, *Geometry of Polynomials*, American Mathematical Society, Providence, R.I., 1966.

133. T. S. Huang, "Two-Dimensional Windows," *IEEE Trans. Audio Electroacoustics* AU-20 (1972), pp. 88–89.

134. J. V. Hu and L. R. Rabiner, "Design Techniques for Two-Dimensional Digital Filters," *IEEE Trans. Audio Electroacoustics* AU-20 (1972), pp. 249–257.

135. Y. Kamp and J. P. Thiran, "Maximally Flat Nonrecursive Two-Dimensional Digital Filters," *IEEE Trans. Circ. and Sys.* CAS-21 (1974), pp. 437–449.

136. E. Cheney and H. Loeb, "On Rational Chebyshev Approximation," *Numer. Math.* 4 (1962), pp. 124–127.

137. T. S. Huang, J. W. Burnett, and A. G. Deczky, "The Importance of Phase in Image Processing Filters," *IEEE Trans. Acous., Speech, and Sig. Proc.* ASSP-23 (1975), pp. 529–542.

138. E. Fornasini and G. Marchesini, "Algebraic Realization Theory of Two-Dimensional Filters," in *Variable Structure Systems*, edited by A. Ruberti and R. Mohler, Lecture Notes in Economics and Mathematical Systems, Springer-Verlag, New York, 1975.

139. M. Fliess, "Un Outil Algebrique: Les Series Formelles Non Commutatives," in *Mathematical System Theory*, edited by G. Marchesini and S.K. Mitter, Lecture Notes in Economics and Mathematical Systems, Springer-Verlag, New York, 1976.

140. M. Fliess, "Sur Certaines Familles de Series Formelles," doctoral dissertation, University of Paris VII, 1972.

141. B. F. Wyman, "Linear Difference Systems on Partially Ordered Sets," in *Mathematical System Theory*, edited by G. Marchesini and S.K. Mitter, Lecture Notes on Economics and Mathematical Systems, Springer-Verlag, New York, 1976.

142. E. W. Kamen, "A New Algebraic Approach to Linear Time-Varying Systems," *J. Comp. Sys. Sci.,* to appear.

143. E. D. Sontag, "On Linear Systems and Non-Commutative Rings," *Math. Sys. Th.* 9 (1976), pp. 327–344.

144. Y. Genin and Y. Kamp, "Counterexample in the Least Square Inverse Stabilization of 2D-Recursive Filters," *Electronics Letters* 11 (1975), pp. 330–331.

145. Y. Genin and Y. Kamp, "Two-Dimensional Stability and Orthogonal Polynomials on the Hypercircle," *Proc. IEEE* 65 (1977), pp. 873–881.

146. E. Artin, "Uber die Zerlegung Definiter Funktiones in Quadrate," Abh. aus dem Math. Seminar der Universitat Hamburg, vol. 5, 1927, pp. 100–115.

147. N. K. Bose, "An Algorithm for GCF Extraction from Two Multivariable Polynomials," *Proc. IEEE* 64 (1976), pp. 185–186.

148. N. K. Bose, "Test for Two-Variable Local Positivity with Applications," *Proc. IEEE* 64 (1976), pp. 1438–1439.

149. W. A. Pendergrass, S. K. Mitra, and E. I. Jury, "Spectral Transformations for Two-Dimensional Digital Filters," *IEEE Trans. Circ. and Sys.* CAS-23 (1976), pp. 26–35.

150. A. R. Modarressi and N. K. Bose, "A Multivariable Polynomial Nonnegativity Test," *Proc. IEEE* 64 (1976), pp. 283–285.

151. A. Fettweis, "Principles of Multidimensional Wave Digital Filters," presented at 1976 IEEE Arden House Workshop on Digital Signal Processing, Harriman, N. Y., February 1976; also preprint, Ruhr-Universität Bochum, Bochum, W. Germany.

152. D. S. K. Chan, "Computation Issues in the Implementation of 2-D Filters," presented at 1976 IEEE Arden House Workshop on Digital Signal Processing, Harriman, N. Y., February 1976.

153. A. G. Constantinides, "Spectral Transformations for Digital Filters," *Proc. IEEE* 117 (1970), pp. 1585–1590.

154. E. D. Sontag, personal communication.

155. A. M. Bush, "Some Techniques for the Synthesis of Nonlinear System", Tech. Rept. 441, Res. Lab. Elec., Massachusetts Institute of Technology, Cambridge, Mass., March 25, 1966.

156. T. Marzetta and J. H. McClellan, personal communication.

157. A. V. Balakrishnan, "Linear Systems with Infinite Dimensional State Spaces," in *Proc. Symp. on System Theory*, Polytechnic Inst. of Brooklyn, Brooklyn, N. Y., April 1965.

158. J. L. Lions, *Optimal Control of Systems Governed by Partial Differential Equations*, Springer-Verlag, New York, 1971.

159. J. S. Baras, R. W. Brockett, and P. A. Fuhrmann, "State-Space Models for Infinite-Dimensional Systems," *IEEE Trans. Aut. Control* AC-19 (1974), pp. 693–700.

160. B. F. Wyman, "Time Varying Linear Difference Systems," presented at 1976 IEEE Conference on Decision and Control, Clearwater Beach, Fla., December 1976.

161. B. F. Wyman, "Time Varying Linear Discrete-Time Systems: Realization Theory," to appear.

162. M. Morf, B. Lévy, and S.-Y. Kung, "New Results on 2-D Systems Theory. I: 2-D Polynomial Matrices, Factorization, and Coprimeness," *Proc. IEEE* 65 (1977), pp. 861–872.

163. S.-Y. Kung, B. Lévy, M. Morf, and T. Kailath, "New Results in 2-D Systems Theory. II: 2-D State-Space Models—Realization and Notions of Controllability, Observability and Minimality," *Proc. IEEE* 65 (1977), pp. 945–961.

164. P. E. Barry, R. Gran, C. R. Waters, "Two Dimensional Filtering—A State Estimation Approach," presented at 1976 IEEE Conference on Decision and Control, Clearwater Beach, Fla., December 1976.

165. M. Strintzis, "Comments on Two Dimensional Bayesian Estimates of Images," *Proc. IEEE* 64 (1976), pp. 1255–1257.

166. N. K. Bose, "A Criterion to Determine if Two Multivariable Polynomials Are Relatively Prime," *Proc. IEEE* 60 (1972), pp. 134–135.

167. N. E. Nahi and M. H. Jahanshahi, "Image Boundary Estimation," *IEEE Trans. Comp.,* to appear.

168. H. H. Rosenbrock, *State-Space and Multivariable Theory*, J. Wiley, New York, 1970.

169. W. A. Wolovich, *Linear Multivariable Systems*, Springer-Verlag, New York, 1974.

170. P.-L. Chow, "Perturbation Methods in Stochastic Wave Propagation," *SIAM Review* 17 (1975), pp. 57–81.

171. E. J. Burr, "Sharpening of Observational Data in Two Dimensions," *Austral. J. Phys.* 8 (1955), pp. 30–53.

172. E. Wong, "Detection and Filtering for Two-Dimensional Random Fields," presented at 1976 IEEE Conf. Dec. and Control, Clearwater Beach, Fla., December 1976.

173. J. W. Woods, "Markov Image Modelling," *IEEE Trans. Aut. Control* AC-23, No. 5, Oct. 1978, pp. 846–850.

174. M. S. Murphy and L. M. Silverman, "Image Model Representation and Line-by-Line Recursive Restoration," *IEEE Trans. Aut. Control* AC-23, No. 5 Oct. 1978, pp. 809–816.

175. N. E. Nahi and S. Lopez-Mora, "Estimation of Object Boundaries in Noisy Images," *IEEE Trans. Aut. Control* AC-23, No. 5, Oct. 1978, pp. 834–846.

176. E. Wong and M. Zakai, "Recursive Filtering for Two-Dimensional Random Fields," *IEEE Trans. Inf. Th.* IT-21 (1975), pp. 84–86.

177. D. P. Peterson and D. Middleton, "Linear Interpolation, Extrapolation, and Prediction of Random Space-Time Fields with a Limited Domain of Measurement," *IEEE Trans. on Inf. Th.* IT-11 (1965), pp. 18–30.

178. M. I. Fortus, "Formulas for Extrapolation of Random Fields," *Theory Prob. and Appl.* 7 (1962), pp. 101–108.

179. E. Wong, "A Likelihood Ratio Formula for Two-Dimensional Random Fields," *IEEE Trans. Inf. Th.* IT-20 (1974), pp. 418–422.

180. E. Wong and M. Zakai, "Martingales and Stochastic Integrals for Processes with a Multidimensional Parameter," *Z. Wahrscheinlichkeitstheorie* 29 (1974), pp. 109–122.

181. E. Wong and M. Zakai, "Weak Martingales and Stochastic Integrals in the Plane," *Annals of Prob.* 4 (1976), pp. 570–586.

182. R. Cairoli and J. B. Walsh, "Stochastic Integrals in the Plane," *Acta Math.* 134; (1975), pp. 111–183.

183. E. Wong and M. Zakai, "Differentiation Formulas for Stochastic Integrals in the Plane," Univ. of Calif., Berkeley, Elec. Res. Lab. Memo. No. ERL-M-540, Sept. 5, 1975.

184. R. B. Washburn and A. S. Willsky, "Multidimensional Stochastic Differentiation Formula," MIT Elec. Sys. Lab., Rept. No ESL-R-693, October 1976.

185. E. Wong and M. Zakai, "An Extension to Stochastic Integrals in the Plane," *Annals of Prob.,* to appear.

186. E. Wong and M. Zakai, "Likelihood Ratios and Transformation of Probability Associated with Two-Parameter Wiener Processes," Univ. of Calif., Berkeley, Elec. Res. Lab. Memo No. ERL-M-571, Dec. 2, 1975.

187. E. Wong, "Recursive Causal Linear Filtering for Two-Dimensional Random Fields," *IEEE Trans. Inf. Th.,* Vol. IT-24, No. 1, Jan. 1978, pp. 50–59.

188. A. O. Aboutalib, M. S. Murphy, and L. M. Silverman, "Digital Restoration of Images Degraded by General Motion Blurs," *IEEE Trans. on Aut. Control* AC-22 (1977), pp. 294–302.

189. G. C. Papanicolaou, "Asymptotic Analysis of Transport Processes," *Bull. Amer. Math Soc.* 81 (1975), pp. 330–392.

190. A. S. Willsky, "The Use of Group-Theoretic Concepts in Solving Problems in Estimation and Control," presented at 1976 IEEE Conf. Dec. and Control, Clearwater Beach, Fla., December 1976.

191. J. Yeh, "Wiener Measure in a Space of Functions of Two Variables," *Trans. Amer. Math. Soc.* 95 (1960), pp. 443–450.

192. W. J. Park, "A Multi-Parameter Gaussian Process," *Ann. of Math. Stat.* 41 (1970), pp. 1582–1595.

193. P. Y. Kam, "Modeling and Estimation of Space-Time Stochastic Processes," Ph.D. dissertation, Massachusetts Institute of Technology, 1976.

194. P. Y. Kam and A. S. Willsky, "Some Modeling and Estimation Problems Involving Space-Time Stochastic Processes," presented at 1976 IEEE Conf. Dec. and Control, Clearwater Beach, Fla., December 1976.

195. P. Y. Kam and A. S. Willsky, "Estimation of Time-Invariant Random Fields via Observations from a Moving Point Sensor," in *Proc. 1977 Joint Aut. Control Conf.*, Catalog No. 77CH1220-3CS, IEEE, New York (1977), pp. 1428–1433.

196. R. B. Washburn, Ph.D. dissertation, Massachusetts Institute of Technology, 1978.

197. P. Lévy, "A Special Problem of Brownian Motion and a General Theory of Gaussian Random Functions," in *Proc. 3rd Berkeley Symp. on Math. Stat. and Prob.*, vol. 2, Univ. of Calif. Press, Berkeley, 1956, pp. 133–175.

198. H. P. McKean, "Brownian Motion with a Several Dimensional Time," *Th. Prob. and Appl.* 8 (1963), pp. 335–354.

199. R. L. Sengbush and M. R. Foster, "Optimum Multichannel Velocity Filters," *Geophysics* 33 (1968), pp. 11–33.

200. R. L. Lillestrand, "Techniques for Change Detection," *IEEE Trans. Comp.* C-21 (1972), pp. 654–659.

201. D. P. Looze, P. K. Houpt, N. R. Sandell, and M. Athans, "On Decentralized Estimation and Control with Application to Freeway Ramp Metering," *IEEE Trans. Aut. Control* 23 (1978), pp. 268–275.

202. D. Slepian, "Linear Least-Squares Filtering of Distorted Images," *J. Opt. Soc. Amer.* 57 (1967), pp. 918–922.

203. S. M. Melzer and B. C. Kuo, "Optimal Regulation of Systems Described by a Countably Infinite Number of Objects," *Automatica* 7 (1971), pp. 359–366.

204. W. S. Levine and M. Athans, "On the Optimal Error Regulation of a String of Moving Vehicles," *IEEE Trans. Aut. Control* AC-11 (1966), pp. 355–361.

205. K. C. Chu, "Optimal Decentralized Regulation for a String of Coupled Systems," *IEEE Trans. Aut. Control* AC-19 (1974), pp. 243–246.

206. J. H. Davis and B. M. Barry, "A Distributed Model for Stress Control in

Multiple Locomotive Trains," Preprint No. 1976-9, Dept. of Math., Queen's University, Kingston, Ontario, 1976.

207. P. Dersin, S. B. Gershwin, and M. Athans, "Sensitivity Analysis of Optimal Static Traffic Assignments in a Large Freeway Corridor, Using Modern Control Theory," Rept. ESL-R-671, MIT Elec. Sys. Lab., Cambridge, Mass., 1976.

208. P. K. Houpt and M. Athans, "Dynamic Stochastic Control of Freeway Corridor Systems. I: Summary," Rept. ESL-R-608, MIT Elec. Sys. Lab., Cambridge, Mass., 1975.

209. J. M. Tribolet, "A Survey of Seismic Migration by Wave Equation Techniques," Area Exam. Paper, Dept. of Elec. Eng. and Comp. Sci., Massachusetts Institute of Technology, November 1975.

210. R. Bajcsy and M. Tavakoli, "Computer Recognition of Roads from Satellite Pictures," *IEEE Trans. Sys., Man, and Cyb.* SMC-6 (1976), pp. 623–637.

211. R. D. Reasenberg, I. I. Shapiro, R. D. White, "The Gravity Field of Mars," *Geophys. Res. Letters* 2 (1975), pp. 89–92.

212. J. E. Potter and E. J. Frey, "Rotation-Invariant Probability Distributions on the Surface of a Sphere, with Applications to Geodesy," MIT Exper. Astron. Lab., Rept. RE-27, May 1967.

213. A. Rockmore and A. Macovski, "A Maximum Likelihood Approach to Image Reconstruction," presented at 1977 Joint Automatic Control Conf., San Francisco, Calif., June 1977.

214. T. P. McGarty, "The Estimation of the Constituent Densities of the Upper Atmosphere by Means of a Recursive Filtering Algorithm," *IEEE Trans. Aut. Control* AC-16 (1971), pp. 817–823.

215. A. B. Baggeroer, "Space-Time Random Processes and Optimum Array Processing," Pub. of Naval Undersea Center, San Diego, Calif., 1973.

216. W. R. Hahn and S. A. Tretter, "Optimum Processing for Delay-Vector Estimation in Passive Signal Arrays," *IEEE Trans. Inf. Th.* IT-19 (1973), pp. 608–614.

217. H. Tennekes and J. L. Lumley, *A First Course in Turbulence,* MIT Press, Cambridge, Mass., 1972.

218. J. Capon, R. Greenfield, and R. Kolher, "Multidimensional Maximum Likelihood Processing of a Large Aperture Seismic Array," *Proc. IEEE* 55 (1967), pp. 192–211.

219. A. M. Yaglom, *An Introduction to the Theory of Stationary Random Functions*, Prentice-Hall, Englewood Cliffs, N. J., 1962.

220. U. Frisch, "Wave Propagation in Random Media," in *Probabilistic Methods in Applied Mathematics*, vol. 1, Academic Press, New York, 1968.

221. D. Middleton, "Multidimensional Detection and Extraction of Signals in Random Media," *Proc. IEEE* 58 (1970), pp. 696–706.

222. T. P. McGarty, "On the Structure of Random Fields Generated by Multiple Scatter Media," Ph.D. thesis, Massachusetts Institute of Technology, 1971.

223. P. M. Fishman and D. L. Snyder, "The Statistical Analysis of Space-Time Point Processes," *IEEE Trans. Inf. Th.* IT-22 (1976), pp. 257–274.

224. S. R. Croopnick, "Orbit Prediction in the Presence of Gravitational Anomalies," Charles Stark Draper Lab. Rept. T-536, Cambridge, Mass., 1970.

225. P. P. Varoutas, L. R. Nardizzi, E. M. Stokely, "Two-Dimensional E-Filtering Applied to Image Processing," *IEEE Trans. Sys., Man, and Cyber.* SMC (1976), pp. 410–419.

226. K. Ito, "Isotropic Random Current," in *Proc. Third Berkeley Symp. on Math. Stat. and Prob.*, vol. 2, University of California Press, Berkeley, Calif., 1956.

227. Invited sessions WA1 and WP1 on Seismic Date Processing and Interpretation, in *Proc. 1975 IEEE Conf. on Dec. and Control*, Catalog No. 75CH1016-5CS, IEEE, New York (1975), pp. 1–8, 111–127, 875.

228. R. H.-S. Kwong, "Structural Properties and Estimation of Delay Systems," Ph.D. thesis, Massachusetts Institute of Technology, 1975.

229. J. W. Woods and C. H. Radewan, "Kalman Filtering in Two-Dimensions," *IEEE Trans. Inf. Th.* IT-23 (1977), pp. 473–482.

230. E. Wong, *Stochastic Processes in Information and Dynamical Systems*, McGraw-Hill, New York, 1971.

231. D. J. Hall, R. M. Endlich, D. E. Wolf, and A. E. Brain, "Objective Methods for Registering Landmarks and Determining Cloud Motions from Satellite Data," *IEEE Trans. on Comp.* C-21 (1972), pp. 768–776.

232. D. Middleton, "A Statistical Theory of Reverberation and Similar First-Order Scattered Fields. I: Waveforms and the General Process," *IEEE Trans. Inf. Th.* IT-13 (1967), pp. 372–392.

233. D. Middleton, "A Statistical Theory of Reverberation and Similar First

Order Scattered Fields. II: Moments, Spectra, and Special Distributions," *IEEE Trans. Inf. Th.* IT-13 (1967), pp. 393–414.

234. D. Middleton, "A Statistical Theory of Reverberation and Similar First-Order Scattered Fields. III. Waveforms and Fields," *IEEE Trans. Inf. Th.* IT-18 (1972), pp. 35–67.

235. D. Middleton, "A Statistical Theory of Reverberation and Similar First-Order Scattered Fields. IV: Statistical Models," *IEEE Trans. Inf. Th.* IT-18 (1972), pp. 68–90.

236. J. W. Woods and C. H. Radewan, "Reduced Update Kalman Filter—A Two-Dimensional Recursive Processor," presented at Johns Hopkins Conf. on Inf. Sci. and Sys., Baltimore, Md., March 31– April 2, 1976.

237. J. W. Woods, "Two Dimensional Markov Spectral Estimation," *IEEE Trans. Inf. Th.* IT-22 (1976), pp. 552–559.

238. D. R. Cunningham, R. D. Laramore, and E. Barrett, "Detection in Image Dependent Noise," *IEEE Trans. Inf. Th.* IT-22 (1976), pp. 603–610.

239. A. K. Jain, "Linear and Nonlinear Interpolation for Two-Dimensional Image Enhancement," in Proc. 1972 IEEE Conf. on Dec. and Control, Catalog No. 72CH0705-4SCS, IEEE, New York (1972), pp. 59–62.

240. M. G. Woolfson and V. D. Vande Linde, "Gray Level Processing and the Recognition of Embedded Patterns," *Proc. 1972 IEEE Conf. on Dec. and Control*, Catalog No. 72CH0705–4SCS, IEEE, New York (1972), pp. 54–58.

241. A. K. Jain, "A Fast Karhunen-Loeve Transform for a Class of Stochastic Processes," *IEEE Trans. Comm.*, to appear.

242. A. K. Jain and D. Lainiotis, "Optimum Feature Extraction via a Fast Bi-Orthogonal Expansion for a Class of Image Data," in *Proc. 1975 Conf. on Inf. Sci. and Sys.*, Dept. of Electrical Engineering, The Johns Hopkins University, Baltimore, Md., April 1975.

243. K. Fukunaga, *Introduction to Statistical Pattern Recognition*, Academic Press, New York, 1972.

244. A. M. Yaglom, "Second-Order Homogeneous Random Fields," in *Proc. 4th Berkeley Symp. Math. Stat. and Prob.*, vol. 2, University of California Press, Berkeley, Calif., 1961, pp. 593–622.

245. L. C. Wood and S. Treitel, "Seismic Signal Processing," *Proc IEEE* 63 (1975), pp. 649–661.

246. T. Dalenius, J. Hajek, S. Zubrzycki, "On Plane Sampling and Related Geometrical Problems," in *Proc. 4th Berkeley Symp. Math. Stat. and Prob.*, University of California Press, Berkeley, Calif., 1961.

247. P. A. Meyer, *Probability and Potentials*, Blaisdell, Waltham, Mass., 1966.

248. N. K. Bose, ed., "Special Issue on Multidimensional Systems," *Proc. IEEE* 65 (1977), pp. 819–992.

249. E. I. Jury, V. R. Kolavennu, and B. D. O. Anderson, "Stabilization of Certain Two-Dimensional Recursive Digital Filters," *Proc. IEEE* 65 (1977), pp. 887–892.

250. J. H. Justice, "A Levinson-Type Algorithm for Two-Dimensional Wiener Filtering Using Bivariate Szegö Polynomials," *Proc. IEEE* 65 (1977), pp. 882–886.

251. F. C. Schoute, M. F. ter Horst, and J. C. Willems, "Hierarchic Recursive Image Enhancement," *IEEE Trans. Circ. and Sys.* CAS-24 (1977), pp. 67–78.

252. N. K. Bose, "Problems and Progress in Multidimensional Systems Theory," *Proc. IEEE* 65 (1977), pp. 824–840.

253. A. S. Willsky and P. Y. Kam, "Recursive Estimation of Signals Subject to Random Propagation Delays," submitted to *Appl. Math. and Optimization.*

254. M. G. Strintzis, "Tests of Stability of Multidimensional Filters," *IEEE Trans. Circ. and Sys.* CAS-24 (1977), pp. 432–437.

255. M. G. Strintzis, "BIBO Stability of Multidimensional Filters with Rational Spectra," *IEEE Trans. Acoust., Speech, and Sig. Proc.* ASSP-25 (1977), pp. 549–553.

256. Y. Genin and Y. Kamp, "Comments on 'On the Stability of the Least Mean-Square Inverse Process in Two-Dimensional Digital Filters,'" *IEEE Trans. Accoust., Speech, and Sig. Proc.* ASSP-25 (1977), pp. 92–93.

257. S. B. Gershwin, P. Dersin, and M. Athans, "Sensitivity Analysis of Optimal Static Traffic Assignment in a Freeway Corridor System," in *Proc. 1977 Joint Aut. Cont. Conf.*, Catalog No. 77CH1220-3CS, IEEE, New York (1977), pp. 457–465.

258. P. Y. Kam and A. S. Willsky, "Estimation of Time-Invariant Random Fields via Observations from a Moving Point Sensor," submitted to *IEEE Trans. Aut. Cont.*

259. D. P. Panda and A. C. Kak, "Recursive Least Squares Smoothing of Noise

in Images," *IEEE Trans. Acoust., Speech, and Sig. Proc.*, ASSP-25 (1977), pp. 520–524.

260. H. R. Keshavan and M. D. Srinath, "Interpolative Models in Restoration and Enhancement of Noisy Images," *IEEE Trans. Acoust., Speech, and Sig. Proc.* ASSP-25 (1977), pp. 525–534.

261. J. E. Wall, Jr., "Control and Estimation of Large-Scale Systems Having Spatial Symmetry," Ph.D. dissertation, Massachusetts Institute of Technology, 1978.

262. M. G. Strintzis, "Conditions for Stability of Nonanticipative Two-Dimensional Recursive Filters," *IEEE Trans. Aut. Cont.* AC-22 (1977), pp. 594–597.

263. B. Lévy, S. Y. Kung, and M. Morf, "New Results in 2-D Systems Theory, 2-D State-Space Models—Realization and the Notions of Controllability, Observability and Minimality," presented at Monterey Conf. on Multidimensional Systems, Monterey, Calif., November 1976.

264. D. Goodman, "Some Stability Properties of Two-Dimensional Linear Shift-Invariant Digital Filters," *IEEE Trans. Circ. and Sys.* CAS-24 (1977), pp. 201–208.

265. E. Wong and E. T. Tsui, "One-Sided Recursive Filters for Two-Dimensional Random Fields," *IEEE Trans. Inf. Theory* IT-23 (1977), pp. 633–637.

266. J. B. Bednar and C. H. Farmer, "An Algorithm for the Inversion of Finite Block Toeplitz Matrices with Application to Spatial Digital Filters," in *Proc. Comp. Image Proc. and Recog.*, vol. 2, Columbia, Mo., August 1972, pp. 9–3–1–9–3–10.

267. B. Lévy, M. Morf, and S. Y. Kung, "New Results in 2-D Systems Theory. III: Recursive Realization and Estimation for 2-D Systems," in *Proc. 20th Midwest Symp. on Circuits and Systems*, Western Periodicals, Co., North Hollywood, Calif. (1977).

268. T.-L. Chang, "Limit Cycles in a Two-Dimensional First-Order Digital Filter," *IEEE Trans. Circ. and Sys.* CAS-24 (1977), pp. 15–19.

269. S. R. Parker and L. Souchon, "Synthesis of N-Dimensional Recursive Digital Filters by Taylor Series Expansion," *IEEE Trans. Circ. and Sys.* CAS-24, (1977), pp. 28–34.

270. E. W. Kamen, "Decomposition of Two-Dimensional Transfer Functions into One-Dimensional Components," submitted to *IEEE Trans. Acoust., Speech, and Sig. Proc.*

271. R. Cairoli and J. B. Walsh, "Martingale Representations and Holomorphic Processes," *Ann. Prob.* 5 (1977), pp. 511–521.

272. P. M. Narendra, L. G. Williams, and W. G. Chaplin, "Automated Image Enhancement Techniques for Second Generation FLIR," Rept. on Contract No. DAA653-76-0195, Systems and Research Division, Honeywell, Minneapolis, Minn., May 1977.

273. M. S. Bartlett, *The Statistical Analysis of Spatial Pattern*, Chapman and Hall, London, 1975.

274. J. M. Mendel, "White-Noise Estimators for Seismic Data Processing in Oil Exploration," *IEEE Trans. Aut. Cont.* AC-22 (1977), pp. 694–706.

275. J. M. Mendel, N. E. Nahi, L. S. Silverman, and H. D. Washburn, "State Space Models of Lossless Layered Media," in *Proc. 1977 Joint Aut. Cont. Conf.*, Catalog No. 77CH1220-3CS, IEEE, New York (1977), pp. 86–98.

276. J. W. Bayliss and E. O. Brigham, "Application of the Kalman Filter to Continuous Signal Restoration," *Geophysics* 35 (1970), pp. 2–23.

277. N. Crump, "A Kalman Filter Approach to the Deconvolution of Seismic Signals," *Geophysics* 39 (1974), pp. 1–13.

278. N. Ott and H. G. Meder, "The Kalman Filter as a Prediction Error Filter," *Geophysical Prospecting* 20 (1972), pp. 549–560.

279. S. L. Wood, M. Morf, and A. Macovski, "Stochastic Methods Applied to Medical Image Reconstruction," in *Proc. 1977 IEEE Conf. on Dec. and Cont.*, Catalog No. 77CH1269-OCS, IEEE, New York (1977), pp. 35–41.

280. L. B. Jackson, "An Analysis of Limit Cycles Due to Multiplication Rounding the Recursive Digital (Sub) filters," in *Proc. 7th Allerton Conf. on Circuit and System Theory*, sponsored by the Dept. of Elec. Eng. and the Coordinated Science Laboratory of the University of Illinois, Urbana-Champaign, October 1969, IEEE Catalog No. 69 C 48-CT, pp. 69–78.

281. I. W. Sandberg and J. F. Kaiser, "A Bound on Limit Cycles in Fixed-Point Implementation of Digital Filters," *IEEE Trans. on Audio and Electroacoustics* AU-20 (1972), pp. 110–112.

282. T. Claasen, W. F. G. Mecklenbräuker, and J. B. H. Peek, "Frequency Domain Criteria for the Absence of Zero-Input Limit Cycles in Nonlinear Discrete-Time Systems with Applications to Digital Filters," *IEEE Trans. on Circ. and Sys.* CAS-22 (1975), pp. 692–696.

283. A. N. Willson, Jr., "Limit Cycles Due to Adder Overflow in Digital Filters," *IEEE Trans. on Circ. Th.* CT-19 (1972), pp. 342–346.

284. E. D. Sontag, "Linear Systems over Commutative Rings: A Survey," *Richerche di Automatica* 7 (1976), pp. 1–34.

285. G. Marchesini and E. Fornasini, "Realization of Bilinear Input-Output Maps and Their Characterization by Formal Power Series," in *Mathematical Systems Theory*, edited by G. Marchesini and S. K. Mitter, Lecture Notes in Econ. and Math. Sys., No. 131, Springer-Verlag, New York, 1976.

286. J. Burg, "Maximum Entropy Spectral Analysis," Ph.D. dissertation, Stanford University, 1975.

287. T. G. Stockham, Jr., T. M. Cannon, R. B. Ingebretsen, "Blind Deconvolution through Digital Signal Processing," *Proc. IEEE* 63 (1975), pp. 678–692.

288. A. V. Oppenheim, R. W. Schafer, and T. G. Stockham, Jr., "Nonlinear Filtering of Multiplied and Convolved Signals," *Proc. IEEE* 56 (1968), pp. 1264–1291.

289. A. H. Jazwinski, *Stochastic Processes and Filtering Theory*, Academic Press, New York, 1970.

290. R. W. Brockett and R. A. Skoog, "A New Perturbation Theory for the Synthesis of Nonlinear Networks," in *Mathematical Aspects of Electrical Network Analysis, SIAM-AMS Proc.*, Vol. 3, American Mathematical Society, Providence, R. I. (1971), pp. 17–33.

291. A. S. Willsky, "A Survey of Failure Detection Methods in Linear Dynamic Systems," *Automatica* 12 (1976), pp. 601–611.

292. D. L. Gustafson, A. S. Willsky, J.-Y. Wang, M. C. Lancaster, and J. H. Triebwasser, "A Statistical Approach to Rhythm Diagnosis of Cardiograms," *Proc. IEEE* 65 (1977), pp. 802–804.

293. A. V. Oppenheim and R. W. Schafer, *Digital Signal Processing*, Prentice-Hall, Englewood Cliffs, N. J., 1975.

294. J. L. Massey, "Shift Register Synthesis and BCH Decoding," *IEEE Trans. Inf. Th.* IT-15 (1969), pp. 126–127.

295. R. Johnston, "Linear Systems over Various Rings," Ph.D. dissertation, Massachusetts Institute of Technology, 1973.

296. M. Morf and T. Kailath, "Recent Results in Least-Squares Estimation Theory," *Ann. of Econometrics*, to appear.

297. E. I. Jury, "Stability of Multidimensional Scalar and Matrix Polynomials," *Proc. IEEE*, to appear.

5

Some Issues in Nonlinear System Analysis

5.1 Introduction

Most of the discussion to this point has dealt with the analysis and synthesis of linear systems, perhaps distorted by nonlinear effects such as quantization. However, there has been much work on the analysis and design of systems that are fundamentally nonlinear in both digital signal processing and in control and estimation theory. It is beyond the scope of this book to consider the research in this area at any depth, and we refer the reader to the references and to the literature in the two disciplines for the full story. In this chapter we limit ourselves to a brief look at two particular directions of research whose common thread is the use of algebraic concepts to study nonlinear systems possessing particular types of structure. The philosophy underlying these results is that many of the concepts and techniques from linear system theory can be adapted for the analysis of certain nonlinear systems. Not only is this philosophy useful in allowing one to solve certain nonlinear problems, it is also valuable in providing insight into the properties of linear systems. One gets a clearer picture of which system properties carry over to nonlinear systems with particular structure and which properties are fundamentally tied to linearity.

5.2 Basic Concepts in Homomorphic Filtering

In digital signal processing Oppenheim [1, 2, 37] abstracted the key concept in linear system analysis—superposition—and developed what he termed *homomorphic signal processing*. The basic idea is as follows [37]. Let X and Y be spaces with two operations defined on each—a binary operation

$$x_1, x_2 \in X, \qquad x_1 * x_2 \in X,$$
$$y_1, y_2, \in Y, \qquad y_1 \circ y_2 \in Y, \tag{1}$$

and an operation of scalar action

$$c \in R \text{ or } C, x \in X, \qquad c \cdot x \in X,$$
$$c \in R \text{ or } C, y \in Y, \qquad c \cdot y \in Y. \tag{2}$$

A homomorphism is then a map H from X to Y that preserves these operations; that is it satisfies a generalized superposition principle

$$H(x_1 * x_2) = H(x_1) \circ H(x_2), \qquad H(c \cdot x_1) = c \cdot H(x_1). \tag{3}$$

If the operations (1) and (2) satisfy the axioms of a vector space (for example, all the operations are commutative), then (3) looks very much like a linear system. In fact, one can show in this case [1] that any such system can be represented as the cascade of three homomorphic systems

$$H = D_y^{-1} \circ L \circ D_x, \tag{4}$$

where L is a standard linear system, and D_x and D_y are called *characteristic systems*. They translate the operations in X and Y into usual vector addition and scalar multiplication.

Let us look at an example of this. Let X be the space of input sequences in which each input is strictly positive. We make X into a vector space with the operations

$$[(\alpha \cdot x_1) * (\beta \cdot x_2)](n) = x_1(n)^\alpha x_2(n)^\beta; \tag{5}$$

the system D_x is clearly seen to be the map

$$x(n) \longrightarrow \log [x(n)] \tag{6}$$

with inverse

$$\xi(n) \longrightarrow e^{\xi(n)}. \tag{7}$$

One can similarly define vector space operations in which X consists of all nonzero complex numbers or all those of modulus one [1, 37], although there are some difficulties due to the nonuniqueness of the complex logarithm [1, 37].

Having this framework, one can consider the filtering of signals corrupted by multiplicative effects. That is, suppose we observe

$$z(n) = x(n)u(n) \tag{8}$$

(all quantities assumed positive), and we wish to recover x from z. If we take the logarithm of both sides

$$\xi(n) = \log z(n) = \log x(n) + \log u(n), \tag{9}$$

we can use linear techniques to filter $\xi(n)$, yielding the output $\eta(n)$, and we then obtain the desired filtered version as

$$\hat{x}(n) = e^{\eta(n)}. \tag{10}$$

For applications of multiplicative homomorphic processing, we refer the reader to [2, 37]. When $\log(x)$ and $\log(u)$ are Gaussian random variables (when x and u are *lognormal* variables [9, 12–16, 20])—the filtering of $\xi(n)$ is simply a Kalman filter (this result is developed thoroughly in [20]). The continuous-time version of this multiplicative noise model has been studied in [2], and its stochastic analog was developed in [9]. Let us examine this case at some length. Let $w(t)$ be a two-dimensional Gauss-Markov process satisfying the equation

$$\dot{w}(t) = Aw(t) + v(t), \tag{11}$$

where $v(t)$ is a two-dimensional white noise process

$$E(v(t)) = 0, \qquad E(v(t)v(\tau)) = Q\delta(t - \tau). \tag{12}$$

Suppose we transmit the frequency-modulated signal[1]

$$x(t) = \exp\left[\int_0^t [w_1(s) + jw_2(s)]\,ds\right]. \tag{13}$$

Due to some effect, say atmospheric turbulence [21], the received signal is corrupted by multiplicative noise

$$r(t) = \mu(t)x(t), \tag{14}$$

where

$$\mu(t) = \exp(\eta_1(t) + j\eta_2(t)) \tag{15}$$

and η is a two-dimensional Brownian motion process

$$E(\eta(t)) = 0, \qquad E(\dot{\eta}(t)\dot{\eta}(\tau)) = R\delta(t - \tau). \tag{16}$$

Because of the continuity of $r(t)$, there is no difficulty in taking the complex logarithm [9]; essentially, continuous monitoring of phase allows one to unravel it and determine the number of revolutions, as well as the value of the phase modulo 2π. In this case $r(t)$ is equivalent to the observations

$$d\xi_1(t) = w_1(t)dt + d\eta_1(t), \qquad d\xi_2(t) = w_2(t)dt + d\eta_2(t). \tag{17}$$

Using standard Kalman filtering techniques, we can obtain the least-squares estimates $\hat{w}_1(t)$ and $\hat{w}_2(t)$. However, the best estimate of x is not

$$\exp \int_0^t [\hat{w}_1(s) + j\hat{w}_2(s)]ds,$$

essentially because the integral of a best estimate is not the best estimate of the integral. In this case we can obtain the desired estimate as follows. Let

$$\rho_1(t) = \int_0^t w_1(s)ds, \qquad \rho_2(t) = \int_0^t w_2(s)ds. \tag{18}$$

Then by adjoining these integrals to w_1 and w_2 to form a four-dimensional "state," we can again design a Kalman filter (with measurements (17)) and obtain the best estimates $\hat{w}_1(t), \hat{w}_2(t), \hat{\rho}_1(t)$, and $\hat{\rho}_2(t)$. Then the desired estimate is

$$\hat{x}(t) = \exp\left(\hat{\rho}_1(t) + j\hat{\rho}_2(t)\right). \tag{19}$$

The details of this development are given in [9, 12]. These references also show that the solution of the discrete-time version—that is, when we observe only $r(k\Delta)$, where r is as in (14)—is much more difficult, essentially because the ambiguity in the complex logarithm cannot be resolved in this case.

In digital signal processing, multiplicative homomorphic systems represent only half the picture. One can study systems in which vector addition is the operation of convolution, and multiplication by an integer n corresponds to convolution of a signal with itself n times [1, 2, 37] (multiplication by a noninteger is a generalization of this [1, 2, 22]). The key to the development of homomorphic filtering techniques for convolutional noise is the z-transform of signals. Let X be a vector space of signals under the operations of convolution as vector addition and scalar multiplication as defined above. Then we have the following transform relations

$$(x_1 * x_2)\,(n) \longleftrightarrow X_1(z)\,X_2(z),$$
$$(\alpha \cdot x_1)\,(n) \longleftrightarrow X_1(z)^\alpha, \tag{20}$$

and we see that homorphic convolution systems look like multiplicative homomorphic systems in the frequency domain. This allows one to develop a rather complete theory of convolution-homomorphic filtering [2, 22, 37]. Techniques such as homomorphic deconvolution have found application in speech analysis [3, 37], dereverberation of signals such as those arising in seismic applications [2, 22, 23, 37], and in several other disciplines [2, 37].

5.3 Analysis of Bilinear Systems and Relationships with Homomorphic Systems

A recent direction of research in control and estimation theory has been the study of bilinear systems [5–16, 38]; the multiplicative homomorphic system (11)–(16) represents one of the simplest examples. Consider (13). We can easily obtain a stochastic differential equation for x:

$$\dot{x}(t) = (w_1(t) + jw_2(t))x(t). \tag{21}$$

If we regard w_1, w_2 as inputs—controls and/or noises—we see that the right-hand side of (21) consists of a product of inputs and the state; that is, it is a bilinear function of the two. Generalizing this, we obtain the class of bilinear systems

$$x(t) = \left[A_0 + \sum_{i=1}^{N} A_i u_i(t) \right] x(t), \tag{22}$$

where the A_i are known $n \times n$, possibly complex-valued matrices, the u_i are scalar inputs, and x is either an n-vector or an $n \times n$ matrix.

The question of the control, estimation, and stability of bilinear systems such as (22) has received a great deal of attention in the recent past and has applications in a wide range of disciplines [5, 12, 14–16, 24, 38]. We will not examine the control or stability issues here. Rather, we content ourselves with a brief look at the estimation problem to uncover some of the main issues in bilinear signal processing. In the scalar case (21) one can readily obtain a representation for $x(t)$ of the form (13). However, in the vector case this is not true in general. In fact, the solution of (22) has the representation

$$x(t) = \exp\left\{A_0 t + \sum_{i=1}^{N} A_i \int_0^t u_i(s)ds\right\} x(0) \tag{23}$$

if and only if all the matrices A_0, A_1, ..., A_N commute (a very restrictive condition). The commutativity or noncommutativity properties of these matrices play a central role in the analysis of bilinear systems, and the introduction of concepts from the theory of Lie algebras and Lie groups allows one to study these systems in great detail [5, 6, 8–17, 25, 26].

Let us see what this noncommutativity can do by examining a problem motivated by (11)–(16). If we examine those equations and consider only the phase effects (w_2 and η_2), we see that this problem is the estimation of a phase given noisy measurements of that phase. By performing a transformation on the measurement, we obtain a noisy measurement of the angular frequency, and we can apply standard Kalman filtering techniques to estimate the angular frequency and its integral. Then the desired phase estimate is just the complex exponential of the estimate of the integral. A natural extension of this problem is the consideration of rotation in three dimensions. We follow [5, 12, 14–16]. Suppose we have a satellite equipped with an inertial platform. The orientation of the satellite with respect to an inertial frame can be described by specifying inertial coordinates of a body-fixed orthonormal basis. The resulting set of three 3-vectors, called the *direction cosine matrix $X(t)$*, has the property

$$X'(t) X(t) = I, \quad \det X(t) = 1. \tag{24}$$

Let $w(t)$ be the angular velocity of the body with respect to inertial space, given in the coordinates of the body frame. Then, the evolution of the direction cosine matrix is described by the bilinear equation

$$\dot{X}(t) = \left[\sum_{i=1}^{3} R_i w_i(t)\right] X(t), \tag{25}$$

where

$$R_1 = \begin{bmatrix} 0 & 0 & 0 \\ 0 & 0 & 1 \\ 0 & -1 & 0 \end{bmatrix}, \quad R_2 = \begin{bmatrix} 0 & 0 & -1 \\ 0 & 0 & 0 \\ 1 & 0 & 0 \end{bmatrix}, \quad R_3 = \begin{bmatrix} 0 & 1 & 0 \\ -1 & 0 & 0 \\ 0 & 0 & 0 \end{bmatrix}. \tag{26}$$

Suppose that our only observation of satellite attitude is from the inertial platform; that is, we observe the direction cosine matrix $M(t)$ of the body with respect to the platform, which is supposed to remain fixed in inertial space (in which case $M = X$). However, because of various errors (such as gyro drift) the platform drifts, and our actual observation is

$$M(t) = X(t)V(t), \tag{27}$$

where the platform misalignment term $V(t)$ is the direction cosine matrix of inertial space with respect to the platform. As described in (14), this can be modeled by a bilinear equation of the form[2]

$$\dot{V}(t) = V(t)\left[\sum_{i=1}^{3} R_i v_i(t)\right], \tag{28}$$

where the v_i represent gyro drift and for simplicity are taken to be white.

Now compare (25)–(28) with (13)–(15), using (21) and an analogous equation for μ. We see that we have a direct analog of the phase (one-dimensional rotation) problem, including a multiplicative noise model (27). If only one w_i and the corresponding v_i are nonzero, then this problem precisely reduces to the phase estimation problem [9]. Suppose we now assume that w obeys an equation such as (11). Then by the matrix equivalent of the complex logarithm (again we have no mod 2π difficulties because of our continuous observation), we can essentially differentiate $M(t)$ to obtain noisy measurements of w corrupted by the gyro drifts v_1, v_2, v_3. This problem is somewhat more complex than the earlier one because one must take care in using stochastic calculus and, more importantly, because rotations in three dimensions do not commute [16, 27]. However, one can carry the analysis through to obtain a measurement equation of the form

$$z(t) = w(t) + M(t)v(t), \tag{29}$$

where $v' = (v_1, v_2, v_3)$ [16]. The effect of the gyro drifts on our measurement of angular velocity depends on our attitude; this dependence can be seen from the presence of $M(t)$ on the right-hand side of (29).

Using (29), we can design a Kalman filter to estimate w. However, we run into a problem in estimating X. Recall that in the one-dimensional problem, we augmented the state of our Kalman filter with the estimate of the integral of w, but in the three-dimensional case the integrals of components of w are not simply related to X, again because of the noncommutativity of rotations in three dimensions. In fact, in this case the problem of optimal estimation of X is infinite dimensional [14]. Thus in the one-dimensional case we obtain a decomposition much like (4). We can convert our multiplicative process into a linear one and operate on it with optimal linear techniques. However, the reinjection of the resulting filtered process becomes extremely complex. One must use approximate methods [12, 14] except in special cases. The case in which all the A_i commute is much like the scalar case and involves looking at the integrals of certain quantities [9, 12]. In addition, if the A_i obey certain (somewhat less restrictive) noncommutativity relations, one can obtain a finite-dimensional optimal procedure by considering several types of iterated integral [14, 15, 17].

Let us say a few more words about the relationship between homomorphic filtering (HF) and bilinear signal processing (BSP). Recall that HF is based on the existence of certain algebraic properties between input functions and output functions—the validity of a superposition rule. In HF one designs a filter consisting of three parts: (1) a projection system, which unravels the signals so that one can use (2) a linear filter, followed by (3) an injection of the resulting process to yield the desired output. In the scalar example of BSP, as described in (11)–(19), we obtain a system of exactly this form—a HF (logarithm-linear (Kalman) filter-exponential); and we obtain essentially the same results for the model (22), (27) if the A_i commute. However, in the general case we cannot obtain the entire picture. We can unravel the signal and perform linear (and perhaps nonlinear [14, 15, 17]) processing, but the reinjection process is much more difficult. Perhaps one of the keys to the difference between HF and BSP is the difference in their starting points. In homomorphic filtering the fundamental assumption involves the algebraic structure of the relation between input trajectories and output trajectories (superposition). For bilinear systems analysis the starting point is (22), which imposes an algebraic (multiplicative) restriction on the time rate of change of the state or output; that is in some sense (22) represents an incrementally homomorphic model, in which the fundamental assumption involves algebraically compatible dynamics (as opposed to input-output relation). When the A_i commute, (22) also yields a multiplicative input-output relationship, and in the other special cases considered in [14, 15, 17] the restrictions on the A_i yield other tractable input-output relations, but in these cases the optimal filters are not homomorphic (since after we unravel the received signal we perform a nonlinear filtering operation). In the general case, however, the algebraic structure of (22) still allows one to perform a great deal of analysis [5, 10].

5.4. Concluding Remarks on Algebraic Techniques for Nonlinear Systems

The use of algebraic and geometric concepts and techniques to study systems with algebraically compatible dynamics or input-output relations has increased greatly over the past few years as new theories and applications have been uncovered [5–19, 24–36]. Recently certain nonlinear systems having Volterra series representations have been studied with great success [6, 10, 11, 14, 17, 33, 34] using techniques and ideas that have grown out of the study of bilinear systems [5, 7]. Nonlinear systems have also been studied using techniques adapted from the theory of multidimensional systems (see chapter 4). In addition, motivated by many of the same issues that prompted Oppenheim's study of generalized superposition [1], several researchers [18, 19, 28–34] have examined systems whose state dynamics possess some but not all of the algebraic structure of linear systems. Several researchers [35, 36] have studied controllability, realizability, and related properties for systems that possess particularly nice input-output descriptions, much along the lines of Oppenheim's generalized superposition. Such analyses have yielded new insights into the properties of linear systems, and many of the powerful tools of linear system analysis are being extended to other dynamical systems, establishing the foundations for a synthesis and analysis theory for special classes of nonlinear systems. It is this key idea—the use of algebraic tools to synthesize and analyze nonlinear systems with structure—that is the major common theme of the nonlinear systems research in the two disciplines.

5.5. Notes

1. Here we are allowing both the usual type of modulation on the phase and a homomorphic modulation on the amplitude.

2. Technically one must include a correction term in (28) if one interprets it as an Ito stochastic equation. This is not difficult, but it does obscure our point with technicalities (which certainly are very important). See [16, 27] for the details. Note that (28) can be interpreted rigorously if one uses Stratonovich calculus [8, 14].

5.6. References

1. A. V. Oppenheim, "Generalized Superposition," *Information and Control* 11 (1967), pp. 528–536.

2. A. V. Oppenheim, R. W. Schafer, and T. G. Stockham, Jr., "Nonlinear Filtering of Multiplied and Convolved Signals," *Proc. IEEE* 56 (1968), pp. 1264–1291.

3. A. V. Oppenheim and R. W. Schafer, "Homomorphic Analysis of Speech," *IEEE Trans. Audio Electroacoust.* AU-16 (1968), pp. 221–226.

4. T. G. Stockham, Jr., T. M. Cannon, R. B. Ingebretsen, "Blind Deconvolution through Digital Signal Processing," *Proc. IEEE* 63 (1975), pp. 678–692.

5. R. W. Brockett, "System Theory on Group Manifolds and Coset Spaces," *SIAM J. Contr.* 10 (1972), pp. 265–284.

6. R. W. Brockett, "Volterra Series and Geometric Control Theory," *Preprints IFAC 1975*, Boston, Mass., August 1975.

7. P. d'Alessandro, A. Isidori, and A. Ruberti, "Realization and Structure Theory of Bilinear Systems," *SIAM J. Contr.* 12 (1974), pp. 517–535.

8. R. W. Brockett, "Lie Theory and Control Systems Defined on Spheres," *SIAM J. Appl. Math.* 25 (1973), pp. 213–225.

9. J. T. Lo and A. S. Willsky, "Estimation for Rotational Processes with One Degree of Freedom. I–III," *IEEE Trans. Aut. Contr.* 20 (1975), pp. 10–33.

10. D. Q. Mayne and R. W. Brockett, eds., *Geometric Methods in System Theory,* Reidel Pub. Co., Dordrecht, Holland, 1973.

11. R. W. Brockett, "Nonlinear Systems and Differential Geometry," *Proc. IEEE* 64 (1976), pp. 61–72.

12. A. S. Willsky, "Dynamical Systems Defined on Groups: Structural Properties and Estimation," Ph.D. dissertation, Massachusetts Institute of Technology, 1973.

13. J. T. Lo and A. S. Willsky, "Stochastic Control of Rotational Processes with One Degree of Freedom," *SIAM J. Contr.* 13 (1975), pp. 886–898.

14. S. I. Marcus, "Estimation and Analysis of Nonlinear Stochastic Systems," Ph.D. dissertation, Massachusetts Institute of Technology, 1975.

15. A. S. Willsky and S. I. Marcus, "Estimation for Bilinear Stochastic Systems," MIT Elec. Sys. Lab. Rept. ESL-R-544, Cambridge, Mass., May 1974.

16. A. S. Willsky, "Detection and Estimation of Signals in Multiplicative Noise," *IEEE Trans, Inf. Th.* IT-21 (1975), pp. 472–474.

17. S. I. Marcus and A. S. Willsky, "Algebraic Structure and Finite-Dimensional Optimal Nonlinear Filtering," *SIAM J. Math. Anal.,* to appear.

18. R. W. Brockett and A. S. Willsky, "Finite Group Homomorphic Sequential Systems", *IEEE Trans. Aut. Contr.* AC-17 (1972), pp. 483–490.

19. M. K. Sain, "The Growing Algebraic Presence in Systems Engineering," *Proc. IEEE* 64 (1976), pp. 96–111.

20. C. Johnson and E. B. Stear, "Optimal Filtering in the Presence of Multiplicative Noise," in *Proc. Fifth Symp. on Nonlin. Est. Th. and Its Appl.,* San Diego, Calif., September 1974; Western Periodicals, North Hollywood, Calif.

21. E. V. Hoversten, R. O. Harger, and S. J. Halme, "Communication Theory for the Turbulent Atmosphere," *Proc. IEEE* 58 (1970), pp. 1626–1650.

22. R. W. Schafer, "Echo Removal by Discrete Generalized Linear Filtering," Tech. Rept. 466, Research Laboratory of Electronics, Massachusetts Institute of Technology, Cambridge, Mass., February 1969; also Ph.D. thesis, Massachusetts Institute of Technology, 1968.

23. L. C. Wood and S. Treitel, "Seismic Signal Processing," *Proc. IEEE* 63 (1975), pp. 649–661.

24. R. Mohler, *Bilinear Control Processes,* Academic Press, New York, 1973.

25. J. Wei and E. Norman, "Lie Algebraic Solution of Linear Differential Equations," *J. Math. Phys.* 4 (1963), pp. 575–581.

26. J. Wei and E. Norman, "On Global Representations of the Solutions of Linear Differential Equations as a Product of Exponentials," *Proc. Amer. Math. Soc.* 15 (1964), pp. 327–334.

27. J. T. Lo, "Signal Detection on Lie Groups," in *Geometric Methods in System Theory,* edited by D. Q. Mayne and R. W. Brockett, Reidel Pub. Co., Holland, 1973.

28. Y. Rouchaleau, B. F. Wyman, and R. E. Kalman, "Algebraic Structure of Linear Dynamical Systems. III: Realization Theory over a Commutative Ring," *Proc. Nat. Acad. Sci.* 69 (1972), pp. 3404–3406.

29. E. D. Sontag, "Linear Systems over Commutative Rings: A Survey," *Ricerche di Automatica* 7 (1976), pp. 1–34.

30. E. W. Kamen, "On an Operator Theory of Linear Systems with Pure and Distributed Delays," in *Proc. 1975 IEEE Conf. on Dec. and Contr.,* Catalog No. 75CH1016-5CS, IEEE, New York (1975), pp. 77–80.

31. R. Johnston, "Linear Systems over Various Rings," Ph.D. dissertation, Massachusetts Institute of Technology, 1973.

32. M. A. Arbib and E. G. Manes, "Foundations of Systems Theory: Decomposable Systems," *Automatica* 10 (1974), pp. 285–302.

33. M. Fliess, "Sur la Réalisation des Systèmes Dynamiques Bilinéaries," *C.R. Acad. Sci. Paris* 277 (1973), pp. 923–926.

34. M. Fliess, "Sur Divers Produits de Series Formelles," *Bull. Soc. Math. France* 102 (1974), pp. 181–191.

35. R. E. Kalman, "Realization Theory of Multilinear Systems," in *Mathematical Systems Theory*, edited by G. Marchesini and S. K. Mitter, Lec. Notes in Econ. and Math. Sys., No. 131, Springer-Verlag, New York, 1976.

36. G. Marchesini and E. Fornasini, "Realization of Bilinear Input-Output Maps and Their Characterization by Formal Power Series," in *Mathematical Systems Theory*, edited by G. Marchesini and S. K. Mitter, Lec. Notes in Econ. and Math. Sys., No. 131, Springer-Verlag, New York, 1976.

37. A. V. Oppenheim and R. W. Schafer, *Digital Signal Processing*, Prentice-Hall, Englewood Cliffs, N.J., 1975.

38. A. S. Willsky and S. I. Marcus, "Analysis of Bilinear Noise Models in Circuts and Devices," *J. Franklin Inst.*, 301 (1976), pp. 103–122.

6

Concluding
Comments

In this monograph I have examined a number of broad research areas
that have attracted workers in two disciplines, digital signal processing
and control and estimation theory. The goal of this study has been
to explore these areas to gain perspective on relationships among the
questions asked, methods used, and general philosophies adopted by
researchers in these disciplines. When I began this study I felt that
such a perspective would be extremely valuable in promoting collaboration and interaction among researchers in the two fields. I think that my
initial feelings have been thoroughly substantiated. Not only are there
numerous examples of questions in one discipline that can benefit from
the point of view of the other but a number of new issues naturally arise
from combining the two points of view.

Each discipline has its own distinct character, and clearly these will and
should be maintained. On the other hand, each discipline can gain from
understanding the other. State-space methods have their limitations, such
as in specifying useful digital algorithms and structures. On the other hand,
state-space methods provide extremely powerful computer-aided algorithms for noise analysis, optimal design specification, and so on. State-
space ideas also allow one to consider multivariable and time-varying
systems. All these aspects of state-space theory may prove of value to people involved in digital signal processing. On the other side, researchers in
digital filtering have answered many crucial questions related to turning

design specifications into implementable designs. The deep understanding that workers in digital signal processing have concerning the problems of digital implementation is something that researchers in control and estimation would do well to gain. Thus it seems clear that a mutual understanding will prove beneficial to all concerned.

I have raised numerous questions and have speculated on various possibilities throughout this book, and it would be an impossible task to summarize these questions and speculations here. Rather, I will mention only one or two questions from each area. These may not prove to be the most exciting or promising problems, but I feel that they are representative and summarize the tone of this monograph.

1. *Stability analysis.* What is the effect on overall stability of the finite arithmetic constraints of a digitally implemented feedback controller?

2. *Parameter identification, linear prediction, least squares, and Kalman filtering.* Can state-space and recursive filtering methods be used to model and identify time-varying models of speech? Do stochastic realization and recursive maximum likelihood methods offer useful tools for pole-zero modeling of speech?

3. *Synthesis, realization, and implementation.* Can state-space realization and filter structure concepts be combined to obtain useful realizations for multivariable or time-varying digital filters? Can state-space noise analysis methods aid in roundoff analysis of digital filters? Can we develop design techniques (for feedback controller design) that directly take the constraints (storage, speed, word length) of digital implementation into account?

4. *Multiparameter systems, distributed processes, and random fields.* What role do state-space methods (if they exist) play in the analysis and synthesis of two-dimensional filters? Can Lyapunov theory (if it exists) aid in understanding the effects of finite arithmetic in two-dimensional systems? What role should two-dimensional recursive estimation and detection techniques have in image processing? Can two-dimensional concepts provide any insight and/or results for distributed parameter, space-time, or decentralized control problems?

5. *Some issues in nonlinear system analysis: Homomorphic filtering, bilinear systems, and algebraic system theory.* Is this algebraic point of view a useful approach to the analysis and synthesis of nonlinear systems and filters? Homomorphic filtering has found widespread application; can the same be said for other algebraic concepts?

Whether these issues or the others raised in this book have useful answers is a question for the future. I believe that many of them do, and I hope that others will think so as well.

Appendix 1

A Lyapunov Function Argument for the Limit Cycle Problem in a Second-Order Filter

Consider the second-order filter in figure A.1. The ideal (undriven) dynamics of this filter are

$$x(k + 1) = Ax(k), \tag{1}$$

where

$$x(k) = \begin{pmatrix} x_1(k) \\ x_2(k) \end{pmatrix}, \qquad A = \begin{pmatrix} a & b \\ 1 & 0 \end{pmatrix}. \tag{2}$$

Suppose we implement the filter using a single magnitude-truncation quantizer [3] following the summation. Denote this quantization operation by $Q(\cdot)$ In this case the actual dynamics are

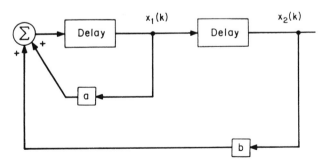

A.1
A second-order filter.

$$x(k + 1) = F(Ax(k)), \qquad F\begin{pmatrix}\xi_1\\\xi_2\end{pmatrix} = \begin{pmatrix}Q(\xi_1)\\\xi_2\end{pmatrix}. \tag{3}$$

Let us look for a quadratic Lyapunov function

$$V(x) = x'Bx, \qquad B = \begin{pmatrix}b_{11} & b_{12}\\b_{12} & b_{22}\end{pmatrix}. \tag{4}$$

In fact, let us assume that B proves the asymptotic stability of (1), that

$$B > 0, \qquad B - A'BA > 0. \tag{5}$$

We compute

$$\Delta V(z) = F(Az)'BF(Az) - z'Bz \tag{6a}$$

$$= (F(Az)'BF(Az) - z'A'BAz) + (z'A'BAz - z'Bz). \tag{6b}$$

From this it is clear that we have asymptotic stability if[1]

$$F(Az)'BF(Az) - z'A'BAz \le 0, \qquad \forall z, \tag{7}$$

or if (a somewhat stronger condition)[2]

$$F(\xi)'BF(\xi) - \xi'B\xi \le 0, \qquad \forall \xi. \tag{8}$$

Equation (8) is equivalent to

$$b_{11}[Q^2(\xi_1) - \xi_1^2] + 2b_{12}\xi_2[Q(\xi_1) - \xi_1] \le 0, \qquad \forall \xi_1, \xi_2. \tag{9}$$

Using the fact that $|Q(\xi_1)| \le |\xi_1|$, we can see that (9) holds if and only if $b_{12} = 0$. Thus we must find conditions on A such that there exists a diagonal B, satisfying (5):

$$b_{11} > 0, \qquad b_{22} > 0, \qquad B - A'BA > 0. \tag{10}$$

Equation (10) can be further reduced to the following equations (after we normalize $b_{11} = 1$, which we can do simply by scaling B):

$$0 < b_{22} < (1 - a^2), \qquad -b^2 + (b^2 + 1 - a^2)b_{22} - b_{22}^2 > 0.$$

We can rewrite the second inequality as

$$(a^2 - b^2 - 1)b_{22} < -b_{22}^2 - b^2, \tag{11}$$

and the possibilities are given in figure A.2. If $(a^2 - b^2 - 1) > 0$, either we have no region in which (11) holds (b), or the region is for negative

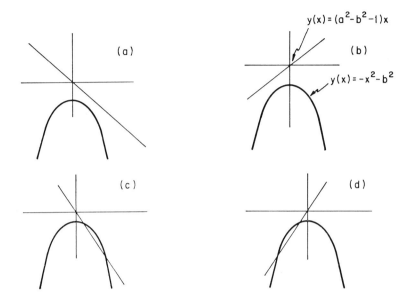

A.2
Inequality (11).

values of b_{22} (d), which violates the first inequality in (11). Thus we must have

$$a^2 - b^2 - 1 < 0; \tag{12}$$

in fact, we must have case (c), which means that there must be two real solutions to (11) when the inequality is made into an equality. Some algebraic manipulations yield the inequalities

$$0 < b_{22} < (1 - a^2), \tag{13a}$$

$$\sigma(a, b) \triangleq a^2 - b^2 - 1 < 0, \tag{13b}$$

$$\rho(a, b) \triangleq (1 - a^2 + b^2)^2 - 4b^2 > 0, \tag{13c}$$

$$\frac{-\sigma(a, b) - [\rho(a, b)]^{1/2}}{2} < b_{22} < \frac{-\sigma(a, b) + [\rho(a, b)]^{1/2}}{2}. \tag{13d}$$

Using (13b), we see that (13c) is equivalent to

$$1 - a^2 + b^2 > 2|b| \quad \text{or} \quad |a| < |1 - |b||, \tag{14}$$

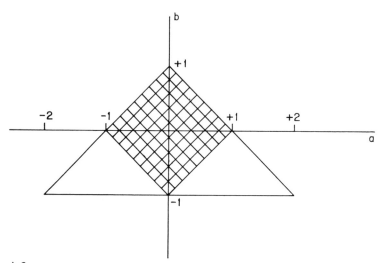

A.3
The stability result.

and under this condition both (13b) and (13c) hold. Then we can find a
value of b_{22} if and only if the inequalities (13a) and (13d) overlap. Combining these, we find that the region of (a, b)-space for which we can use this
technique to prove stability is

$$|a| < 1 - |b|, \qquad |b| < 1, \tag{15}$$

which is illustrated in figure A.3. The triangle is the region in which the
linear system (1) is asymptotically stable, and the cross-hatched area is
(15). In the remaining part of the triangle one must use a nondiagonal B,
and this technique will not work. This is not to say that we cannot find
Lyapunov functions that will prove stability in these regions of (a, b)-
space in the one-magnitude truncator case but rather that we will have to
work harder to find them if they exist (either by working directly with
(6a) or by looking for nonquadratic Lyapunov functions). This derivation
illustrates the type of argument that one can make using Lyapunov functions and also the difficulties and the limitations of the technique.

Notes

1. This is the criterion used by Willson (see p. 5) for the overflow problem.
2. This is not stronger if A is invertible, which is true if and only if $b \neq 0$.

Appendix 2

The Discrete
Fourier Transform
and Circulant
Matrices

Circulant matrices appear in several places in chapter 4. In this appendix we indicate some of their properties. Suppose we have a block-circulant matrix A

$$
A = \begin{bmatrix} A_0 & A_{N-1} \cdots & A_1 \\ A_1 & A_0 & A_2 \\ \vdots & & \\ A_{N-1} & A_{N-2} & A_0 \end{bmatrix},
$$
(1)

where each A_i is $P \times Q$. Consider the equation

$$
y = Ax,
$$
(2)

where y is an NP-vector, partitioned into P-vectors

$$
y' = (y_0', \ldots, y_{N-1}'),
$$
(3)

and x is an NQ-vector, partitioned into Q-vectors

$$
x' = (x_0', \ldots, x_{N-1}').
$$
(4)

Combining (1)–(4), we obtain

$$
y_i = \sum_{j=0}^{N-1} A_j x_{i-j},
$$
(5)

where all subscripts are to be interpreted modulo N. Hence the right-hand side of (2) is nothing more than a cyclic convolution. Let us take the discrete Fourier transform of the sequences $\{y_i\}$, $\{x_i\}$, $\{A_i\}$ where, for example,

$$\tilde{y}(l) = \sum_{i=0}^{N-1} y_i W_N^{-il}, \qquad l = 0, \ldots, N-1, \tag{6}$$

and

$$W_N = e^{j2\pi/N}. \tag{7}$$

In the transformed domain we now have N decoupled sets of equations

$$\tilde{y}(l) = \tilde{A}(l)\tilde{x}(l), \qquad l = 0, \ldots, N-1, \tag{8}$$

and we have effectively block-diagonalized the block-circulant matrix A. If $P = Q$ and each of the A_i is circulant, then each of the $\tilde{A}(l)$ is circulant, and we can diagonalize each of them by iterating this development. Thus we can use the FFT to diagonalize A. In addition, if we write

$$\tilde{y}' = (\tilde{y}(0)', \ldots, \tilde{y}(N-1)') \triangleq Ty, \tag{9}$$

$$\tilde{x}' = (\tilde{x}(0)', \ldots, \tilde{x}(N-1)') \triangleq Sx \tag{10}$$

(here $S = T$ if $P = Q$), we observe that

$$TAS' = \operatorname{diag}(\tilde{A}(0), \ldots, \tilde{A}(N-1)). \tag{11}$$

Therefore, in this case, the calculation of Ms, where M is the matrix of eigenvectors of A (and s is any arbitrary vector), can be performed using the FFT.

Index

Aboutalib, A.O., 155, 156
Adaptive estimation and control, 25, 53, 55n, 92, 169
   on-line identification for, 25, 92
   self-tuning regulators for, 53
   use of techniques for, in image processing, 169
Aggarwal, J.K., 112–114, 124, 153–155, 163
Akaike, H., 49, 54
Algebraic system theory, 92, 136, 137, 214–222
   algebraic theory of fast transforms, 92
   linear systems over rings, 92
   for nonlinear systems possessing structure, 137, 214
   for bilinear systems, 219, 221
   described by bilinear input-output functions, 137
   described by Volterra Series, 137, 222
   (*See also* Bilinear systems; Homomorphic filtering)
   on partially-ordered sets, 136
   on time sets with algebraic structure, 136
   See also Multivariable polynomials; Realization theory; State space models

All-pole modeling. *See* Autoregressive models; Linear prediction; Speech processing
Analog-digital transformations. *See* Design
Anderson, B.D.O., 117–119
Anderson, G.L., 170
Andrews, H.C., 131, 138, 144, 148, 150, 165, 166, 168, 186, 187
Angel, E., 164–167, 173, 186, 188
Ansell, H.G., 118, 136
Array processing. *See* Seismic signal processing; Space-time processes
Assefi, T., 154, 155, 168
Astrom, K.J., 25, 54
Asymptotic stability, 2, 3, 6, 7
   basic concept of, 2, 3
   for wave digital filters, 6
   See also Limit cycles; Lyapunov techniques; Stability
Atal, B.S., 26
Atashroo, M.A., 52
Attasi, S., 131, 133–135, 159, 161, 166, 167, 174, 186
Attitude estimation. See Bilinear systems
Autocorrelation method, 28–31, 33–37, 42, 43, 56n